Wrestling Year C

Connecting Sunday Readings with Lived Experience

Wesley White

In Medias Res, LLC
Publisher
Onalaska, WI

Wrestling Year C
Connecting Sunday Readings with Lived Experience

© 2025 by Wesley White

ISBN 978-0-9911005-4-5

White, Wesley
Wrestling Year C: Connecting Sunday Readings with Lived Experience/ Wesley White

1. Religion / Biblical Meditations / Spirituality
2. Christian Rituals & Practice / Worship & Liturgy
3. Revised Common Lectionary

Dedicated to:
Shai White-Gilbertson and Brandon White
Nathan and Nicholas White
and
Children and Grandchildren everywhere
even unto seven generations down the line

Foreword

For more than 15 years, Wesley White has been my mentor, my disturber, my advocate, my co-conspirator, and the editor and prime-critiquer of nearly all my writing. Through my own trials and triumphs, Wesley has been a most resolute companion. He is as generous with his time as he is with his wisdom. It is my holy privilege to call him friend.

Wesley White is a straight, white man who spends his privilege in the interest of justice and peace. He has the rare ability to understand, at profound levels, the experiences and struggles of the marginalized. His discerning eye and clear-thinking, combined with his magnanimity and humility, make him a precious gift, indeed.

These sublime characteristics are embodied in and resonate throughout Wesley's writing. I am delighted that, in publishing his daily lectionary reflections, Wesley is sharing his prescient insight with a broader audience. And now, with the addition of Year C, the cycle is complete and a wellspring of theological acumen waits to be plumbed. I hope you will come to appreciate and rely on this resource as much as I do.

In a world of populously-palatable "me and Jesus" devotionals, Wesley's reflections stand out as a daily challenge to raise our gaze and to look with clarity and intention at the world around us—especially at those people we are least inclined to see and those situations we are most inclined to ignore. He brings together the best of the Wesleyan (John, that is) tradition, which balances piety and mercy.

A Word of Caution: If you read a particular reflection and don't quite understand it, try again. Wesley's work demands that you rejigger your thinking. It's worth it!

A Word of Hope: I implore you to do more than just read these pages for your own theological edification. Please take these words into your being and let them transform your doing—for Christ's sake.

Amy

Preface

This book is the result of a 5-day-per-week blog over 13 years. Small bits can add up. Small acts can add up. Small opportunities can add up.

For this third year of comments, I note some small keyboard symbols that have been helpful through the years in keeping me open to openness: *, ~, ?, <, >, ^, !, ( ), +, and … .

*

Readers of my previous writings will know that I have used an idea from Rustrum Roy in his 1979 Hibbert Lectures, *Experimenting with Truth*. Roy uses an unfamiliar cloud-of-dots symbol ⁙ to represent "God." I use an asterisk "*" between a "G" and a "D" rather than a random pattern of dots, but the intent is the same—to blur or thin the boundaries within which G*D has been trapped by language. An asterisk stands for "more can be found elsewhere, so look in another place for what is not here."

Over the years, I have extended that to concepts such as Neighb*r and Creati*n. Of course, it needs to be extended to every virtue, such as L*ve and M*rcy. There is mystery and more held in each word. Each word needs its breathing space, and an "*" has been a useful marker to visually indicate, "Don't think you know what you are saying when you use this word, as there is more here than meets the eye or ear."

Do note that allowing space for words to have a life of their own is different than our tendency to say more than we know. Honoring "more" is not the same as intentionally adding just a little to be persuasive and bias things in your direction. The distinction here is between the * of a creative "Breath/Wind/Word" in Genesis 1:2 and the manipulation of a "snake" in Genesis 3:4–5.

I invite you to try adding an * into your writing at various places to remind yourself, if not your reader, that you are aware of language being too constrictive at points, and we wrestle the best we can with the tools we have at hand.

~

This marker of an approximation or equivalency is another way of indicating the importance of connotation. When we get down to it, we say what we mean to the best of our ability, but our ability has limits. We set up word pictures for one another and need some vehicle to remind ourselves that we may have come close to expressing our meaning, but the reality of Babel, version 17.4 (to mention only one iteration of many), needs to be taken into account.

Whether a loose approximation (~) or tight (≈), our description of an experience, especially a heightened one, is at best an approximation of what we experienced. A ~, along with an *, opens the necessity of parable and midrash to further investigate our understanding of "that which invites us into a larger perspective".

The tilde is also a way to notate alternating current. A key benefit of alternating current is an ability to use a transformer to change voltage. An opportunity for transformation is something that can easily take place in liminal space where approximation allows one insight to be used in a variety of ways, transformed as appropriate. Here is where teaching to the pupil and moving from stage to stage in our life/spirit growth finds fertile ground.

In alphabets, a ~ changes the sound of letters—"N" is different than "Ñ". When sounds change, words change. A Word change is an opportunity to hear the old in a new way and to be repurposed.

?

Raising questions goes beyond the famous slogan of the 1960s, "Question Authority." Questions are at the heart of starting a new creation. "What would happen if . . . ?" questions remind us that all we think is settled, isn't. Questions fine-tune a gross approximation: Is it more compassionate this way, or this? Is justice clearer with this decision, or this?

When questions are deemed unpatriotic or heretical, whether to friend, nation, or church, we know that it won't be long before things fall apart. Questions balance competing visions and lead to better decisions. When questions are outlawed, outlaws reign.

One of the best ways to practice wisdom is to go out of your way to find a question appropriate to the situation. It is easy to play a modern game of cynically raising one question after another, but not so easy to follow the way of the Cynic to the heart of the matter—simplicity. Jesus has been seen as a Jewish Cynic, and his simplicity is "G*D and I are One" (holistically, not numerically).

A worthy practice is to ask a question of every pericope and follow where it goes.

< >

These symbols of "less than" and "greater than" are perennial polarities as we find the truth and the perversion of each in its turn. It is worth learning about polarities and paradox theory as we are always dealing with multiple truths that are interdependent and complementary of one another. In an interconnected creation, no one truth stands alone; each needs the other to be seen for what it is and is not. An escalating defense of one pole blocks a needed reformation and renewal through a healthy flow. Here is one polarity that often surfaces in this series of wrestlings with the lectionary—Humility and The Image of G*D.

These twinned virtues are often not linked in what has come to be known as orthodox or traditional Christianity. More usual is the linking of Humility's shadow of Humiliation and The Image of G*D's shadow of Idolatry of should and pride.

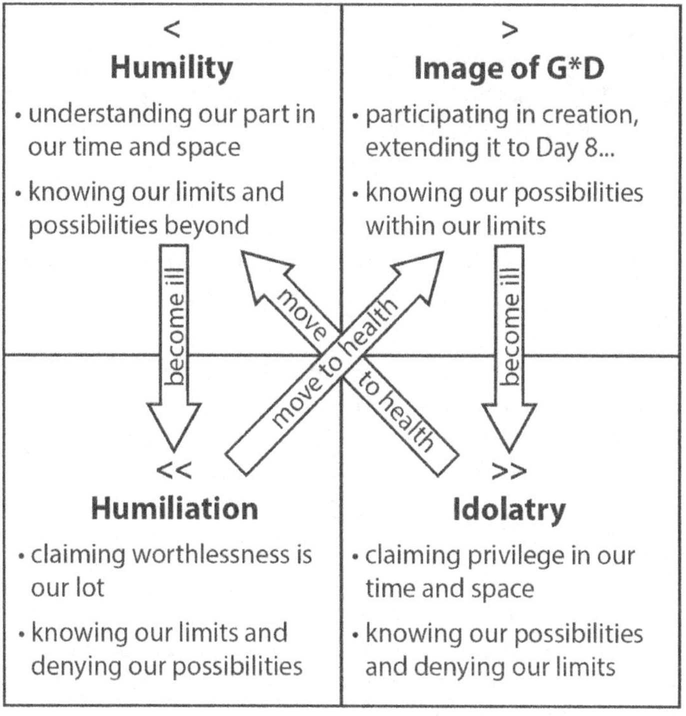

Here, we will begin with the lower left quadrant, the dark of the deep pre-Word of Creation. Here, everything remains potential.

Some would begin this story a bit later in the all-too-usual camp of Fallen Nature. It is true that there is a stumblebum within us that seems to know how to shame and humiliate us in a split second. Ancient images of shapelessness, traitor, and worm are all too close to the surface of our experience. We don't engage; we betray and we discount. Again and again, we meet an enemy only to find out it is both our communal structure and our own proclivities. Here we wrestle with sin.

There is no known antidote for this in its own terms. Humans are "wormy" (with apologies to Brother Worm). If this were the only story to be told, we would have hung our heads and disappeared eons ago. We have developed hierarchies of worminess from whoever is today's scapegoat for all that is wrong to some imagined divine right of kings. This has kept us going, but only in place as we repeat history *ad nauseum*. Our purpose seems to store pie-in-the-sky for some later imagined heaven, forgetting it is wormy pie and who wants to look forward to that.

It actually takes a long journey to go a short way back to a healthy humility that manages energy, keeps connections, and honors the presence of more than is in evidence. Somewhere along the way, we sense a mustard-seed-sized amount of creation bubbling inside us. It is a carbonated bubble wriggling to be set free from the constraints of being in the belly of a worm. It can be capped for a long time, but it will out.

We may first sense this in folks who are assured of their being. While being dismayed about how they get away with not first hanging their head or heart, that little G*D bubble, Creati*n bubble, expands within our wondering about only reading the wormy parts of our Bible and Tradition.

A mystery of conversion, whether long and developmental or short and quantum-leap, enters. It can be prepared for or not. Either way, the moral arc of the universe also has an Image of a G*D track that allows for Neighb*rs and S*lf. Here, recognition of our Neighb*r as loved and our S*lf as loved, binds us together and to G*D. This assurance binds each part of creation together as more than worms—as Images of G*D, as Beloveds.

This is not to say that everyone in a community is at the same place. Even as we might claim the old term of "perfection" for some experience of wholeness, we are still within a wormy context, an empire of one sort or another that tempts us to leap tall buildings, be adulated for the goodies it can provide, or claims our life is to accumulate, accumulate, accumulate.

Within our everyday we easily and eventually presume on being an Image of G*D and turn that into our only persona. It doesn't take much for us to say one little bit more than we know, and then we feel a need to buttress our claim with more and more justification for being right. It doesn't take long for us to begin defending G*D, where no defense is needed, and then we pit my defense against your defense.

We have again met the enemy, and it is power. Power is our idol, and taking care of G*D takes a great deal of it.

Once in the grip of our *idol du jour*, we are at the flip-side of humiliation—pride. We can spend just as much time here as we did in humiliation.

The dysfunction of perpetual schism in search of a final truth only brings us back to a deepest-dark. Again, there becomes nothing left to lose, and our search for freedom from knee-jerk righteousness is found in the last place we would expect to find it—humility.

In humility, we find again our partnership with G*D, not our defense of G*D. Here we find an image that calls us back together, internally and communally. We can no longer lose G*D to prove we have the absolute best interpretation of life, and we can no longer lose ourselves as a minion in thrall to a jealous G*D.

As you know by now, every virtue has its vice. In hanging on to the virtue of humility, we turn it into a technique rather than a fruit of a larger spirit. It isn't long before we have ritualized humility and turned it into sacrifice. From this, there is an almost inevitable progression to some bloody atonement that requires intentional humiliation.

And around we go, again and again and again. We try to set up methodologies that will short-circuit our awareness of where in this cycle we are and simply keep us a humble image of G*D. The briefest look at a life journey or our corporate history will show our better angels continually undermined by trying to stay in one spot as though there were only one way to be humble (check out Moses' humility) or an image of G*D (check out Jesus' description of a job description for Holy Spirit as recorded in John 13–17).

Hopefully, each time through, we are engaging in a deeper humility and a wider, more inclusive imagination.

Every time through a creation cycle brings new insight. Our experiences change and prepare us with courage to practice what we are now seeing. This is a place of Joy that doesn't regret "being too late smart," but knows it is for "such a time as this" that we are now ready to make a journey to a next level or stage of life. Others were gifted with responsibility in the past to call out, "Danger! This way!" and others will be so gifted tomorrow. Today, though, this is our year to manage.

On our best days and in our everydays, Humility and an Image of G*D can rise and reset our relations with our self, one another, and creation. These helpful gifts are fragile and need nurturing as they live on the doorstep of humiliation's hovel or teeter on pride's precipice.

In Humility and in an Image of G*D may we find ancient understandings of prevenient grace and theosis for all.

The movement from ⇢ the prideful humiliation of a deep too satisfied with itself ⇢ to image a creating, evolving, and partnered G*D and Image of G*D ⇢ open to idolatry that can only be rescued by humility and ⇢ too soon lost again to humiliation seems to be a form of perpetual motion—both unstoppable and manageable.

The greater and lesser symbols can also be placed over one another in such a way as to see everything closing down > and, in the midst of such decay, a new line of life opening up < that will continue past every other ending we can project. There is a comment about this in Psalm 66:1–9. Check it out with your own story of a life.

If we have the imagination to see this overlap as the end-points of Ouroborus, you can see additional great cycles and polarities herein encapsulated. Here is a shorthand way of asking us to see beyond the literal and the given—another form of an *.

∧

A caret also fulfills a variety of functions: a proof-reading mark to insert punctuation or text, a circumflex accent that changes pronunciation and thus the meaning of a word, a signifier of exponentiation (multiple multiplications) when superscript is not available; in some computer systems, it is an *escape character* that changes the significance of a subsequent character; and more particularized usages.

The ∧ is similar to an * in helping us remember to look beyond a first level of understanding and leave space for a new way to look. If we are looking beyond the present, there needs to be a variety of tools that help us do so. In some ways, we could begin piling up a whole series of superscripted superscripts to help us escape the trap of thinking we know what we are saying and how we are being heard:

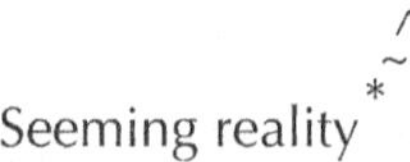

Seeming reality

An appreciation of provisionality is a blessing.

!

At first blush, the ! seems like a signed, sealed, and delivered ? that straightens everything out and removes us from the provisional, from looking for more.

The ! is a marker that seems to say, "This is settled." We know from past experience and our subsequent understanding of change and growth that this is a powerful hint to us that this is a special place where attention needs to be applied.

Where it is sarcasm, we need to ask what led to this breaking of relationship and how it might be mended. Where it is surprise, we need to wonder why we're surprised because this is a great spot to continue our growth. Where it reinforces force to bend us to its will, we need to step back and look from seven generations out, how well it is going to stand up, and whether this is just false bravado.

Merriam-Webster online says the first known use of this symbol was in 1824. It didn't make the keyboard until 1970, according to Smithsonian online. It is overdone these days of hyper-individualism where our personal perspective seems so unique and significant.

Mark !s well, for this is a starting point where one of the other more open signs can probably be put to good use.

( ) or [ ]

As you note in this series of Wrestling Years, I am overfond of parenthetical statements that allow for a clarifying image or expansion of a particular line of thought. These admittedly break the flow and nearly always require going back to the beginning of the sentence to start again with a particular picture in mind and read it while skipping the parentheses.

This not only allows me a bit of room to play, it keeps the reader from comfortably plowing ahead as though some end-point may be reached. It is a stop-and-smell-the-roses type interruption. Hopefully, there will be a consideration of what other trail might be fruitfully tracked down as a result of different experiences and referents.

Whenever you are in the presence of a liturgy (whether secular or religious) it is an intriguing exercise to take out your pencil and add parentheses to see what the extras are that begin to say more than they can bear.

For instance, from the United States Archive:

> We (the People of the United States), in Order to form (a more perfect) Union, (establish) Justice, (insure) domestic Tranquility, (provide for the) common defence, (promote the) general Welfare, and (secure the) Blessings of Liberty (to ourselves and our Posterity), do (ordain and) establish this Constitution (for the United States of America).

Now we can look at what follows to see who it is that is being cared for and who isn't. What is it about the historic setting of this document that needs remembering when applying it to today? If you were to read that series backwards, would the emphasis be on Justice or Liberty?

Looking at the sequence also lets us see that the word "defense" is not capitalized, like the rest of the terms. What might we make of the significance of this in light of the hyper-militarism of this day and a dramatic imbalance that favors "defense" over "Welfare"?

Another instance comes from the beloved *Book of Common Prayer*:

> Almighty God, (whose beloved Son willingly endured
> the agony and shame of the cross for our redemption):
> Give us courage, (we beseech thee, to take up our
> cross and follow him; who liveth and reigneth with
> you and the Holy Spirit, one God, now and for ever).
> *Amen.*

It is a blessing to be able to see a space wherein more can be added. It is also a blessing to be able to see what has been added. Here, a prayer is for courage. Questions can now be asked about what courage is needed. Is it to be about a process of active redeeming, which is different than simply repeated cross-carrying? Is it courage to live out of a life understood to have been freed? If we follow Jesus, do we also participate in a next step of an evolving creation or is it just following orders as cannon-fodder for the church?

We are not to just note these special characters and where they are placed, but to be free enough to add them where they need to be present.

+

Hopefully, the point has been made about these wonderful little jots and tittles of keyboard symbols, and you can add your own understanding of what a + means for you.

If you need some assistance in this, I refer you to a book of excerpts of the writing of Richard Rohr, *Yes, and … : Daily Meditations*.

• • •

The ellipsis indicates someone has made a decision that there is more here than needs to be said to make the point. If you trust the source, it is appropriate to say thank you for the work done on your behalf. If you have a question about a source or know from past experience that they are quick to turn everything to their own advantage, it is necessary to check out the source, as, like statistics, an ellipsis can be made to lie or keep secret something the editor does not want revealed.

Each time one of these comes around, we can check our trust level. This is part of active reading, which is just as important as active listening. While it takes more time and energy, it has a much better outcome.

In some sense, there is an invisible ellipsis between words where we can ask, "What's missing here that would better clarify the meaning?" Fortunately or unfortunately, the following comments ask you to use your sense of invisible ellipses on a regular basis. Blessings on your engagement or going on to other parts of life to actively make mercy visible.

What, then, do all these little bits and pieces of unspoken typography come to? For me, they are aids to pause long enough to consider that I don't quite get it and to add in other experiences in a desire to move from a more constricted life and context to a wider one with more elbow room. Hopefully, this allows a more holistic engagement with G*D, Neighb*r, and Creati*n.

A posting by Jim Taylor caught my attention. It resonated well:

> I see myself almost as a transparent membrane between the past and the future—inhaling the past, exhaling the future. Past and future butt together, separated only by the thickness of a single breath.

I put this together with other breath exercises that bring in a sense of healing, peace, joy, or other needed blessing from the future that displaces and exhales some dis/ease, fear, sorrow, or other stuckness from the past.

In these breaths and symbols, I am aided in becoming a mobile thin-space.

May your wrestlings with, "Is this all it means," bring you an assurance of your blessing. May you rejoice that you are loved as you have been, are, and as you may become.

Notes on Format: Even though there are usually four scriptures designated for each Sunday of the church year, they are presented here in book order rather than calendar order. While tempted to use the Jewish order for the Hebrew readings, I will stick with a traditional Protestant Christian ordering. This allows reading the over-arching story as a devotional book while also providing a relatively easy way to find the four readings. If there is a question about what the pericopes for a given date are, go to *lectionary.library.vanderbilt.edu/* for the chapter and verse and to *textweek.com/* for all manner of resources regarding the readings.

An Appendix contains a chart of the seasonal variants used in this book. I look forward to hearing how you have improved on these alternative names for the Sundays and a few other moments in a Church Year. In this and other ways, we encourage one another to engage and modify tradition through current experience.

What some have called poetry, because of a visual presentation of phrasal fragments strung together, is usually a modified Cut Up process used by William Burroughs. I simply call these Fragments.

Mercy and Joy abound
take plenty
and some to pass around

Wesley White . . . May 2015 . . . October 2025 . . .

Additional lectionary comments are found at kcmlection.blogspot.com.

An archive of unedited comments is found at wesleyspace.net.

*For the greatest benefit,
remember to read the Biblical text
immediately before proceeding to the comment.*

Genesis 1:1–2:4a
Hopeless Hope Vigil

A Vigil is a religious ritual prior to a special event and/or a watchfulness in place of sleep.

How much can be presumed for an Easter Vigil?

Do we already know the outcome, and so are trying to heighten an experience through sleep deprivation, a variant of drug use? This can lower the liminal threshold to move us toward extraordinary significance that sets our experience of resurrection above even a first Mary-at-the-grave experience.

Do we continue Absent Saturday and deepen that with a time to officially recognize our hopeless condition? This might raise the bar of surprise, so we will attend to a new way forward for our life and our life together.

Liturgically, Easter Vigil is a spoiler alert for Easter Day. It is the beginning of the Easter season, sort of a reverse Ash Wednesday.

And so we begin with a creation story here at what is supposed to be a new creation through resurrection rather than an original Word.

Try retelling Easter as a creation story. In the beginning when G*D was resurrecting Jesus the grave was formless void and darkness covered the deeps of Sheol, Hades, and Hell while light was gently breaking from within a stone-cold tomb . . . . (Your turn to take it further—you might try this with a group doing a progressive story where one person starts and the next carries the story one step further and around it goes.)

As you move through this series of reflections, it will be helpful to have some Vigil time before attending to your reading of the pericope, letting it sit for awhile so you can have a fresh appreciation of both the finality of death and Jesus' visit to those who had gone before (be careful with this one though and don't mistake not having heard the name Jesus with any lesser engagement with life). Having remembered and anticipated—now it is time to receive and act.

Genesis 7:1–5, 11–18; 8:6–18; 9:8–13
Hopeless Hope Vigil

The Ark holds clean and unclean, preserving both.

Presumably, the clean and unclean parts of human experience are also preserved. Seemingly, Noah contains both, as his pre-ark righteousness is as real as his post-ark drunken stupor.

Is one dove left mateless when its mate does not return? Is the raven continuing to soar, or did it do an independent alighting?

It is the little absences that niggle at the mind. A raven was loosed and never reported back. Did it die or remain mateless in another landing spot? Likewise, with a dove that never returned to the ark. Was it ready to lay an egg and begin evolving into a subspecies on a mountain further?

While a new covenant connection can be made between a rainbow and an empty grave, those are after-the-fact reflections. Here we are vigiling—between absence and resolution.

This may be a time to reflect on that which comes prior to these passages. Remember back to the prior instructions to Noah—take two of each kind aboard. Included in this instruction are both clean and unclean kinds. Without being able to see an olive branch, Noah proceeds.

Without seeing an open grave, may we proceed to engage those our culture deems unclean and carry them in the ark of our life and care. In this way, we are recapitulating an important part of our Noachian tradition and awaiting a resolution of our drifting present after a dramatic and traumatic loss. This embrace of the unclean is as important a vigiling act as lighting a candle.

Genesis 11:1–9
Energy to Witness

Trying to take control in order to be on top inevitably leads to confusion. Take a look at any political process, even democratic ones, and it becomes apparent that common interest soon loses out to partisanship. We can claim we are after the same goal and even use the same words to describe it, but when the day ends, we are suspicious of the others for wanting to succeed so desperately. We know our suspicion is well-founded because, given half-a-chance, we would be glad to take the lead among equals.

We don't need to have G*D enter the picture to deliberately set folks at odds with themselves; we do plenty well all by ourselves.

The real trick is to keep a focus on our differences that might be mobilized in the same direction. When our differences can be brought to bear on a subject, we are able to make better decisions than when we are assuming we are all on the same page, only to find we are not. This is a huge benefit to a consensus process that intentional interim ministry teaches so well.

A value of Pentecostal language is its appreciation of different languages and the perspectives they bring to the table. To try to share with someone else what is so very important to you, when they obviously speak differently, is to search for our common humanity.

What, then, is so important that you would be willing to learn a new language to be able to share it? Or is it only important enough for you to repeat it and repeat it in your own personal language with no concern whether or not it is heard?

---

god and adam and eve	farsi english and swahili
talked each evening	yuwaalaraay hindi and aymaran
there was agreement	blue white-collared and moneyed
understanding	child teen and adult
and yet	and yet
a babelsnake	a babelfish
was able to confuse	enlightens our differences
them about one another	with a gift of a new brainwave

[Never mind that Douglas Adams claims, "Meanwhile, the poor Babel fish, by effectively removing all barriers between communications, has caused more and bloodier wars than anything else in existence."]

Genesis 15:1–6
Proper 14 (19)

Imagine G*D satiated. G*D has had it up to here with what G*D had thought would be a good thing—sacrifice. Stop, already! The sacrificial system only leads to expectations of getting more—in this case, Abram getting biological descendants.

There is no covering up who we are with the fanciest of offerings. When some cosmic bottom-line is measured, it won't be a matter of how much sacrificial blood is spilt but how much harm was avoided and how much good was initiated.

If we are willing to make this shift from sacrifice, the good of the land will more than flow in to fill whatever good we have sent forth. If we are not willing to make this shift, that which we have not held back (harm) will be as garlic mustard, teasel, and emerald ash borer in the American Midwest—invasive and uncontrolled.

Time's up. Still trying to substitute something in place of seeking justice? Forget it. The argument is over—it's justice or nothing.

---

purell kimcare provon
were too late on the market
for Lady Macbeth and preemptive warriors
who wring bloodless bloody hands

a next entrepreneurial opportunity
is not covering up what is already there
but a preventive cleansing
to keep purell from being needed in the first place

pure-el calls forth a new desire
to be elseways than el has been
and in turn to have el's images
transformed in our lifetime

Genesis 15:1–12, 17–18
Conviction [2]

Remember: "Belief" is not a head trip or an assent to a doctrine or creed. "Belief" is an action. Abram "lived as if" G*D's promise of descendants were true already. This living-as-if was Abram's righteousness.

It is very easy to get caught up in the ritual of slaughtering and dividing animals. Do note that G*D simply requested the presence of animals, Creati*n's witnesses, just as later there will be traditions of Jesus born in a manger with the witness of animals. It was Abram who proceeded to sacrifice the animals and who would later be all too ready to sacrifice Isaac. It is difficult to get rid of our personal and cultural baggage and to mis-hear G*D—it's been going on since Adam.

Note also that G*D came into the picture again after Abram was exhausted from keeping the carrion-cravers at bay. G*D came in the dark of night, in the evening of a next day.

I imagine that the smoking fire pot and flaming torch passed between the pieces of animals asking forgiveness, bringing restoration, and anticipating Ezekiel's valley of dry bones.

May you live-as-if into a new morning of a next day without carrying the burden of personal and cultural needs for sacrifice.

---

walking between the pieces of our lives
the divisions that keep us from being whole
we are worn down and out
even going so far as to defend our divisions
sacrificed for what seemed like good reason at the time
    it isn't until we get to dream-time
    we finally set aside
    needing to be in charge
    able to let flame and smoke
    travel where they will
        can we make sense of it
        beyond a wanted reward
        of nation upon nation
        added to our revenue stream
        nope, we'll settle for any reward
            bloody scenes verify
            our fear of trust
            our need for reward
            to lighten the dark
            we carry even in victory

Our behavior sensitizes us to more or fewer options. Our associations shape our involvement.

When we participate in deceit, we are less able to hear and respond to teachings and opportunities to practice honest dealings. In this way, our behavior limits our reception of a word of health and healing and common-wealth.

A lack of imagination of how we might have a better present and future than we do is as deadly as a famine of bread or a drought of water.

When our behavior pushes us toward a larger hospitality, our ears are opened to our deep-heart's desire. What we hear as G*D's creative word, still enlarging our life, brings with it moments of conversion that can last a lifetime and more.

———————————

let me bring you a little bread
let me under-weigh a little grain

between these two
lie a chasm
requiring
amazing grace
to bridge

let me bring you a little bread
let me pile high a little more grain

Genesis 18:20–32
Proper 12 (17)

How great is the outcry! How great the sin! The inhospitability! The injustice! How tempting to pull it all up, even if it takes any elseway opportunity with it.

How important it is to remember Gomer, as well as Hosea, and their children, who become more than their beginning! In so doing, we hear G*D engaging G*D with an internal dialogue between discontent and promise.

We hear echoes of G*D's self-reflection through the vehicle of Abraham—"Shall I go into Sodom and know her children as my own? Are pity and adoption my hallmarks, or not? If one of my own goes astray, will I take out my loss on others?"

It is so tempting to have our fantasy—you are not mine!—cemented for all time. It is so blessed to have this same fantasy redeemed in real life.

---

it takes two to whore around
whether that be macro
with G*D and Sodom
or micro
any two Gomers and Hoseas

then we freeze-frame a moment
and name it abomination
not yours
not mine
not any

forgetting a first word
is not a last word
yes, you
yes, me
yes, all

so look again
in your bag of tricks
for not only the old
familiar approbation
but a new beginning

Genesis 22:1–18
Hopeless Hope Vigil

Creation stories come in a variety of guises. There are those that build and those that transition. Here is a creation story in reverse.

A chaotic deep is not a given. Here, chaos comes as a deliberate test, not a state of affairs. Promises have been given. Life is moving along.

Then comes G*D, like Mary Poppins with chaos in her wake. Delete my promise and your reward. Kill your son, your gateway to a multitude of descendants (forgetting Ishmael, of course). This command brings dissonance. It is chaotic and a way to madness.

Who is resurrected here? G*D? Abraham? Isaac?

It is easy to see this as a new beginning for Isaac. We can even see it for Abraham (except for those tales that have Sarah giving him the silent treatment because of what he was willing to do). Can you see this as a resurrection of G*D who had forgotten to show steadfast love and, instead, demanded it of another?

Finally, G*D comes around, even as G*D also plays an excuse game, saying they can see that Abraham intended to kill, and that was good enough. Sometimes a resurrection simply puts us back to square one.

Genesis 32:22–31
Proper 24 (29)

Into the midst of trepidation that all Jacob knew was coming to an end (his past had caught up with him, and there would be no choosing of doors to escape), Jacob has a dream realer-than-real.

A wrestling ensues until a hip is dislocated, leaving no way to gain leverage upon a strong foundation. There was only limping around an altar of past success.

The contest had gone on long enough that evening was becoming morning. In the end, there is an end to wrestling. In this end, there is neither victory nor defeat but mutual blessing.

We are renamed, reoriented, reanimated. Imagine what it would be like in your world if a word finally came to you, "You have striven with G*D and Neighb*r, and have lasted."

In coming through, we, too, would want to know our contender's name—that we might rename them. Though a name is not revealed here, Charles Wesley later penned a poem, "Wrestling Jacob", turned into a hymn, "Come, O Thou Traveler Unknown" (386 and 387 in *The United Methodist Hymnal* of 1989). Here, Charles' conclusion is, "thy nature and thy name is Love." Though not included in current versions of the hymn, the 14th and concluding stanza runs:

> Lame as I am, I take the prey,
> hell, earth, and sin with ease overcome;
> I leap for joy, pursue my way,
> and as a bounding hart fly home,
> through all eternity to prove
> thy nature, and thy name is Love.

In days of discouragement, of wars and rumors of war, and of great community splits threatened and happening, a challenge is to reveal in our life the nature and name of Love that will not let us go nor escape our grasp, even should the night darken or the morning be afar.

———————————

You are encouraged to read *Thy Nature & Thy Name Is Love: Wesleyan and Process Theologies in Dialogue*, edited by Bryan P. Stone & Thomas Jay Oord.

Genesis 45:3–11, 15
Guiding Gift [7]

It is after the weeping that we can talk. Before the weeping, there is power to attend to. Power to cut off and send away. Power to accumulate for one's self and one's own. Power to have authority over others.

Use of power eventually brings us to a time of weeping without explanation or excuse—just weeping. What is there to say beyond excuse and justification for the way we exploit the earth and one another?

If we are going to claim we are where we are for the protection of particular people and resources, there must come a prior question of "sacredness". If there is nothing of intrinsic worth within a person or land, there is nothing worth protecting. If there is worth present, our very act of protecting it, weakens it. Quite the paradox.

It is at this point that the story being told has huge holes as well as deep significance. The next five years will see the population reduced to poverty, in debt to the ruler of its day. The farmers will move to share-cropping. The gap between the wealthy and the poor will dramatically increase.

On what basis do we claim a benefit of right of place for ourselves and our own kind?

How might Joseph have wept for the Egyptian poor as well as the desperate straits of his family of origin? Is this not the process of political gamesmanship—weep privately before one group and show strength elsewhere?

Imagine Joseph not closing the door and creating a secret with his brothers. Such openness may have led to rebellion and revolt. It may also have led to an open community that could arrive at a better solution than bigger barns for the wealthy and loss of land for the poor.

Be thankful for a reunited family. Continue mourning for lost nations that will enslave and, in turn, be enslaved.

---

  a lost boy made good
  and did the best he could
   some was made right
   and others went wrong
    rejoicing with fat cats
    requires rejoicing with lean calves
     lost boys are not found
     until all that has been lost is found

Exodus 12:1–4, (5–10), 11–14
Courage Thursday

Tracking a beginning is very tricky.

Was Jesus' last Passover meal a beginning or did it begin with his baptism or temptations or miracles or signs or Temple confrontations or showing up the priestly class?

Does Israel's first month of the year depend on the last of the plagues or did it begin with a babe on the water or a murder or burning bush or a hardened heart?

Where is your marker for your life? Was it an economic turnaround, a lottery ticket, a relationship beginning or ending, a death of a significant person in your life, or your own brush with mortality?

Presuming you can identify your own personal turning point, how do you celebrate it? A feast? With cake and candles? And will others carry that on?

Blessings on identifying your beginning point and the point before that. Eventually, you'll get back to a slight moment before a big bang —how mysterious that there is something rather than nothing. Rejoice and move on.

Exodus 14:10–31; 15:20–21
Hopeless Hope Vigil

Here is yet another creation story—one that moves through the deep of chaos. Where the wind and spirit of G*D once moved over the face of the deep, it now penetrates to the bowels of the deep.

Fear rising from behind us, from all our accumulated yesterdays, makes every situation ultimate. Here we are, caught between a devil and a deep blue sea disguised as a marshy reed sea. We look back, and all our mistakes are hot on our tail. We are about to reap the consequences of each past misstep or return to a slavery that, at least, was known.

Our fear fixates us on our fear. We can only look back over our shoulder and walk in circles. Our fear keeps us from looking ahead, even if it is dangerous. We blind ourselves to what we may yet do today to have a different tomorrow rise in our midst.

A resurrection of escape comes as we put our past behind us for a moment and look onward. A breathing exercise can help us see beyond our current sense of being trapped.

Notice something not quite as it was? Here is an opportunity to breathe in for a slow count to 5 (easy to keep track of on one hand). As we hold for another slow count to 5, we can check to see if there has been a slight shift on the outside or our inside. We can now smoothly breathe out for another slow count of 5. As we wait for another 5, we can do another check. This process can be repeated until we are calm enough to affirm that things, now, are not as they were. I am, now, not as I was.

With this recognition of an ever-so-small shift, we can continue our intentional breathing to affirm on an in-breath, "The past is the past." While holding that breath, we can confirm, "Grass grows through cement." On our slow out-breath that feeds the trees, we can affirm, "A new way is open." As we let that take form, we can affirm, "I am ready now."

At some point, dark waters, breath-by-breath, part. The waters part just enough.

Having made one more transition, we glance back at our fear to see how small it was.

Look. Breathe. 1..2..3..4..5. Wait. Move. Glide across the floor. Onward. Another fear? Look. Breathe ...

Exodus 15:1b–13, 17–18
Hopeless Hope Vigil

Here we celebrate being brought out in order to be brought in.

If that takes the doing-in of others, so be it. When we work from a vision of "warrior", we live with a calculus of some lives deemed more valuable than others. In this way, we set up structures that justify the cost of victory.

It is difficult to discern whether a heroic warrior is endemic to the Universe or if that is a model preferred by people in duress as an acceptable rescuer. Anything less than a warrior means our danger wasn't as great as we made it out to be, and we could have handled it ourselves. In many ways, we prefer to be rescued rather than participate in our own release and journey decisions. When something goes awry, we have a built-in blame target—a too-weak warrior.

It is this dynamic of blame that rises to the fore in the darkness. We have experienced a great captivity to our lost hope, our abandonment. While there was plenty of information that Saviors always fall as their work is always from below, we were never able to incorporate it into our everyday life. We were either never believing it was going to work out or fantasizing about a jump to perfection.

When our expectation of privilege so dramatically failed, we flipped our digital response from participant in life to helpless and lost, needing saving.

A question here: Will anything less than a full-blown victory by a fierce warrior bring long-term health for the individual parts and the whole of Creati*n?

Play these two back and forth:

- G*D, in Jeremiah's mouth, comes out as destruction (once decided, always decided).

- G*D, in relation to Moses, comes out as remover of destruction (twice thought, a different decision).

Now we need to wonder whether one of these models is standard or if they are contextually driven. As I look over the breadth of G*D's story as it comes through the Bible, thinking twice is more often the case. This seems to be because of a prior decision never finally gone back on—steadfast love. Sometimes, the remembering and rethinking of this takes more time than people have in their lives, but rethinking does occur.

Whether Moses or Jeremiah in their settings, or you and I in ours, it is appropriate to ask for a second thought in light of a first thought to experience and enact steadfast love. Imagine what would happen if the church-institutional or any congregation were to re-ask every question they have been faced with in the last 10 years in light of imitating G*D's steadfast love in their context. Would they then be freed to make a different response to a current decision?

---

one messenger reports
Moses tried to calm his God down
think twice was the call

and this great G*D
backed off angry threats
deciding not to destroy

as messengers report
about my life and trials
is G*D calmer for my presence

Exodus 34:29–35
Mountain Top to Valley

When in deep conversation with G*D, self, or other, we aren't always aware of the difference it is making in us. One way or another, deep conversation sets off fires within that cannot be hidden.

There are changes that occur in deep conversation that affect every relationship we have, including with the one with whom we have had a deep conversation. Fear, from ourselves or another, is not an unexpected response to a significant change that has happened.

There really isn't any way to cover over the consequences of a deep conversation. This, of course, is one reason more such conversations don't go on—our preemptive fear cuts them off before change becomes necessary.

Are there some conversations you've been meaning to have that you've avoided for fear, yours or another's, that the result would be devastating to business as usual, would transfigure/transform your life and the life of the world?

If we were dealing with the Seventh Sunday of Epiphany (Genesis 45:3–11, 15), we would look at the issue of how other forms of presence can be as dismaying as Moses'—as when Joseph reveals himself to his brothers. Here, deep secrets that have been kept are a veil that needs to be lifted, not a deep conversation.

From whichever way we come at this issue of having one's face or one's family transfigured, this is a significant issue in a culture of fear —wars, disagreement equated with treason, management by leaks, etc. Transfiguration may be one of our yet-available tools to make a difference.

---

introverted Moses
finds energy
in mountain-top
get-aways

extroverted Joseph
finds energy
in intra-personal
relationships

sparks fly
when energy is found
to light one's face
to light another's

it's time
engage energy
inner and outer
for transfiguration

transformation
of self
for edification
for reconciliation

Numbers 6:22–27
Naming Day

We often talk about the importance of the name of Jesus. In and of itself, it is inconsequential. Let's shift, for a moment, away from naming Jesus to what Jesus might name as his life-work—to reveal Blessing as constituent of a Way with G*D.

Christmas angels and Baptismal doves and Locked Room fires still echo down the years, "Thus you shall bless." Does that sound like Jesus? Listen to him saying to you and to all,

> Bless you.
> I affirm you.
> A light of grace surround you.
> A smile of peace be yours.

This, then, becomes a common journey of those on a Way with G*D.

Don't just bless or glorify Jesus' name. As Jesus reminds us, while saying "Jesus, Jesus, Jesus", it still takes $4+ to get a cup of Starbucks and is no heavenly ticket. Rather, name and live Jesus' way—be blessed and bless.

Numbers 21:4b–9
Relic Day

How to train your *saraph* (fiery, winged dragon) is an age-long question, far older than a recent movie. Here we have sympathetic magic through an analogous form. In other writings, we are commanded not to make idols, but this recounting has the practical effect of another command to "make a serpent" (see 2 Kings 18:4 to see that the made serpent was worshiped as an idol).

Later, a cross-lifted Jesus is remembered and repurposed as an extension of a Snake-On-A-Stick (sounds like a State Fair treat). Do you ever wonder what a G*D prescription for snakes would have looked like in Eden? [Extra Credit: Recount G*D's presence on an exodus from Eden to Abram's place.]

Would you claim that the copper snakes found at Meneiyeh (ancient Timnah) were relics of this pique of G*D sending snakes and later their antidote? Why would finding splinters of a "cross" carry any more weight? (Oh, right, it's our story.) Are we that reliant upon the equivalent of Dumbo's feather to find our way to life? Would such a sacred relic be anything more than a religious placebo?

Knowing the power of suggestion, it is important to not discount this telling of an experience but to listen behind it for an insight into the dynamics of some current situation we are facing. This strange-to-us story has its reality and teaching moment if we are willing to meditate on its use, appropriate and inappropriate.

Deuteronomy 26:1–11
Conviction [1] — Thanksgiving

Are you in a place that G*D chooses to call a "home"?

If so, reflection on an appropriate acknowledgment is in order. What, beyond an investment of your resources (standing for your life), will you incorporate into your affirmation? Be clear about your confession or litany of markers that led you to this place (or vocation/work or family/friends or play/service).

It will be critical to your remembrance of your history to include "the foreigner living with you." The odds are that someone outside of your claim of space is a descendant of a defeated and evicted people with a moral claim, if not legal, on the very gifts you offer to G*D in thanksgiving.

When scripture is honored, it brings with it a larger awareness and disjuncture with the status quo.

What might happen if Thanksgiving met Lent halfway between, say on July 4th, and the three sat down for a beer and reflection on this passage?

- Would there be any repentance amid or prior to rejoicing?

- Would pride or privilege ignore any questions of their place?

- Would the result of their conversation be an enlargement of "home" for either G*D, foreigners, or themselves?

Deuteronomy 30:9–14
Proper 10 (15)

Questions of authority abound. They are the currency of power—held and desired. Those who can most successfully question another's authority are able to claim authority. We contend over our questions.

Is authority a conveyance that moves from captured or established authority to whoever will keep it in place? Is authority an integrated whole rising from within to bless and challenge current authority?

This curious word "authority" plays on several levels. Going back through its usage, it began by meaning to increase and thus to create (to author).

In today's world, authority might be thought of as that which decreases and thus controls. As you think about your life, what authority do you bring—an inner authority to increase or an outer authority to decrease, to rein in? The difference is crucial, and the choices we make regarding our authority are reflections on our engagement with life.

So, take thou authority...

––––––––––––––––––––

a commandment
that is not a commandment
is not too far away
too high or too wide

this commandment
is not a commandment
for it touches our depths
becomes our own

Deuteronomy 30:15–20
Proper 18 (23)

Jesus' statements of "You have heard it said, but . . ." remind us that G*D's nickname is "Freedom". During "Arab Spring", the *New York Times* reviewed 14 days in Egypt. Key is a statement by the then newly released Wael Ghonim. After being kidnapped by government forces and held for 12 days, he said, "This is not the time to settle scores. Although I have people I want to settle scores with myself. This is not the time to split the pie and enforce ideologies."

Here is a choice as stark as those between the scripturally heightened rhetoric of "Life and Good" or "Death and Evil" or "Fire and Water". Here we have "Violence and Retribution" or "Freedom and Cooperation".

We have heard of and lived in cultures of "Power Over", and again we see the gift of "Freedom Growing" from beneath. After remembering an old Egyptian poem, "The Nile can bend and turn, but what is impossible is that it would ever dry up," Professor Mamoun Fandy remarked, "The same is true of the river of freedom that is loose here now. Maybe you can bend it for a while, or turn it, but it is not going to dry up."

The choice to be free, to hear "you have heard it said, but . . ." is basic to life and therefore to G*D and therefore to us as a goal. To not choose beyond enforced consistency is the hobgoblin of little lives (no matter how large they project themselves).

Simply put, we have not been commanded to side with or be wicked, nor have we been given permission to tear down others to aggrandize our self. We are in this together. I rejoice when you can stand tall for the Freedom of G*D [rendered into Ye Olde English as "Kingdom of G*D"] right where you are. It encourages me to stand tall where I am and to return the favor.

A G*D of Freedom again sets before us a choice: settle scores or build new blessings.

Conviction [4]

Here I am working out of ignorance. What is the Passover tradition during the Exodus? Do we go from Egypt to the plains of Jericho without a Passover? Can quail, manna, and sand substitute for lamb, unleavened bread, and bitter herbs? Given the importance of Passover in the Jewish tradition, are there equivalent periods without Christmas, Good Friday, or Easter in the Christian tradition (perhaps the first 100 years)? What about Coke® and Twinkies® for bread and wine? Are rituals dependent upon the congregants, if not the priests, so injustice trumps kosher, as the prophets claim?

I'm not even sure what to make of these questions? Do they go to the heart of something, or are they entirely beside any point?

In most other arenas, I speculate more freely with a modicum of supposed information. Here, without a base to build from, I am stymied.

Time to ask. Anyone, have any info? And, will I believe it if I hear it?

A look could be taken at circumcision or the restart of Passover observances, but right now I'm fixated on the Exodus/Passover question. If we paid attention, we may even find that our various fixations on supposedly better-known pieces of information lead us to equally stuck places. From a point of either too little or too much information, we do not find a fruitful place for midrash.

---

dear g*d help
my unbelief
my disbelief
my ignorance
my surety

and in helping
leave room
for all the above

together
to gather
new life

1 Samuel 2:1–10
Elizabeth and Mary Meet

There is not much new under the sun. Variations upon themes and a periodic mutation that shifts a theme seem to be the order of the day. This is one of the reasons it is important to choose mentors wisely. You will become a variant of them. Were you part of a tradition that would choose a confirmation name from the saints of old? It was a significant exercise to try to discern who would be an intended model for you to draw near to as you encounter new occasions and duties of today.

Are the words from Mary in Luke or Hannah in 1 Samuel unique? No. A more difficult question: Are they mine, as well? Note how a religious or spirit understanding has real-world implications. To come at this from the side, rather than head-on, re-read *Common Sense* by Thomas Paine and see if that helps locate you next to Mary and Hannah. We are talking revolution here.

1 Samuel 2:18–20, 26
Blessed Body [1]

Footnotes are often where the action is. Note verse 20 where the NRSV text reads, "the gift that she made to the Lord", and the footnote has an alternative reading of "the gift that she asked of the Lord."

If we play a bit with another footnote, the *New Interpreter's Study Bible* notes a going back to Samuel's name in 1:20. Saul's name is also found within the letters of "Samuel" which has led some to consider this to have been a beginning birth story for Saul (like the Christmas story is for Jesus) to respond to the question, "Where did his greatness come from?"

The note goes on to indicate this is an ironic situation for the "people", in turn, "asked of" Samuel for Saul when Samuel was the leader they needed, not Saul.

We run into some of that same irony with Christ and Christian. People are always looking for something beyond what is already available to them—loving grace. Here, Christians have to keep justifying their existence in terms of the limits of the Bible, and so few can see that even greater things than Christ's are available through Christians who attend to the revelation of Holy Spirit and change their too-easy judgments about sin and mercy.

I'm sure this kind of thinking makes folks just a little skittery and anxious about heresy. The point here is that you are in good company—Samuel was rejected; Jesus was rejected; you are being rejected because of the openness to new life you bring. So, hang in there, literally and figuratively; there are bigger things to be. Here in Christmas is a foretaste of Easter.

2 Samuel 11:26–12:10, 13–15
Proper 6 (11)

Leadership led astray by its own sense of divine right and might-makes-right is no new story. A little preemption here, a little privilege there, and pretty soon, underlying arrogance and exclusion from responsibility begin to show through.

No matter how you cut it, the missing verses (12:11–12) sum it up —"you think you acted in secret, but the consequences of your actions will be noted."

The national parallels from long-ago to today are striking. There is nothing new under the sun. What may be less noticed is how the responsible parties are not just the leaders but, in a democracy, also you and I. We have conspired together—leaders and people—to steal property, to press our advantage, to dissemble, to plot with lies.

How far can you draw out the parallels before you are accused of meddling and subject to the same end as Naboth and Uriah? Is it worth that end to bring lies to light? How about simply calling out, "Enough! Torture is torture—no matter what any rationale permitting torture might suggest." War is war—no matter how it is justified.

How long can we avoid drawing out the parallels before we lose our ability to follow in Nathan's footsteps? What penalty will we receive if we do not raise the questions? What justification can we give if we allow another to be wounded because we failed to enlighten the leaders through the only means sometimes available, a court jester's tale?

Whether put winsomely like Nathan or bluntly like Elijah, we are to speak truth to power.

1 Kings 8:22–23, 41–43
Guiding Gift [9] — Proper 4 (9)

There are a couple of helpful progressions here.

From the ark surrounded by priests (v 6) to
    the inner sanctuary (v 10) to
       heaven and highest heaven (v 27),
    the presence of G*D expands.

From Solomon, the Lord's servant, (v 28) to
    Israel (v 30) to
       foreigners (v 41),
    all will be heard by G*D.

Where are individual congregations, whole denominations, and generic religion with these expansions? Are we still moving forward or retrenching? It feels like the orthodox and creedal emphases these days are moving us in reverse order, contracting the pattern from creation to my house to having G*D in my pocket and narrowing us from all people to my people to me.

Pray with Solomon and do better than he did after he finished praying.

1 Kings 17:8–16, (17–24)
Proper 5 (10)

In the midst of Baal-worshiping Phoenicians, Elijah found G*D at work. Elijah appealed to the ancient virtue of hospitality—first make me, the traveler, a little something from your less-than-little supply.

When the virtue held, the blessing came; eyes were opened to see an abundance that was overlooked before.

How might we continue to offer the gift of hospitality beyond any scarcity-fear of our own? Has the church lost this gift of hospitality among its own members, as well as an offering for others? What are we afraid of when we turn our LGBTQ sisters and brothers away from the little we have? What are we afraid of when we retreat from literally standing alongside the poor? Are we afraid of contagion or compassion?

This morning, we are training our greeters and ushers in some of the attitudes and actions of hospitality. A part of that will be a sensitivity to be on hospitality-duty (though that is a less than felicitous way of putting it) even when not listed as a greeter or usher for the day.

Do you believe that going out of your way for another is simply what you are to do? Have you been taken advantage of too many times to risk it again? Do you know you have enough, and more, to share?

This gift can be learned from those who do hospitality best—the outcast and the poor. G*D observes this in the "widows". May G*D observe this gift in you and me.

1 Kings 17:17–24
Proper 5 (10)

The woman who fed Elijah might well expect a reward for giving up her last food. She might have felt relief, hope, joy after finding her larder restored and perpetually re-filled. Such privilege!

And then ... it happened ... her son fell sick ... died.

"What have you brought against me? Are my sins not forgiven/forgotten, but punished/retained? Was your secret mission to kill my son?"

These may well have been questions in the mind of Sarah when Abraham took Isaac to a place of sacrifice. They may well be yours, as well.

If this is not just a set-up to show off Elijah, how might we engage it?

Consider these questions to be variants of the religious classification of the "Nones". Their experience of the church does not accord with the aspects of life they consider to be real and of importance to them. A current Elijah would be seen as only bringing condemnation and restriction on life; certainly not life in fullness.

> As you experience your current culture, what sign of new life needs to be given?

> For whom would you "beg of" or what would you "bargain for" from G*D?

> How do you expect your begging or bargaining to be received?

Monotheism is a blood sport. Winner takes all, including the lives of any challengers. The same happens whenever someone messes with our source of happiness that we locate in an external security or affirmation or control.

It is easy to get caught up in an attitude of, "Anything you can do, I can do better".

It is difficult to get out of the implication of genocide once I have tasted the privilege of a promised land or my due. Anything, anything, that gets in the way is fair game to be steamrolled.

---

this land ain't big enough
for both of us, Pardner
sheep and cattle don't mix
so will it be
fence or free

I'll give you 'til sundown
to get out of town, Friend
or it's the OK Corral
where the fastest gun
puts out another's sun

there is no middle ground
you're simply wrong, Pal
my might cancels your right
you have no escape
but to change your shape

so we come to disaster
each divided from each
each lonely in their cave
waiting beyond wind
to recast a win

1 Kings 19:1–4, (5–7), 8–15a
Proper 7 (12)

Just two chapters ago (17:2–4), G*D's presence led Elijah forth to Wadi Cherith, there to be fed by ravens, and mere verses later to be fed for a long time by a widow who only had a handful of flour left (miracle upon miracle). Now, Elijah runs away on his own, only to be fed by angels. This raises questions in our own life about how long ago we experienced being fed and what our expectation is about a next feeding. [This question is real for all aspects of our self—body, mind, spirit, relationships, ...]

It is so easy to forget the blessings that have brought us to a testing moment. So it is that Elijah despairs so much that he could only sleep his life away and couldn't eat. Again, Elijah is sustained, this time by angels (just ravens by another spelling?)

It is so easy to exaggerate one's troubles of the moment and to lose perspective. Sometimes it takes quite a while (40 days plus) and quite a distance (as much as 600 to 1,000 walking miles, depending on terrain) to regather perspective.

Finally comes a bottom-line question: "What are you doing where you are?"

When we hear our poor excuse of a response, a click of recognition can come—"I am not alone. I have a life to live and a task to accomplish." Simple statements; both. And so we go forth to lay the groundwork for a next generation. Whether they are able to prepare for the next after them is beside the point. Our call is ours.

We have gotten ourselves and one another in another fine mess (think Laurel and Hardy). There may be nothing more to do than to find one other to mentor to better health than we have that they might be ready to carry on. To keep our soul alive, we give it to another that they might do what we cannot.

A mantle of power (covering term is "spirit") is very attractive and addictive. It is an equivalent of a ring in Tolkien's major work.

Of course, the implication is that Elisha would use a mantle of power for good, while Golem would use a ring of power for ill.

The first use Elisha makes of the mantle he "earned" by keeping his eye on it is to ease his own travel, to make a way where there wasn't a way, to have dominion over the waters. In so doing, Elisha effectively tests whether the power is a residual one (left-over G*D, unused by Elijah) or has become his that can be used without the mantle (can Dumbo fly without his feather).

Like it or not, we all have more power (whether vested in mantle, ring, money, position, or whatever) than we like to acknowledge. A key question is what are we doing with the power we have, even before a potential doubling of it?

---

tricks and techniques
are still an order of the day
to implement
to demonstrate
to accumulate
power and more power

slogans and mantras
motivational posters
focus our attention
blocking out questions
transforming everything
into a tool my tool

1 Kings 21:1–10, (11–14), 15–21a
Proper 6 (11)

"Sinner" is a temporal categorization. At different times, sin is differently defined. Regardless of a current definition of sinner, sin is usually defined as an act of commission. When sins of omission around a current definition are also considered, we all end up on a sin continuum.

So it is here: Naboth claimed his own identity, and Ahab claimed control over Naboth's identity. In today's rapidly changing experiences of sexual orientation, those who play the scripture card to claim those attracted to others of their same sex are automatically sinners are here represented by Ahab. Those who claim their inheritance of sexual identity are in Naboth's role.

Naboth speaks for women in a patriarchal system, for African slaves brought to the Americas and elsewhere, Native peoples anywhere, or any group dismissed by the powers that be—"I will not give over my identity."

The powers that be who do not allow people a place at a table of community or decision-making will eventually hear, "You have sown the seed of your own destruction."

If you have privilege within a power system, no matter how small it may seem to you, and you remain silent, you are complicit in every form of Ahab against Naboth. Divest from the perk of silence. Speak your support of "Naboth" to your current "Ahab". Do not continue allowing the power of some to define the sin of others.

2 Kings 2:1–2, 6–14
Proper 8 (13)

Just a while ago, we heard that Elijah heard a silence. How would this story be different if Elijah had left in silence instead of in a whirlwind?

As it is, we might re-look at the silence story and understand that G*D was in the earthquake and storm. The problem was that Elijah was so stormy on the inside that the external storms couldn't be experienced in their fullness, only as an extension of himself. Here, the "other" needed silence to be recognized.

Now, with Elijah and the reader prepared for silence, a whirlwind returns. What do you make of a G*D who doesn't stick to one mode of interaction but is constantly tricking us (a little something picked up in a wrestle with Jacob?).

This now-you-see-it-now-you-don't continues with Elisha. The narrator shows us a picture where Elijah is lifted away by a whirlwind, gyring him to heaven. Elisha got distracted by fiery chariots and horses and couldn't take his eyes off them to see the tornadic energy behind them, the whirlwind.

Of course, if we have to make every part of the scriptures cohere, we can always state that there was a whirlwind of fiery chariots and horses rather than have the chariots and horses simply come between Elijah and Elisha as a veil of mystery at every time of death. We are always missing a whirlwind of spirit within another—our own is so blustery and distracting.

At any rate, the mantle of Elijah has fallen from Elisha and all subsequent prophets and is awaiting your picking it up and striding through the boundaries of your life to join the continued work of prophecy—Love Prevails!

2 Kings 5:1–3, 7–15c
Proper 23 (28)

A diseased winner. A star with a visible fault. A sinning saint. However you characterize Naaman, there is no getting away from his accomplishments (G*D granted?) or his limitations (also G*D granted?). If we are going to accord activity or responsibility in one arena, can we keep it from both?

As we listen in, where a king finds their limit and stops acting like a god, we find an opening for a prophet differentiated enough from G*D to know something about the basic healthfulness of seven deep cleansing baths in the Jordan River (note the number as a completedness and the location as a boundary/entrance to a promised land/healing).

It would be easy to leave this matter with an offer of a Thanks Offering. At least note that Naaman will return to another setting in which he will be required to be in the presence of "idolatry", and Elisha gives a blessing to do so.

We struggle with our partnering with G*D while attending to a variety of gods in our life. How we parse out G*D, God, and god makes a difference.

May you be generous in your blessing of "Peace" to those whose lives remain enmeshed in Gods and gods.

2 Kings 5:1–14
Proper 9 (14)

It takes a village to heal a person.
In this village, healing includes

- those who have an inside track to processes that lead to healing,
- those who facilitate getting to the right spot for healing,
- those who are resistant to images of healing because of the bind it puts them in,
- those who have a point to be made through the healing process,
- those who need to be in charge of their own healing,
- those who can talk truth to power,
- those who are healed who need to validate their healing through some shift of a gift to a commodity to be bought and sold, and
- those who take advantage of the healed.

How is it in your village? Are folks mobilized to teach about healing and point a direction where it might be found? Are folks ready to provide the openness needed to allow a new way of understanding? Are folks prepared to give up their control of the healing processes?

Where does some form of universal health care fit into your village? How do we deal with the regularization of healing, we might simply call curing, and how do we set free a gift of healing beyond the limit of cure? Is healing to prove something to enemies, free for all (including enemies), and/or limited to one's own kind?

Having been through this with an individual focus, how do we begin to talk about the healing of systems?

Nehemiah 8:1–3, 5–6, 8–10
Guiding Gift [3]

We can get very ritualistic about special days. Yesterday was both an American presidential inauguration public ceremony and Martin Luther King, Jr. Day. Back much further was Ezra/Nehemiah Day. What is not so easily kept in mind are the movie credits that scroll after people leave the theater. We get what we came for and presume we are entitled to all the work of the many it took to provide it. We are entertained and leave. You might want to try staying all the way through the credits as a spiritual discipline of thanksgiving through a witnessing of names.

The elided verses in today's reading remind us of the mundane (someone built the presentation platform) and the sublime (there were interpreters, translators, to help folks understand what was in that strange and wonderful book of yore). Carpenters and linguists, what a combo, each played their part.

Imagine a movie is being made of your congregation, your community; where would you show up in the credits? This may be where the enduring strength of religion lies: each person doing their part with their gift. Religion begins to slip when the credits are shortened to the pastor and/or board. A community begins to falter when the mayor and/or council become director and no one else need be mentioned. In his 2012 inauguration speech, President Obama had a couple of refrains. One refrain pertinent to this passage (particularly verses 4 and 7) is "We . . . the people." The conclusion of that speech points to the work needed to hear an ancient book in the time of Ezra and Nehemiah come alive for us:

> My oath is not so different from the pledge we
> all make to the flag that waves above and that fills our
> hearts with pride. They are the words of citizens, and
> they represent our greatest hope. You and I, as citi-
> zens, have the power to set this country's course. You
> and I, as citizens, have the obligation to shape the
> debates of our time, not only with the votes we cast,
> but the voices we lift in defense of our most ancient
> values and enduring ideas.

> Let us, each of us, now embrace with solemn
> duty, and awesome joy, what is our lasting birthright.
> With common effort and common purpose, with pas-
> sion and dedication, let us answer the call of history
> and carry into an uncertain future that precious light
> of freedom.

Job 14:1–14
Absent Saturday

Time to get out paper and pencil (or fountain pen—my latest is an inexpensive Hero from China, though I usually use a Blue Lamy Safari 1.1 italic steel nib with Noodler's *Black Swan in English Roses* ink or a Platinum PTL-5000A with a fine gold nib and Diamine *Regency Blue* ink).

Down an edge of the paper, write the following understandings with enough space to allow for a couple of sentences between.

a flower grows only to die

in the dark shadows are absent

dirt is dirt

we die; we expire

there is no awakening the dead

Now, the tough part that may take up to 15 minutes: Reflect and write where you are experiencing these realities. Does the same response show up as a refrain in each setting? Is there a different experience for each? Where do you have several examples clamoring for attention? Where is there only silence?

Attend to your losses, your silences, until you can only sit numb. To do less is to say this Paschal Triduum is fluff, of no consequence, was maybe helpful to someone a long time ago, but not worth attending to today. No numbing loss; no surprise for you at hope's return.

Job 19:23–27a
Proper 27 (32)

prosperity is only such
for its given moment
always there has been a crash

only after said crash
do we find a new prosperity
even more prosperous

a prosperity unimaginable
without a proverbial black Monday
setting its background

look not for a new prosperity
a new heavenly image
without losing the old

it won't be a mere extension
but the more sweet
for being a quantum leap

Psalm 1
Guiding Gift [6] — Proper 18 (23)

• Happy delight: an excellent starting place.

• Yielding fruit in your time: the time for this is always now.

These two let us know we are moving toward a great-better, not yet arrived.

In this psalm is a fine play between the joy of creation and the joy of participation. When these two are active, we anticipate joy beyond joy yet to come.

Remember your joys. Live your joys. Anticipate your joys.

To take a next quantum leap:
remember joy; live joy; anticipate joy.

No matter what order you proceed through this trinity of joy, you will soon find yourself embarking on the other aspects.

An excellent start to the Psalms—an excellent start, period. Now begun, keep it rolling.

Psalm 5:1–8
Proper 6 (11)

It is wonderful to come to an understanding that I have been shown an abundance of steadfast love. Whether this abundance comes from G*D, Creati*n, Neighb*r, You, Myself, or even a mistake of mine Enemy, it is wondrous to behold.

Then comes the tricky part of what to do with such abundance. My temptation is to store it away in a big barn and to get an even bigger one, if necessary.

Once in a while, I can restate verse 8 into a more expansive reading of living with abundance: "Lead me, G*D, in justice straight from you to me to my enemies that your abundant love might be known in their lives as well."

The rest of the Psalm, as written, continues to divide those who have already received a touch of abundance from those who have not yet received that gift. The Psalmist seems to carve this moment of division into stone—the currently blessed are blessed forever, and the unblessed will ever be so.

If one can postulate a greater receptivity on the part of the Psalmist, from unheeded to heeded, what keeps them from granting the possibility of change and growth to those now deemed enemies? Would the Psalmist recognize a woman with ointment, surprising Pharisees and Jesus with an anointing, or would the door have been especially barred to her ever having such an opportunity?

Here, abundance turns out to be a curse inasmuch as it asks a huge change in relationships that is not easy to live into. May you be blessed with such a curse and the wisdom to better use it.

Psalm 8
Naming Day — New Year's Day — Live Together

From the Bottom Up

      9 - O G*D, partner, Wow!

      8 - Birds above and fish below sail their course,

      7 - beasts near and far continue their way.

      6 - We engage all that sets our context

      5 - and revel in our connection—

      4 - bringing to mind how care-full we are.

      3 - Under every light, we open again

      2 - to hear a new word beckon a new picture—

      1 - tomorrow and today together.

Psalm 14
Proper 19 (24)

The plans of the poor are easy to dismiss, mock, and confound, as they have more long-term hope than short-term power to affect a *status quo* that relies on their poverty for the economic engine of the day.

This does not suggest that there are no consequences for such oversight.

We all have heard about overthrow and revolution, whether from an external source we call G*D or the boiling over of pain from below. Such oversight (either planned misuse of the poor or their structural invisibility) runs counter to the explicit preference for the poor known in verse 5 as "the upright".

Our "devouring" of one another is one more sign that we have strayed into external sources for our happiness, our joy of life, our meaning. We cannot stop using others and removing their "Thouness". This blocks our participation in a common goal to accompany one another home to ourselves and home to G*D.

Who will bring this wholeness to our time and space? Who will re-introduce compassion to our culture? This is still a good question. Does your Pentecostal awakening contain this question that puts you back on the street rather than huddling with friends? Perhaps it is for such a time as this that this question resurfaces—Are you the one we have been waiting for to lead us one step closer to "Zion's" wholeness?

Psalm 15
Proper 11 (16)

The question of who is "in" is never-ending. It is far more informative to ask, "Who won't be welcome?" To this question, there is an easy one-word response: "Nobody."

A basic presumption here is that being made in the image of G*D means that everyone will eventually wrestle their way through the various dualistic choices set before them to choose that which is not split from itself—steadfast love with the rest of creation. To separate from others will be no more thinkable than chopping off your hand for a misdeed or going back to one misapprehension or another. Body, mind, spirit, and relationships are all in this together, and placing the blame on a hand for an intention's error is both inappropriate and ineffective.

So, see the blessing in others and accept the opportunities set before you when little things count as much as big things.

To be honorable, through and through, means living from and into the heart—from our heart to the heart of another (whether that be G*D or Neighb*r). So, how are we doing with our basic job description?

Blessed are those who . . .

   walk blamelessly (who are poor in spirit)

   speak truth from their heart (who mourn)

   do no evil to friends (who are meek)

   do not reproach neighbors (who hunger and thirst for righteousness)

   stand by their oath (who are merciful)

   do not lend money at interest (who are pure in heart)

   do not take a bribe against the innocent (who are peacemakers)

   shall not be moved (who are persecuted for their mercy)

Psalm 16
Hopeless Hope Vigil — Proper 8 (13)

My job is to be protected; your job is to protect.

Kudos to the protector and all those claiming to protect.

As long as I am protected, I'll think and say what will continue the protection, because I am held by that bond.

So far, that is working well, pleasantly enough for me, if not for all.

Tell me what I need to do to keep your protection, and that check is in the mail.

The path of life is that of protection. In your protection is my joy; in your meting out of my protection, I find pleasure forevermore.

————————————————

- Protection of my life is crucial to its continuance.
- Protection of my life limits my growth.

Blessings on telling one protection from the other and choosing well in this moment and the next.

Psalm 17:1–9
Proper 27 (32)

Verses 1–7 are an excellent affirmation of both our intent to walk in paths of mercy and our actual success in doing so. We celebrate where our talk and our walk reinforce one another.

This could be the introduction to every time of confession—we come from good stock, G*D stock. It is out of a spirit of an inter-connected and inner-connected Creati*n that we enter any acknowledgment of wandering into individualized protection and its attendant misuse of people and resources.

It is worth some contemplative time between verses 7 and 8 to see what is going on that we shift from an affirmation of partnership into a begging posture.

This is important as this is just the first part of the Psalm. In spending time here, we can find our way back to a partnership that does more than ask G*D to ambush any crouching-in-wait for us. We can actually end with a desiring that their limited vision for "more" be fulfilled. This blessing of an abundance for our enemies, lives our "talk" and brings them to a better place from which to see the limitation of "more". From here, we continue an invitation to be joined in a common vision based on better relationships with one another and all of creation.

May your next morning awakening find a renewed vision of a current day in which justice for all will be revived and a restoration of the outcast and overlooked will remake our communal home.

Psalm 19
Guiding Gift [3] — Hopeless Hope Vigil

What if creation around us is telling the glory of G*D, and we have our nose stuck so far inside our economic fears that we can't smell anything beyond decay?

What if time is telling the glory of G*D, and we are so caught in fearing a future better, but different, than our modicum of control of the past that we can't experience anything but the disorientation from riding a centrifuge repeating itself ever more quickly?

What if fear is telling the glory of G*D, and we are so caught in little preoccupying anxieties that we miss the mystery of the blessing of a larger threat focusing us and moving us beyond our fears?

What if we miss these gifts and are only left with our errors?

Well, we will have missed a gift of being able to act on the basis of resurrection and new life. We will have missed our opportunity to let kings know they are naked and to run idolaters of money and institutional survival far enough out of their comfort zone for them to catch a glimpse of life beyond their usual accumulated patterns of control and power. We will have missed the joy of simply doing what is helpful for the time and space we have available to us.

"What if" can lead us to "what now", and herein we find revival. Go ahead; make your day—be glory.

Psalm 22
Consequence Friday

One might almost think that a goodly portion of the Paschal Triduum is based on Hebrew Scripture quotes, repurposed with a twist, to make Jesus a G*D. Quoting the Psalms might make us want to take a look at them in their own right, but with these quotes, it is more likely the Gospel writers were redefining the Psalms rather than honoring them.

At best, we can play along with Nikos Kazantzakis' *Last Temptation of Christ* and remember the first temptations after Jesus' baptism were all responded to with quotes from the scriptures of Jesus' time. The quotes drive us back to the originals.

Do note the Jewish tradition to read this Psalm on Purim, a celebration of the saving of a later exiled community. Thus, Psalm 22 is a communal psalm, not an individual one; it is a psalm of community restoration, not about a Messiah.

For this year, re-view the last verses (30–31),

In such a time as this,
so live today
that a people yet unborn
will have echoes of steadfast love and
affirmations that new life is already present
if they are willing to risk their personal life for the benefit of all.

What begins as a complaint of utter forsakenness goes through a process of remembrance that hearkens back and back to a time of deeper belonging.

Now, with both that memory and a current dilemma, we work our way through all our usual patterns. Finally, again, we re-engage our previous relationship with G*D and Universe. We return to a proclamation of creation's community where, together, we are in this endeavor of living, and we cannot leave any behind—particularly those who have been systematically reduced by conspiracy and circumstance, the poor.

This remembrance and proclamation hold us through the rest of this fragment of a Psalm. With these, we have set a foundation for the concluding verses of that which is still to come—a wider fulfillment of preemptive mercy, prevenient grace, and saving justice. Each of these is a small and yet quantum step beyond personal privilege and power.

Psalm 23
Assured [4]

The *New Community Bible* notes this Psalm "glides easily from the metaphor of the shepherd to the metaphor of the host."

We, too, find ourselves in the everyday world with all its ups and downs. Since we are patterning people, we are able to see a thread of life running through everything, even death. We sense a shepherd, some cosmic assurance that all manner of states of being shall be well and weller again. We are hosted.

Sometimes we consider the end of this Psalm to be some heaven we arrive at. This shifts a bit with a translation from the Septuagint, "I will return …" to replace "I will live (dwell) …." Having been pursued in everyday life to be a host, we will return with friends and enemies to feast together at table.

By the end of the Psalm, we can find our sense of being hosted shifting, and we find ourselves as hosts. To dwell in some metaphoric house of G*D is not a resting place for us, but is to bring us to a place of responsibility for said house and to learn to be a good host. Note that hosting does not begin at the door, but with an engagement of people before that, so they can see our care for them and all. This is a generic invitation that turns specific over time. "Come, let us reason together; let us live in peace together."

What is usually seen as a Psalm of comfort in a time of distress is also a call to being a H*st. Imagine living in a world where we host one another.

It will help if you look up the word "host" and follow its derivation. It seems the root is "enemy" and later becomes "host of guests/visitors/strangers/foreigner/enemies" and a root for "hospital". If "host" can move from a horde of enemies to caring for them, imagine this Psalm recording a journey of your life from estranged to caring.

Isn't that a Lenten journey worth the travel? Let us be a H*st to Creati*n and one another (friend or enemy), and we will find we have also H*sted G*D.

Psalm 23
Assured [4]

I am willing to be led out
from my thieving fear
for getting things
is never over
       want wants more
       and more and more
       until want wants more than more
       and we lie exhausted
even in a green pasture
we are too tired to eat or drink
and so we rest and fast
until we want no more
       now restored
       all those wants are seen
       as a darker than dark valley
       able to be faced and entered
this new vision
is a great comfort
upon which I can rest
rod and staff
       from grabbing what I want
       I notice an overflowing table
       with forks and spoons and knives
       to dine gracefully slow
there is time for thanks
there is time for greeting
there is time for leading
there is time for time
       my heart's cup overflows
       goodness and mercy for all
       in each house
       may it be
and how did this happen again
slow abundance
generous hearts
who knew
       these shepherd my greed
       guard my wanting
       through each night
       into this day

Psalm 24:7–10
Old Welcomes New

The first part of this Psalm identifies you as a locus of G*D's blessing and justice. Both of these are public in nature. As such, the tradition of visibility in the communal gateway is important.

This background then leads us to the second-half of the Psalm with its injunction: "Gates, lift high your heads!"

You are a gate. Each of us is a gate, a thin place. When one claims a blessing or engages to set right a wrong, other gates are encouraged. When we see other gates living from their blessing and risking being just, we are encouraged.

Such mutuality assists us in opening a wider blessing and deeper justice.

———————————

hey you
pay attention

out of the past
arises this moment

open to a better tomorrow
riding to meet us all

Psalm 25:1–10
Needed Change [1] — Proper 10 (15)

What promise are you looking for?

Two typical ones are—
   1) being triumphant or
   2) living faithfully.

The beginning of this psalm seems to be most interested in winning over others to join us in having picked or been picked by the most powerful god or totem.

Key words here include trouble, shame, guilt, guarded life, and some sense of eternal truth beyond local reality.

If these become less important, we can jump to the end of this pericope to focus on what it takes for us to develop and continue in a sense of being a part of a larger whole—being humble.

Here, the focus becomes our faithfulness, our promise fulfillment, our covenant, our word. This doesn't focus on guilt or prevailing. Rather, we look at simply using our gifts.

Psalm 27

Conviction [2]

"Waiting for the Lord" can be a passive waiting for something to happen or a spring-loaded readiness to act at a kairos moment ripe for intervention. A key question is, "What is meant by 'living in the house of the Lord'?"

Is this a readiness and willingness to praise and sacrifice? Is this a readiness and willingness to prophesy justice? If it is a bothness, which takes precedence when both are present? We suggest prophecy trumps praise (reference John Wesley's sermon *On Zeal*).

Here we see waiting as an active state. Living in the house of the Lord is to live in the image of "the Lord"—a creator and a co-creator and a re-creator—"a lover," if you will. This progression is where we find risk, partnership, and mercy—three important qualities that define the beauty of G*D, of Creati*n, of Ourselves.

---

my light
shining down the future's broadening way
pointing to fulcrum spots today
where the past might be moved
from fate to fortune

my salvation
putting a hand out
taking a hand in hand
joining lives
revealing goodness

my strength
stable
resilient
fearless
confident

Psalm 29
Beloved

The voice, spirit, presence of G*D is over water. A slight sound, a breeze, is magnified. G*D is positioned to be reflected.

It might be asked, what are we if not water, enhanced? Some bone, some minerals, some nano-electrolytes, but mostly water, and here we speak and act G*D in our time and place—reflective glory created with a glory of our own.

Over rivulet and flood, G*D hovers. Over time and space, we hover. Nested beings—Christmas has brought an angel hovering over witnesses hovering over a babe hovering over nations hovering over angels. Epiphany has brought us a star hovering over a manger, hovering over creation, hovering ....

In each part and whole is blessedness found. No one remains lost in chilly exile. Baptism of Jesus, yes. Baptism of all, yes.

---

virtual water
sprinkled water
poured water
engulfing water

where is the presence of G*D missing
if we go to the ends of the earth
there is water
if we ascend to the heights
there is water
if we descend to sheol
there is water

my baptism is your baptism
your baptism is my baptism
our baptism is creation's baptism
in our beginning is our end
and through it all—baptism

Psalm 30
Assured [3] — Proper 9 (14)

Where is the breath of life? That needs to be our orientation. To put one's trust in any given source presumes that it will continue to be a source of inspiration.

Those who are able to help liberate in one direction often find themselves caught enslaving several other directions. Some are good at giving food to the hungry and not so good at freeing prisoners. Some can uphold an orphan and turn their back on someone bowed down.

This is part of a gift of community we find it difficult to deal with. We set up generic leaders who aren't able to handle some particulars and are not able to delegate. This results in gaps in our common good.

So it is important to identify who has the breath of life in a particular direction and to follow them and to follow someone else when another breath is needed. Blessings upon your discernment.

---

if I kick off this mortal coil
and leave my praise
to my dust
will it?

what pride I
continue to exhibit
as though my praise
could be left behind

were it so
and my dust
praised forth
what then?

for one thing
morning
time to hang up
sackcloth

so caught in weeping
so ignorant of joy
my mourning must be peeled
away from my need

arise sackcloth
dance dust
expand soul
silence anger

weeping may linger
joy may tarry
prosperity may plead
dust may profit

Psalm 31:1–4, 15–16
Absent Saturday

Save me in your steadfast love.

When life gets desperate, we pull out our last gasp. Beyond our ability to hope any longer is some even deeper understanding beyond our understanding that a cosmos-wide force of love will find an unexpected encounter with our life, even as does that of an elusive neutrino.

Finally, without expectation, we simply ask to have our grief observed. Not even acknowledged, just impassively, peripherally glimpsed.

Today is an opportunity to practice absence to such a degree that we will be filled with an assurance of being beloved, anyway. Whenever a smidgeon of hope arises, respond to it as to any distraction, momentarily present and set aside. To be distracted by hope before encountering steadfast love will weaken our resolve to live steadfastly, no matter what.

In some ways, this pericope is the exception to the sense of absence needed in this day. Don't let that distract you, tempt you out of absence too soon. Your dark day of the soul is needed, even as it is a trial.

Psalm 31:9–16
Premature Fear Sunday

Palms:
    Hey, Hey, Hey!
    Steadfast Love, Forever!
    G*D Answers!
    Salvation – Present!
    This Is the Day for Rejoicing!
    We Bless the Blessed in a House of Blessing!

Passion:
    i am in distress
    wasted by grief
    a life of sorrow
    years of sighing
    misery sapped
    bones rubbery
    i am scorned
    a horror
    a dread
    fled from
    death's equivalent
    broken
    schemed against
    plotted against!
    can i trust
    any hand
    any love?

and so?
    are you expecting to find what you bring to the table?
    might a day of rejoicing in the midst of danger,
       yet be appreciated?
    which is foreground, which background?

Psalm 32
Conviction [4] — Proper 6 (11)

Keeping silence, keeping secret, keeping closeted, wastes body and soul. A silent, secret groaning, prelude to an earthquake or a volcanic eruption, persists at a sub-seismic level.

Whether this comes from an eternal heavy hand or an internal fear or learned response, our strength withers and our reserves dwindle.

Life-deniers have their moments but not their day.

Life-affirmers find their assurance, their belovedness, around every corner.

Celebrate, sing, be glad in Life, rejoice, shout for Joy, raise the roof! The silenced, secreted, closeted have nothing to lose but their chains! They shall find and be found and feast—a fresh start!

Psalm 32:1–7
Proper 26 (31)

We do indeed desire an understanding that will enable us to live. A part of the religious struggle is how to use this desire. Is it limited to control of our lives and our environment? If so, how does it ever grow, for the way in which we use control is to limit change? Is it intended to be continually ahead of us, and so our task is more to learn how to learn than it is to memorize the overload of what has come down to us? If so, how do we deal with the constancy of change that will lead us beyond creedal words? How do we deal with our response to change being to slow it down to manageable bits?

It seems we can either deal with "decrees righteous for ever" or with "understanding", but not both at the same time. To stand between them is to put one at risk of cognitive dissonance and every other kind of soul-wrenching experience that can be imagined.

In some sense, there needs to be a division between G*D and ourselves, as well as a unity. G*D needs "forever" space, and we need growth-in-learning space. It is important not to confuse these two. Sometimes G*D needs reminding about forever, and we need reminding about the importance of now. Sometimes we even need to remember for one another.

Likewise, we can't try to hold together an image of G*D being a hiding place as well as one that surrounds us with glad cries. We are no longer hidden if being exulted over. We cannot be celebrated while still being hidden away.

---

trouble and anguish have come	to a larger vision of tomorrow
and come and come	nearer and nearer
again and again	we turn again and again
we wonder how can we last	until it is vision no longer
finding a beauty of righteousness	then external decrees
again and again	and internal understanding
brings us closer and closer	again and again
to a delight larger than failure	dance with one another

Psalm 33:12–22
Proper 14 (19)

[This reflection brings in Psalm 50:1–8, 22–23,
an alternate to the Isaiah pericope for the day.]

G*D among us, authorizes the heavens and earth with authority
to judge.

G*D in the heavens, looks down upon us and is appealed to by
us.

As we play back and forth between the location of G*D, we might also play with our own location. Are we looking to be high and lifted up, the greatest of the disciples, the most favored of nations, the sacrificers of others? Are we after being servants, the ones who offer their lives for others, the cross-bearers, the thanksgiving-givers?

Here we have an interplay between the prophets and the priests whose hearts, while intended to be oriented in the same direction, lead them to different realms of authority and thus different realms of action.

Ironically, the active role of thanksgiving shifts out of its usual categories. The prophets shift the focus to thanksgiving and away from sacrifice as a way of exhibiting thanksgiving. The priests shift the focus to sacrifice, intended to eventually lead to thanksgiving as a state of being.

Prophets claim the way to peace is peace, the way to thanksgiving is thanksgiving.

Priests claim the way to peace is war, the way to thanksgiving is sacrifice.

These are highly overdrawn caricatures, as there are always false prophets around, as well as priests of integrity. They do call for us to think about them again and to use the everyday issue of location as a meditation/contemplation opportunity to reflect on where we stand and to what end. May we continue to grow in wisdom as we look about from our current location and courageously move on to see things from a different perspective.

Psalm 36:5–10
Guiding Gift 2

G*D's steadfast love is showered all over the place. It doesn't make any difference where or who one is or whether we are talking about a human being or a mountain—that love is a given background.

Why then the plea that it continue? Is it not rock solid? Why in particular would those who know G*D need continual assurance? Are we the most tempted to ignore it? Are we the most likely to subvert it into power for ourselves? Are we aware of how much we are in debt to it, and can't ever quite hold our heads up on our own?

For folks who claim to know something so extraordinary as a source of steadfast love, we seem to keep losing our way within it. We imagine it to be limited, and we need to scramble for our share. We suspect that the future may be different than the past and that we will find ourselves not being uniquely privileged by our knowledge. We fear that it is too good to be true, and since we obviously need it, it may, as obviously, lead to greater and greater expectations that we cannot live up to, and we will lose love.

Why might you plead for more steadfast love for folks who are exactly as we are? Might it be an attempt to lull G*D into setting us as the standard, thus protecting our rights forever? We are, obviously, upright of heart—was there ever a doubt—and if that is the criterion, we get the love we need. Too bad about those others who don't do as we do.

---

extend to heaven
an upright heart
until
an upright heart
becomes heaven

Psalm 36:5–11

Clarification Week: Monday

If this is a week to actually reflect on what we will not give up on —steadfast love even in the face of death, the persistence of prevenient grace, an engagement with pre-emptive mercy, and so much more—this whole Psalm needs reflecting on as a whole.

This bit of praise and hope is sandwiched between sin and destruction. To cherry-pick this section as we enter into a week of value clarification doesn't do justice to the depth of choice constantly before us.

———————————

with too flattering an eye
we gaze upon all we intend
covering over all consequences
not hearing the cry of our intendee

with no feedback loop
our refuge rebuffs refugees
we measure bounty by our stomach
not hearing the growl in others

our faith and wisdom
require humility and listening
to push us into greater justice
and pull us back from inattention

Psalm 37:1–9
Proper 22 (27)

How do we pursue a journey to awareness of the presence of G*D in the face of our present situation, demanding our attention be limited to it? When captured by Babylon, Capitalism, Preemptive War, Drugs, Sex, Niceness, Comfort, or Whatever—how do we sing a different song that releases accumulated hatred? How do we sing Dylan's *It Ain't Me, Babe* to those who and that which would claim our soul?

A sense of detachment/assurance works wonders in this setting. We don't fret at what might be done to us; we don't become envious and do the same to others. All of this (me and my situation) will soon fade. This leaves a clearer vision of the possibility of doing good in the midst of subversions of a blessed Creati*n.

So we engage patience and walk away from wrath. We participate in creative acts of parabolic living and active non-violence. We do this in regard to both ourselves and others.

Psalm 37:1–11, 39–40
Guiding Gift [7]

In honor of the acrostic structure of this psalm:

Avoid the wicked heart of wrongful gain
Avarice cannot sustain eternity

Build trust into the land of the commons
Brighten your heart's desire beyond desire

Commit to bettering the next seven generations
Confide with one another in the light of day

Depend on a long-term source of assurance
Defend the vulnerable no matter the cost

Evenly approach temptation and blessing
Eager to enact your hope through deep care

Finally know privilege is a place of absence
Finally throw your lot with the poor

G*D is a map of refuges for renewal
Go, walk and talk together, honestly

Psalm 40:5–10
Creation's Conception

Creati*n's birthday is another time to celebrate a covenant service. While doing so, it is also important to keep alert to the temptation to idolize our relationship with G*D—where G*D cannot be aspired to, only obeyed, and we are entirely at G*D's behest.

The Wesleyan Covenant Service includes sentiments such as:

I am no longer my own, but thine.
Put me to what thou wilt, rank me with whom thou wilt.
Put me to doing, put me to suffering.
Let me be employed for thee or laid aside for thee,
  exalted for thee or brought low for thee.
Let me be full, let me be empty.
Let me have all things, let me have nothing.
I freely and heartily yield all things to thy pleasure and disposal.
And now, O glorious and blessed God, Father, Son, and Holy Spirit,
  thou art mine, and I am thine.
So be it.
And the covenant which I have made on earth,
  let it be ratified in heaven.
Amen.

While finding this to be personally meaningful in a non-attached way, in its prescribed form, there is no wrestling through to an agreed-upon meaning, there is only signing on. As long as this is a relational document revealing steadfast love, it continues to bear some fruit. When it becomes a control mechanism to not step outside some currently perceived "covenant", "plan", or "G*D's will", our sense of beloved community goes askew, and we settle for hierarchy instead of partnership.

To see what this service looked like to generations before us, go to this link:

wesley.nnu.edu/fileadmin/imported_site/Wesley_Covenant-1781.pdf

While you are there, be sure to note some of the phrases such as, "Adventure yourselves with Christ." What do you think that meant way back when? What does it mean to you now?

Psalm 42 and 43
Hopeless Hope Vigil — Proper 7 (12)

> I say to G*D, "Why have you forsaken me?"
> I say to my soul, "Why are you cast down?"

As with all "why" questions, there is no adequate singular response.

I suppose it is good to know this vigil that begins the Easter season is drawing to a close. As with any therapeutic intervention, this vigil may not come to anything before it is time to close. So, why, again, are you here? Why are you so in need of an Easter that you are vigiling through the night or awake before the dawn?

"Why? Well, why not? It can't hurt."

You've paid deeply to come this far. And yet, is it always an option to not hold on any longer, but fold. Blessings on your decision to come back for another session and deal with things before the 50th minute of a 55-minute appointment.

Anytime after Pentecost will also be a good time to ask these questions. Not long after an exciting release from a locked room, we begin to recognize how difficult it is to continually live at a peak experience.

Asking these questions prepares us to better distinguish between feeling forsaken/cast down and being blessed/lifted up/moving ahead.

Psalm 45
Creation's Conception

Verses 4–5 bring us a deep divide in our spirituality. There doesn't seem to be an easy way for more than individuals to come to grips with the tension between our better and worse tendencies.

> Glorious and triumphant, ride on
> for the cause of truth, gentleness and justice;
> let your right hand show marvelous deeds.
>
> Your arrows are sharp,
> the enemies of the king lose heart;
> nations fall beneath your feet.
> [*The New Community Bible*]

In no time at all, we find our ideals of truth, gentleness, and justice brought low by the domination of those who are not us. We are even ready to leave our ancestors behind in favor of the power of sons for generations to come—"In the place of ancestors you, O king, shall have sons; you will make them princes in all the earth."

While the definition of beauty shifts from time to time within a culture and between cultures, the thrust here is that boys are powerful kings and girls are beautiful queens who beget more powerful boys to become kings.

Remind yourself again about "truth, gentleness, and justice." How will you practice that in a culture for which it is happy talk and not for intentional implementation?

Psalm 46
Hopeless Hope Vigil — Evaluation Day

To be a preparer of a better way is indeed a high calling. It is one within the reach of everyone.

Sometimes we strive for some better part, to be the hero/heroine of whatever situation we are in. Sometimes that is not only possible, but achievable. For a given time and place, we are the obvious catalyst to move things along. More often, we would do better to cast around for simply a next baby step that someone else will be able to build on, bring to fruition.

It is amazing how often this role of the preparer of a better future revolves around acts of forgiveness. Time and again, the gift of radical forgiveness is needed to clear space for a better time to come. It is this forgiveness that provides a better picture of salvation and ways in which it might become clearer and stronger in our living.

In this last moment of Lent or the Church Year, we might cast our hearts and minds back over the past year to see the proportion of our experience that found us humbly preparing a better way compared to those moments when we were a dominator, a final capstone put in place. My hunch is that we will all find ourselves more often in the role of preparer. Now that we have cast back, we might be able to more forthrightly and joyfully fill more of that role in the year ahead. This will lead to a greater fulfillment by this time next year.

---

there is a river	streams pre-river	gathering
whose streams make glad	sea post-river	holding
habitations of the heart	play their part	connected
whose strong flow	along a way	river-wise
sees us through to dawn	of new life	courageous

Psalm 47
Our Turn to Witness

Psalm 47 is paired with Psalm 93 for this Feast Day. You are feasting with others, are you not?

"Highness" is emphasized in both Psalms. Whether talking about the quality of being or a title, we have a long heritage of *up* being better than *down*. In so many ways, the children's game of King of the Mountain is a model of life. Capturing the high ground brings a tactical edge (at least until drones came along). We still use some arbitrary moral high ground as a basis from which to whip up the winds of war.

This natural law of *up* naturally claims that G*D must be the highest of all highnesses. If we can't quite get there, we can be associated with what we claim can be at the pinnacle.

As we easily consider ascension as separation from, it might be worth raising a question about any purpose of being above and beyond. Such a position can help question any *status quo*. When looked at from the perspective of subjected people, the *status quo* is better than anything worse, even if not as helpful as something else. Coming at life from a generational perspective rather than an individual one allows a questioning of present authority. Ascension can give the distance needed to better evaluate where we have been and come to an insight into where we might yet be. Ascension allows a look over the next range of hills.

This can cut several ways. We may look into a new land and claim there are giants there; retreat! We may also look beyond a border and see a new community worth all the trouble it takes to get to.

Are you willing to ascend or just leave that to Jesus?

Psalm 49:1–12

Proper 13 (18)

Steadfast love endures.

This may mean that "a little dab will do you"—sort of like one of those funeral jewelry pieces where you can keep a bit of the cremains of a loved one close to you.

This may mean that you need to constantly enlarge your ability to receive more and more of this steadfast love because it just keeps coming, and we can't give it away quickly enough. When we don't keep up with being as steadfast in loving others as G*D is steadfast in loving us, the only way stored love can be released is with our death.

I don't mean to lessen the lesson about real resources that need to be distributed, but part of the reason we feel we never have enough resources is because we haven't given away enough.

------

mortals cannot abide in their pomp
  so says the psalmist
pomp?
  I ain't got no stinkin' pomp!
pomp?
  I stay to myself, no bandwagon here
pomp?
  with my old beat-up hat?
pomp?
  with my distain of all things fashionable?
pomp?
  hmmm
pomp?
  oh, where I invest my wealth and honor
pomp?
  yep, I got me some pomp
pomp
  nope, it won't abide
pomp
  nor will I—even covered in my pomp
pomp
  and you?
pomp?

Psalm 50:1–8, 22–23
Proper 14 (19)

Some folks appreciate a firm boundary more than others. For those who do, marking such a boundary with fire helps keep it in sight and at a distance.

Here, the important boundary may be better seen as beauty—a beauty of interconnections, a beauty of wholeness, a beauty of creation and creativity.

This beauty is to stimulate two complementary responses, thankfulness and responsiveness.

All too often, these get covered over by whatever seems to offer greater control or power, or falter in the face of a fear that there will be a consequence if not done correctly.

This is the fire that precedes our living beautifully as an image of a steadfast love. We don't see that love in ourselves and turn to burning our bridges before even setting foot on them. Our response to beauty is not more beauty, but cynically putting it down wherever it might shine through.

It might be said that the firm boundary we are afraid we might cross, so we set it ablaze, is actually a false boundary constructed so we don't ever have to realize how beautiful we are and how able we are to respond mercifully even before such is needed.

May you be blessed this day with a clear vision of the beauty of life, your part in it, and many expressions of thankfulness.

Psalm 51:1–10
Proper 13 (18)

1) G*D does not need to "create" a clean heart in us. That comes with the territory of creation and life ("It is good"). We do find ways to hide that clean heart away under a patina of dust and ashes as we fail to or refuse to keep our house in order. We do need assistance to learn a discipline of creative dissonance that recoils not from difficult choices and moves gayly forward where angels fear to tread.

It is quite alright to acknowledge failure in keeping the energy of life strong. But it is overly prideful to elevate ourselves to chief of sinners and to have our sins against Neighb*rs discounted as only a sin against G*D.

Relax, we are in good hands.

2) Scripture comments on scripture. This needs more attending to than our desire for consistency and justification can always handle. In this case, the last two verses, probably a late addition, cast this Psalm in the light of the plural, the communal, and not just the singular, personalistic way we too easily have a first read.

If we can remember to constantly see our personal foreground in a context of a communal background, we will more accurately assess where we can actually change what we can and add our weight to that of others to change what, alone, we couldn't.

Attend—we have good hands.

Psalm 51:1–17
Self-Recognition Day

Would you attribute steadfast love to your neighbor or environment? If you could see a way clear to do so, you might begin this psalm with:

> Have mercy, O Neighb*r, according to your steadfast love.
> Have mercy, O Creati*n, according to your steadfast love.

Imagine that this lack of imagination is the reason we have a tradition of imposing ashes. We don't see mercy in one another and, sure enough, it is never there when it is needed.

We are willing to break our heart and have a contrite spirit before G*D, but not before Neighb*r or Earth. Until we can include these, despising continues. What a blessing it would be to all concerned to be able to enlarge expressions of mercy.

While mercy is difficult to measure in others, we should be able to see what this would mean if we added yet another starting spot:

> Have mercy, (your name here), according to your steadfast love.

Where will your ashes of remembrance take you? All the way to re-membering mercy?

Psalm 52
Proper 11 (16)

Psalm 52 sets two dramatically different approaches to life—devouring and trusting—against one another. Implication, it is better to trust—it is to one's long-range benefit.

Leaving that duality behind for the moment, I am intrigued with the image of "a green olive tree in the house of God." The flourishing of ourselves (our tree-ness) is like the flourishing of steadfast love or mercy. This is what is called for, regardless of whether or not we ever gloat over those who limit such G*D-ly qualities.

It helps to remember Jeremiah 11:16—

> The Lord once called you, "A green olive tree, fair
> with goodly fruit"; but with the roar of a great tempest
> he will set fire to it, and its branches will be con-
> sumed. (NRSV)

If flourishing is to continue, it needs to continue to deepen and strengthen its roots, or it, too, will fall.

The image of a green olive tree is not a cause for pride but an investment in deeper roots to have greener leaves and more bountiful fruit. When satisfaction sets in, roots wither, ever so slightly at first, and fruits are reduced. It's not easy being green.

---

laughter at doing well
enhances such doing
even when all about
are mourning

by our laughter
we scorn not others
but enlarge our life and see
more reason for laughter

our laughter brims over
surely goodness and mercy
are with us now
and anon

My soul bonds with you; your right hand seals the deal.

A lovely image. Does the parent or the child get the most out of being held breast to breast? That's probably the wrong question to ask, as they get different things from the same encounter—from each according to their love; to each according to their need.

What, these days, is your soul clinging to? Is it returning the favor of upholding you?

What, these days, are you upholding that is in the clinging stage of life?

How is it when parting comes? Do we contemplate the other in various moments? Do we sing about having become accustomed to their face? Do we faint when we consider the distance between?

I am presuming these have their correspondences in the life of each part of the relationship. Do you think G*D meditates on you when you have gone down the road with half the inheritance? Do you think G*D is directing the music of the spheres to sing you a lullaby when you are in a strange bed? Do you think G*D faints from desire for you?

This intersection of interdependence and mutual admiration is worth looking at.

Psalm 65
Proper 25 (30)

The Lord of hosts, the G*D of Gods, pours out G*D's nature in the form of rain. Much in the Psalms can be traced back to a competition with various Rain Gods. This makes sense in a dry climate or one reliant upon agriculture.

We experience this refreshing and growing rain as a gift of resurrecting, reviving, and restoring community—the rain of G*D, the reign of forgiveness, the rein on our destructive tendencies.

Of course, there is torrential rain, monsoon rain, hurricane rain, typhoon rain, and the like, that erodes and floods out. But here we are in a thankful mood that catches a glimpse of the presence of G*D in the fertility of rain that satisfies our longings and lifts our fainting souls.

As folks made in G*D's image, we, too, are to become at least a shower of blessing in others' lives. This is our happiness and our praise.

May you be poured out as daily as the bread that sustains G*D, Neighb*r, and Creati*n.

Imagine this: You are G*D's mirror.

When your community, or any, is invited to see the wonder of G*D, they will be glancing in your direction. Your stumbles and recoveries are an asset more wonderful than we can fully appreciate. While it is very easy to swing from one to another—original-sinner stumbles or heroic recoveries—the larger truth is that we are simply an image of G*D, creating life as we go along.

As we stand revealed as a stubborn stumbler and a resilient recoverer, we are a great encouragement—nothing is forever, and a new creation is already popping up.

I remember here a model proposed by Dr. Egon Gerdes that sets us in the midst of a Fun House of hiding and closings, of revelation and openings.

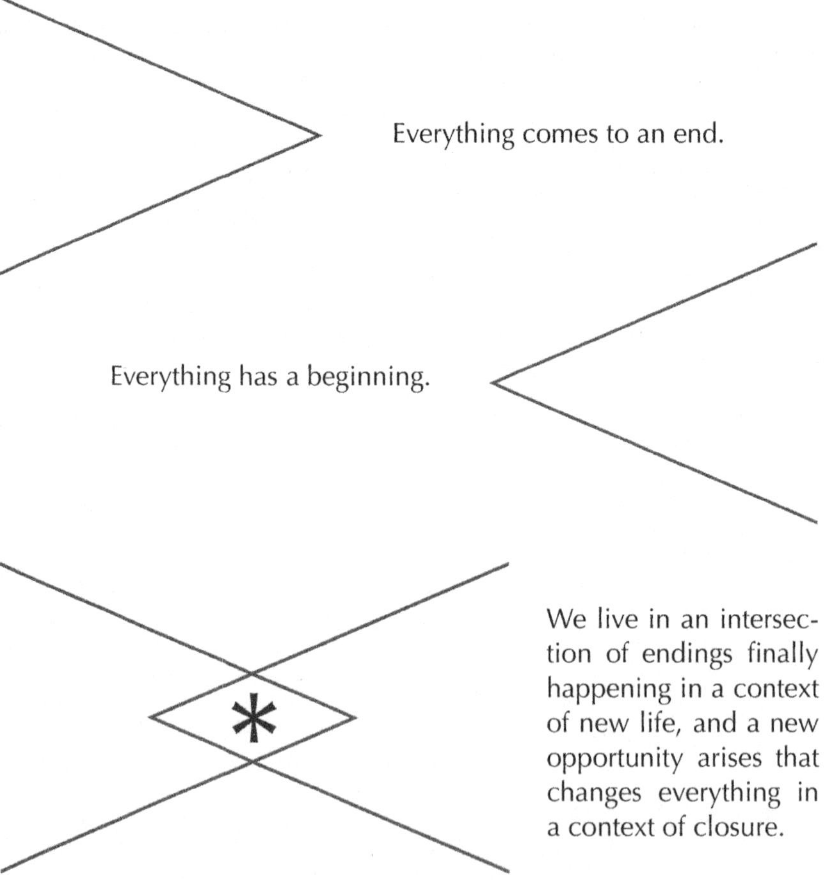

Psalm 66:1–12
Proper 23 (28)

"The theme of this psalm is not obvious . . . ." [*The Jewish Study Bible*]. So we continue the mystery of dreams. "The exodus-conquest theme may hint at the theme of the return from exile and re-entrance to Judah (... a common symbol for the return in post-exilic times...)" [*ibid.*]

Praise G*D.

1) We have been kept among the living while bad things happen to ordinary people.
2) We have been tested by fire.
3) We have been grounded like a bird in a net, trapped with no way out.
4) We have been subdued.

—— (dream-like jump) ——

1) We have come to a spacious, prosperous place.

When we can't explain the various incongruities of life, we are tempted to put it all on G*D—the pains and the joys, the testings and the blessings. None of this "proves" G*D. What lies behind our insistence on making sense of the world, even if it takes projecting experiences onto G*D? It would seem we are still in the midst of a dream.

Keep singing for a better tomorrow. When we find ourselves there, perhaps then we will see beyond our multiplicities of experience and better understand this and other praise psalms.

Psalm 67
Assured 6

How very good and pleasant it is when kindred live together in unity. Note, this is far, far different than living in uniformity.

When this is not only our intention but our experience, we claim that G*D's graciousness and mercy are evidenced in our midst.

Where have our intentions run awry and amok? First, look for who is not included in our unity. The prophets would have us look first to the poor, the outcast, the weak, and the minority, in whatever forms those take. Given the sweep and the specificity of their vision, it is important to note both the big issues of poverty that affect everyone (including those currently rich) and the personal issues of those we have a particular affinity with.

Just as each of us has a different set of gifts to add to the common good, so each of us has a different set of sensitivities to a person or group who is left out of unity. The deal here is not to claim everyone needs a particular gift to belong or that everyone needs to be focused on the same brokenness of unity. These simply lead us back into more or less sophisticated forms of uniformity.

Interested in a good and pleasant life? It can't be done in isolation from the unity issue.

A parallel is found in the American pursuit of happiness. If we don't care for the unity issues inherent in a common defense of all and the general welfare of all, we will miss the mark of happiness.

Note: To follow this unity/uniformity discussion, you may find an article by Joan Chittister to be helpful—

"Sometimes contradiction is the most Catholic thing."
nationalcatholicreporter.org/fwis/fw081105.htm

Psalm 70
Clarification Week: Wednesday

Here we find another way to glorification, that of the *via negativa*.

Poor and needy, I have G*D on speed-dial!
"Deliver help. Be speedy, not slow."

"Forsaken, forsaken by G*D."
Jesus cries again, "Forsaken", and is dispirited.

Be destroyed to the uttermost, be deeply shamed and confused—still claim your center, your glory, your belovedness, your simply unlikely birth. It is from this center that we proceed, anyway. As generations before us have affirmed in one way or another, "Called or not, G*D is present."

When in a ticklish situation, it is helpful to find a focus of foundation that can re-center our vision of where we are and what is going on. When such a focus returns, it is amazing what options are still open.

Here, the Psalmist understands that life around her is very tenuous. Boxed in and threatened, what is there to hold on to? There is no historical precedent to fall back on for consolation, nor plan to move through. There is no expectation that we can do anything to change the course of events.

Paying attention to the present, particularly, seems to hold no direction that might bear fruit. So, wherever one looks, there is nothing but a hope pitted against a hope.

What is left is miracle and wonder. This is both a diminution of G*D and an expansion. Whatever gap is left, is G*D. G*D leaps gaps and is beyond prediction and repetition of previous encounters.

Settling into there being no option, all of a sudden, there is. And praise flows as Butch and Sundance jump with fear and trembling.

When we shift our attention from only G*D to partnering with G*D, this psalm might sound something like this:

Yes, G*D, we are in this together.
We bolster one another past guilt and shame.
Your expansion of love delivers us from small living, and
  our expansion of love rescues you from bad press.
It is good to listen to one another.
In walking and talking together we find refuge and
  provide refuge.

When the wicked would mishandle us and others
  we find our solidarity and a way through.
Holding one another in hope goes so deep
  we can imagine no time before it was not so.
Praise for you, praise for me, praise for we.
Hopeful Refuge and Refuge of Hope
  we stand together and fall together and rise together.
This is enough.

Psalm 71:1–14

Clarification Week: Tuesday

We are full of conditional love—only take care of me and I'll look after you.

When our hope and praise are dependent upon our own well-being, we need to be in conversation with Job.

Blessings to you in the midst of continual dangers. Your task is to take responsibility for your own hope. May you always be able to see beyond whatever threat you are sensing.

So why would you "deliver the needy" when they identify their need? To receive honor?

Why would you have your heart and resources go toward the weak? To receive praise?

Why would you stop oppression and violence? To receive tribute?

If you are able to avoid these limitations, why would we want to put them on G*D?

It may be as simple as these understandings and engagements:

- Justice is available and achievable.
- Prosperity for all is available and achievable.
- Defense of one another is available and achievable.

- Which part of a current injustice are you called to call out and shift?
- Which part of a current ecological harm are you called to call out and shift?
- Which part of a current political/economic shallowness are you called to call out and shift?

Be a light. Shine in dark corners.

Psalm 77:1–2, 11–20
Proper 8 (13)

I call to mind the deeds of G*D;
Wonders of old are as fresh as my memory.

You created in multiple images (as many as the gods).
You were disappointed in your creation.
You threw your creation out.
You pursued your exiled creation.
You did not kill your creation when your creation killed.
You dispersed language groups.
You were flooded with despair and flooded in return.
You used famine to direct migrations.
You chose the youngest and least to lead.
You raised dynasties.
You were frustrated by leaders.
You exiled peoples.
You were their hope, delayed as it has been.

And, now, in a day of my own trouble—I look to you?
Yes, and to myself and my friends and to creation itself.

I cry.
I cry aloud.
I call to mind.
I grin.
I laugh.
I go around again.
Dance with me, G*D
  a larger dance than my day's trouble—
  or yours.

Psalm 78:1–2, 34–38
Relic Day

The importance of verse 2 cannot be overstated. This very didactic, deuteronomic Psalm about interpreting past events is best seen as
an extended parable or poetic presentation of the past. Essentially,
history is an opportunity for a midrash to assist us in dealing with the
present while still leaving room for a reappropriation of today in light
of its passing and tomorrow's realities.

> I will speak to you in *mashal* (a rhythmical maxim
> expressed in poetic parallelism), in parable, clarifying
> past event and present need.

Like it or not, we are always speaking *mashal*. There is no straight
talk or common-sense understanding. There is no immutable truth or
undying foundation. In the hands of a creative G*D, all is *mashal*, all
is Word. When G*D makes a harmful choice, a new story is told.
Scripture reinterprets scripture.

We can call this reinterpretation repentance or new vision.
Whether we are bloody atoners or "but I say to you" creators, we can
both, thankfully, arrive at verse 38. Here, after acknowledging a lack
of integrity up to this point, we meet a compassion larger than our
limits.

> Compassionate mercy forgives
> does not destroy or let anger loose.

We, too, can participate in this larger compassion. Our starting
place will probably be connected with verse 39 (yes, it will be alright
to extend the passage one verse and into our current life). Remember—we are always dealing with people and a creation that is passing
away, a breath moving on.

> Remember we are but flesh,
> a wind that passes and does not come again.

An appreciation of "vanity" is a vital informant for a healthy
mashal.

Even when comeuppance has arrived for dishonest wealth or deceptive spirituality, we are still trying to wheedle G*D to be on our side and to return us to our most dishonest time when we had the most wealth or the most comfort in ignoring one another.

Bottom line here is, "Sic 'em, God!"

Beneath the bottom line is, "Forgive us so we can get back to our dishonesty."

The pericopes this week are tough for folks to hear, even folks who are diligent in opening themselves to an examen.

Can you be honest about dishonest wealth in your congregation without it leading to a drop in financial giving? Can your fellowship address dishonest spirituality and keep everyone participating? Odds are, if you are not a leader, your talk about these matters will find you ignored or asked to leave. If you are a leader, confronting dishonesty will bring about fewer followers and less money. Is getting back to being honest in church too difficult for the moment? When will it get any better? Is it worth doing anyway?

Examen your self.
Examen one another.
Rejoice when you have come through.
Change when you have been caught out.

Psalm 80:1–2, 8–19
Proper 15 (20)

Hey, G*D!
Stir up your might!
Get out of bed!
Run here!
Save us!

You've done it before. Time to do it again. Your indolence is responsible for our peril, so get a move on.

We're finally and really sorry—yes, you've heard us say that before, but there really is a wolf at the door this time, dressed in pig's clothing no less, eating the fruit of the vine—so help us now and we'll tell everyone what a great gal you are, uhh, great guy, uhh, great god you are.

If I were G*D, I'd go back to bed. However, the persistence of these petitioners is great. I guess I'd get up, but grudgingly. Would I believe them? Nope. I know them too well; they are in my image after all. They continue to want what they want when they want it. So, let's set up the toys for them to knock over again, for someday they'll grow up—at least that hope is still holding, though it is fragile.

How about you? Will you get up for such as are running the world down while expecting a miraculous pick-me-up at the end?

Needed Change [4]

It is so lovely to be innocent.

We are experiencing trouble. We are not in charge, much less cooperating with others. That they've taken over means we aren't getting our way.

So, let's claim a more ideal past than is accurate. Let's look to get back to being in charge, even if we never were. Restoration. Yes, that's the ticket, restoration.

Before being too certain that we can live in perpetual safety, as desired by the closing verse (7), it will stand us in good stead to spend more time with verse 6—"Instead of your blessing we have become a source of contention and derision for the nations."

Does it take two to strive with one another? If we ever acted privileged and mocked our neighbor, did we begin a cycle of strife? Where does responsibility for this contest lie, and will brute victory over them settle us into safety?

Consider what it would mean for our living if we looked ahead to some time of shared lives rather than being restored to a time of being-in-charge—our theocracy instead of theirs.

If we can identify a larger frame, we might be willing to consider repainting our vision on a larger canvas. Hopefully, a next art form (painting) will have room for several creators (painters) and a larger medium (color palette). If nothing else, we may lose some of our innocence and acknowledge a larger context for our smaller desires.

Psalm 81:1, 10–16
Proper 17 (22)

<u>Take one</u>

O that folks would listen to me—that I would be understood for what I meant, not what I said or did or didn't say or didn't do.

G*D seems to feel that having brought folks out of Egypt that G*D would never again have to face the cry, what-have-you-done-for-me-lately. Well, how did that work out?

Never in G*D/Israel connections has so much been offered to so few.

It would appear that if praise is going to be freely given, there must also be the possibility of not following every command performance with a standing ovation.

<u>Take two</u>

Yesterday, my mother had a stroke (bleeding kind, not clotting kind) in a very difficult spot. Surgical intervention is out. Doctor's prognosis for recovery is, "Not good." As a family, we are working on our response. Even as she taught us to know better, we still need to wrestle our way away from playing the resuscitation game.

Hear this Psalm in a mother's voice:

Sing aloud to Mothers Anonymous, our strength;
*shout for joy to every Mother of G*D.*

"I am your Mother, who brought you up out of every trouble you have gotten yourself into. Open your mouth wide and I'll put another gingersnap in it."

But my children did not listen to my voice; even my favorite would not follow my wisdom.

So I gave them over to the school of hard knocks, to follow their own counsel.

O, that my children would listen to me, that each one would walk in my ways!

Then I would quickly subdue their enemies and turn my hand against their foes.

Those who are after my young-ones had better watch out, for a mother's wrath brings doom forever.

"But my prodigal dear, I will still feed you with the finest oyster stew, and with crumbcake from scratch, I would satisfy you."

Psalm 82
Proper 10 (15) — Proper 15 (20)

We have heard of both a Mercy Inn and a Plumb Line. We now hear about G*D holding judgment, doing justice. This is the result of a plumb line of mercy that was unused, set aside for a more pressing issue, and eventually justice was needed to rectify the results of folks being unkind, unmerciful.

If you don't want to face judgment and justice for having gone awry, then show mercy, no matter what the provocation to express something else. Mercy is preemptive Justice. Mercy obviates the need for justice.

If you are among the G*Ds, then your call is to exemplify Mercy so that Justice need not be brought to bear. In the long run, Mercy is the most efficient behavior, even when dealing with the unmerciful. Without Mercy, non-violent resistance is simply a variation on violence and a will to power.

The longer I sit with this, the more untenable Mercy alone is. Second thoughts arise by the dozens, rationalizations for unMerciful behavior leap into being from nowhere, and the satisfaction of revenge is very strong.

Mercy needs a community able to consistently remember Mercy as an option amid a multitude of spiritual disciplines and fruits of spirit. Even then, in our world, Mercy is miraculous in its presence and effect.

Rise up, O G*D; be merciful.

Psalm 84
Old Welcomes New

Pilgrimages can have many purposes. Often, they are a recognition that there is a current disjuncture that needs to be re-visioned or viewed from a new perspective. Prophets are always on a pilgrimage to see again the foundations of the present. This allows them insight into needed adjustments today that better connect yesterday to tomorrow. In this sense, prophets are highly conservative.

In the midst of all the covering of praise, there is a significant hint of interconnectivity in verse 10a that is deeper than a standard "You're so great, G*D, and I'm so nothing."

Consider this statement in place of verse 10a and what it might mean for the rest of the Psalm:

> Better a day together
> than a thousand on my own.

Hopefully, this will take us out of the limitation of locating G*D or needed vision in one place or time or creed. Equally hopeful is that it will renew us to converse together in the cool of the evening, where both G*D and ourselves can reset in the presence of all the hopes and fears that run through our daily streets.

Psalm 84:1–7
Proper 25 (30)

Happy are we when we are satisfied with the goodness of G*D's presence.

While the experience of G*D's goodness is intangible, it does have weight. This weight tilts us ever so little toward expressions of hope.

Can you feel this weight in your life? It is a weight that lifts.

———————————

roaring waves silenced
people's tumult quieted
into this silence
drop signs
it is evening
it is morning
a new day begun

a gentle river
by trees of healing
forgiveness realized
in iniquities' midst
another year in
another year begun
feasting on joy

Psalm 85
Proper 12 (17)

In Hosea we hear of G*D running out of mercy.
Here we hear of G*D's anger to generations.

Look around. There is good warrant for those perspectives.

Steadfast love is not easy work. G*D tires of it and retracts mercy and indulges in anger. Yet, it is our birthright and the image of our creation. Great imagination and deep community are needed for those times when steadfast love falters. May steadfast love be shown you when your love stumbles. May your steadfast love support another in their time of drought. As Red Green has been heard to say, "Remember, I'm pulling for ya. We're all in this together!"

Psalm 91:1–2, 9–16
Conviction [1]

In some ways, Lent is a sheltered workshop. Here, we develop skills while on the job. Here we employ skills developed through repetition.

In the refuge of Lent, we practice knowing all is well and will be well again. We practice living from a position of knowing we are guarded—boldly. We practice living from a perspective of having been borne up—thankfully. We practice living from a platform of steadfast love—mercifully.

Out of this practice come changed lives—as changed as resurrection or other metamorphoses.

It is good to know we have been sheltered in the shadow of trustworthiness. It is good to know we shelter others in this same gift.

Lent for Dummies

Foreword - affirming we are between ashes
Chapter 1 - practicing love when loving is difficult
Chapter 2 - practicing mercy when mercy is difficult
Chapter 3 - practicing thanks when thankfulness is difficult
Afterword - Easter

Psalm 91:1–6, 14–16
Proper 21 (26)

Happy Assurance Day to me! These Psalms remind me of an important vision in my own life in the summer between High School and College. This was a time of very loose ends (and for someone who is constitutionally drawn to loose ends as a good thing, it was even looser than I could handle). Suffice it here to say this was a time of confusion, uncertainty, fear, depression, and wit's end.

Into the midst of all this and more came a visit by a presence I then identified as Roy, director of a church camp where I had just been a counselor. This avatar brought a clear message that cut through all the rest of the junk of my life—"You will always be cared for."

These six words continue to bring me back to the assurance of this Psalm. These six words have carried me through more difficulties and allowed me to take more risks than I then could even begin to imagine. May this Psalm bring back to you moments of assurance that have seen you through. In remembering, may you, too, have a new birth through your own Assurance Day. (Try not to imagine what Hallmark would do to this holiday!)

Here is another example of the traditional wisdom approach—being "just" results in a present happiness of prosperity, and those who don't appropriately acknowledge G*D are doomed. This is a simple enough proposition to be tempting. And then along comes a bad thing happening to a good person, or the reality of death happens again.

Always, there is a question of another way of reading translations. Are we always under G*D or alongside, with some agency of our own?

Is verse 11 from *The New Jerusalem Bible* or that of *The New Revised Standard Version* to hold sway here? Where does our strength lie?

> I caught sight of the ambush against me,
> overheard the plans of the wicked (NJB)

> My eyes have seen the downfall of my enemies;
> my ears have heard the doom of my evil assailants. (NRSV)

The first reminds us that we have a choice about what we are going to do about the information we have at our disposal—using the fruit of knowledge of choice to choose life (avoiding the ambush of unconsidered consequences).

The second is still enthralled by the notion of being cared for so that a general doom as a result of political/economic/religious bullies can be escaped—only the wicked will be removed, and we will be left in Paradise.

How traditional is your engagement with Wisd*m? What questions do you need to ask of this authority in your life?

Psalm 93
Our Turn to Witness

It is comforting to think the world is firmly set. Well, until there is no getting away from Copernicus and Galileo, who helped us see that our firmness is spiraling through an outer arm of a spiral galaxy itself spiraling through one universe—etc.

In some sense, the dark waters are still with us. Chaos might be clapping to say, "Well done, G*D; freedom is as present as continuity."

We continually find ourselves being lifted up to get a new lay-of-the-land. And, seeing a wider context, we set off again with renewed confidence in a dance between now and then and when and here and there and everywhere.

>the majesty of white-capped waters
>sign a fresh breeze
>wrecking the worn-out
>speeding us onward
>
>yes
>precarious
>but
>oh
>so
>exhilarating

Ascension niggles at the seeming solidarity of systems and structures. Surprise is the unshakeable, so don't be surprised at moving on. This, and more, we learn from the waves. This, and more, G*D learns from standing atop the "breakers of the sea" (NJB).

Psalm 96
Blessed Body: Proper I — Proper 4 (9)

Peace is established with justice (beyond law) and righteousness (beyond hospitality). Zeal beyond our usual limits of engagement leads to good deeds beyond economic gain (no, not just that of monetary gain, but any transaction with an expected benefit).

When we have seen the truly unforgivable forgiven, we burst forth with more and more forgiveness for smaller and smaller infractions. Such forgiveness for our own infractions, as well as those of others, continues until premeditated mercy becomes our standard.

When we have seen humble swaddling clothes enrobing a small holiness, we are glorified and begin to see wholeness in larger universals as well as particulars. Our living praise claims an echo of Julian's: "All will be well, all manner of things will be well"—and we begin that wellness where we are.

Peace with justice and righteousness are worth treasuring.

---

let a decree go out—
peace is birthed
justice for all
and righteousness bright

It is posited that to G*D everything else is a potential idol or demon. This is a fragile proposal regarding a presence that "made the heavens". Focusing on idolatry continues a dualistic construct of that which is not us (wrong, part of an axis of evil) and that which is ours (glory and power).

This gets particularly tricky when we raise a question about the idols of G*D—A Chosen People or those chosen by a Chosen One. It is comforting to be seen as teacher's pet, an idol. When we are idolized, we are an object of affection and don't need to do anything in particular but affirm G*D for having the good sense to prefer us.

For the moment, we stipulate that praise is an appropriate response to be made toward G*D. We also raise the question of what else is appropriate, as mono-culturing of any sort poses dangers to the environment. Having a one-note praise would seem to run similar dangers of narrowing responses and analysis and initiation of a new option. Praise can trap us into a repeating cycle of what worked last time to get us what we wanted.

Is questioning as important as praise? What about out-and-out disagreement?

Idols seem to come with the territory of life. Acknowledging this helps us see if it is good to have an idol such as "love your enemy". Does this help us expand our loving?

One gift of identifying the shape of today's idol is that we might more quickly put it away sometime later today in favor of a more appropriate idol that moves us one step further along. It might be said that we mark our spiritual growth by the idols we have dropped by the wayside. Look back and see how far you have come.

Jesus' prayer is fairly localized—bless these and those in their image. Paul's actions are localized for his own benefit. The Psalmist continues this with a focus on those who authorize a high and exalted god as the one true-god.

If we are dealing with resurrection, wherein these limitations?

Well, it has been seven weeks or nine months since we had an anniversary of a resurrection. That's more than twice as long as it usually takes to institute a new habit, a new way of experiencing the world. It wouldn't be unusual for some forgetting to be happening around the edges. Resurrection opens us to life, and these limitations close us.

If we remember resurrection, we may yet participate in it, not just tout it. Here's a paragraph from Richard Rohr's book, *Immortal Diamond: The Search for Our True Self,* that might trigger some alternatives for you.

No matter what your definition, we all want resurrection in some form. And I do believe "the raising up of Jesus" (which is the correct theological way to say it because it was a relational meaning between Jesus and God, and not a self-generated "I can do this") is still a potent, focused, and compelling statement about what God is still and forever doing with the universe and with humanity. Science strongly confirms this statement today—more than ever before—but with different metaphors and symbols, like condensation, evaporation, hibernation, sublimation, the four seasons, the life cycles of everything from salmon to galaxies, and even the constant death and birth of stars from the exact same stardust. God appears to be resurrecting everything all the time. It is nothing to "believe in" as much as it is something to observe and be taught by.

Psalm 98

Blessed Body: III — Proper 27 (32) — Proper 28 (33)

    Perhaps not, "O sing to the Lord a new song", as much as, "G*D sings a new song."

G*D sings a new song, injecting a newness into expected fate.
G*D is intentional in this, working with what is.
Though begun quietly enough, this song is increasingly sung.
Life, no matter how held in abeyance, goes on, again.
Steadfast love and steady trust have set a forward-leaning heartbeat.
Joy breaks free from the personal and bursts onward.
With musical instruments and nature's infinite variety,
Equity's theme becomes transcendent.

    Note: G*D is not G*D without our partnership, and so we, too, sing a new song.

Psalm 98:1–5
Relic Day

Talismans, thin places, rituals—artifacts function as calls to won-der.

What a place we are in; what a wonder-full world!

We echo the call we hear. Together, with others who have heard, we turn our wonder into music.

Sound and sense are refined over the generations until they medi-ate the wonder once spontaneously experienced and responded to. Now we have to instruct others to sing and dance in hope that they will carry on what was important to us.

We find ourselves pointing to where Grandmother's quest was fulfilled, where Grandfather wove new life from old. Rather than at-tend to an insight beyond our ancestors, we settle for protecting the externals and aphoristic morals that mark where G*D once was.

A call to awe and wonder is a dangerous moment. Will we fall into a lockstep litany trapped by holy-ized words and concepts? (A danger of becoming stuck). Will we float away in search of some ec-static novelty? (A danger of becoming unmoored.)

A call to awe and wonder is an opportunity to honor those who have gone before us to build on their experience with our own. To-gether we may be thankful for our times, claim them as ours, and clear space for others to add their own call, their own wonder, their own music.

These various realities, each-by-each, may yet move beyond ei-ther strict harmony or enforced dissonance and make it all the way to joyful noise.

Psalm 99
Mountain Top to Valley

We are not only spoken to by a shining face, but from a pillar of cloud. Where and when, then, are we not in the presence of revelation, of transfiguration?

When following the Seventh Sunday after Epiphany and looking at Psalm 37 (1–11, 39–40), we also find a transfigurational process present in everyday events as well as on a mountaintop or in a desert. Among these events are the times when we do not fret—thus refraining from anger and forsaking wrath. Such a simple formula for dealing with life—don't fret.

Of course, this is easier said than done. There is a helpful practice, though, that is mentioned before an injunction to not fret—be still. This we can practice anywhere, even on mountain tops. Paying attention to one's breath helps "still" happen. From "still" we find renewed patience. This patience makes us appear meek, which is only a cover for transfigured delight veiled lest it scare those not "still".

And so we move from a reference to a pillar of cloud to sitting dandasana. In this stillness, keep what you find.

---

transition
transfiguration
transformation

a trinity of movements
from one state to another
something active appears

yet clarity for each of these
comes in quiet moments
still centers, gentle breaths

without such stillness
there is busy-ness
there is willy-nilly-ness

to have them move ahead
rather than in cycles
gather a clear still eye

Psalm 100
Thanksgiving

With the eyes of your heart enlightened, thanks lives in you.

Thanks that you will be unscattered and thanks that you can help return folks who have been pushed out. Such thanks rise to the surface and become conscious. From there, it is but a matter of applying courage to implement it.

And so, at the end of a long season of growth, we are left with thanks. After all the fear of too much rain or not enough, we are left with thanks. Even in the presence of current difficulties and in anticipation of judgments yet to be revealed, we are left with thanks.

---

thanks revealed
shyly and boldly
pokes its head out
to reveal its heart
in deeds of loving kindness

a bit of feast here
a tun of fun there
a goodwill stop also
a visit when all seemed lost
so thanks travels

as we have been done unto
we are thankful
thankful enough
to actually do well
to do well unto

Preemptive refuge is a tempting appeal to make. It helps us never arrive at a spot of needing healing; we never get bent-over.

This refuge seems to be based on a requisite quality and/or quantity of praise. One measure of this is how much of ourselves we put into praise and calling G*D to the qualities of mercy, grace, slowness to anger, and steadfastness in love.

Or, if we don't quite make it to preemptive refuge, we expect our praise will, at least, cut down on any time between our need and our rescue.

----

come
come quickly
come quickly effectively

so we cry out
and are echoed by all
in the grasp of injustice and cruelty

so we hear others cry out
and we echo their refrain
refuge, pity, vindication

may our cry
involve our lives
beyond G*D's machinery

recognize
recognize now
recognize now presence

Psalm 104:24–34, 35b
Energy to Witness

Always be a bit suspicious when something is left out. This section of the Psalm begins, "...how manifold are your works!" Then, at the end, excludes, "Let sinners be consumed from the earth, and let the wicked be no more."

Are "sinners" and the "wicked" part of the manifold works? Where did these consumed sinners and wicked folks come from? The same place as Cain and Seth's wives? The image of G*D from creation? Where then lies their being excluded, and if they are excluded, who will protest when we, in our turn, are excluded? What feels good from a privileged position now probably won't when a judging eye turns our way.

If we are going to see G*D as a lone-ranger creator, we will soon find ourselves moved aside from partnership with G*D to someone who sits up and begs (v 28). We become dependent upon G*D to the exclusion of being able to stray from the orthodox, official, tradition claimed to be the guarantor of our next handout.

No wonder some feel like they must continually sing praise. A bit of a lapse might bring being lumped with those sinners not cared a whit for? This is dangerous territory when we stop to consider some imaginary gap between creation and sin and whether praise can bridge it.

Thus, we don't mention sin and wickedness in verse 35a. We need to ban even half-a-verse that takes the focus off of verse 31, "Glory to Yahweh forever! May Yahweh find joy in his creatures!" [*NJB*].

Pentecost is not about praise, praise, praise in a secluded room. It is about face-to-face encounters with that which is different and finding a common link between them. A too-happy Psalm puts more focus on tongues of fire and less on tongues of reconciliation.

For now, imagine a wind blowing ships hither and yon. Imagine them running with that wind, tacking into it, or furling their sails. When wind interacts with life, there are all these little decisions to make. Blessings on your hearing a new wind blow and responding well, no matter from whence it arises or what you have to change.

Psalm 107:1–9, 43
Proper 13 (18)

> Some wandered desert wastes;
> G*D led them to a living community.
> (verses 4 & 7)

Troubles make the most verdant of places seem dry and desolate. Whether those troubles are imposed from the outside or arise from within, we find ourselves further and further removed from a source of comfort.

If we look to amass as much as possible for ourselves, it turns to smoke. If we attempt to rule over one other or many, our vanity will soon be visible for all to see. If we forget the interdependence of creation carefully called forth day-by-day, we engineer our own desolation.

Our hope is that of returning to community, where sharing and collaborating are practiced.

Sharing and Cooperating are two virtues a modern America has ceased to teach beyond rules of politeness that become formality of going through the motions of saying, "I'm sorry." Civics courses are long gone. This is not an elegy for their return, as we only learned the external forms of community, not the deeper joy of embodying community. This is a mourning that we still have so far to go for basic respect of one another.

In a "living community", we are able to realize a relationship between those with water rights and those thirsty unto death; those with a stuffed pantry and those not able to replenish calories spent to simply survive one more day. Here, we learn how well we all can be through sharing and collaboration. Here, we learn the direct line between the rich becoming richer and the poor becoming richer. A living community does not abide the heresy that the rich become poorer if the poor become richer. Rather, "trickle-up" is true.

When we are together and forget to gather all together, we begin moving back into the desert where one more difficult lesson needs the learning. Those who are wise give heed to sharing and collaboration (behaviors that reveal the presence of steadfast love).

Give heed.

Again and again, attend.

Psalm 111
Proper 23 (28)

Verse 7 identifies a key element of G*D's intended results and reminds us of an epiphany regarding Pentecostal reconciliation between the languages and experiences of human varietals—truth and justice.

In all of Creation Days 1–7, we see the externals of light and life and reptiles and rest are recorded. What is not reported at that time, but later noted here, is that each day has its part to play in revealing truth and justice, including this day.

Light is created . . . . *To reveal truth and justice.*

Water is separated . . . . *To reveal truth and justice.*

Plants are seeded . . . . *To reveal truth and justice.*

Time proceeds . . . . *To reveal truth and justice.*

Fish swim, birds fly . . . . *To reveal truth and justice.*

Animals procreate, humans create . . . *To reveal truth and justice.*

Even rest pauses . . . . *To reveal truth and justice.*

Today we are . . . . *To reveal truth and justice.*

Want to keep your saltiness? To shed light into the darkness still around us?

Verse 5 may be what you are looking for—"It is well with those who deal generously and lend, who conduct their affairs with justice."

The communal and parallel behaviors of sharing and fairness go a long way to keeping steady hearts in the presence of fear-producing events, such as those who would gnash their teeth at you or otherwise attempt to throw you to lions.

Facing some duress? It's probably not something you can handle on your own. If it is, it probably isn't duress? If it is duress, you may want to remember its antidotes: sharing and fairness. These are not short-term cures for anything, but they are long-term health for one and for all.

Psalm 113
Elizabeth and Mary Meet — Proper 20 (25)

It is one thing to look far down as G*D-of-all-G*Ds observes a faint image from afar. [Verses 5–6]

It is quite another to move beyond observation to engagement. [Verses 7–8]

Mary could have quite easily turned her experience with Gabriel into an observation game. Hmm, how interesting; I'll just let this be and see what happens.

Instead, Mary takes an intentional trip to see another who had a similar experience, though from a desire for a child rather than just having one awkwardly show up. This trip shifts Mary from passive recipient to active participant. An affirmation by another does wonders to set us on the path of our gift, asked for or not, and whether or not the general populace would agree. An affirmation can lead to a magnificent job description, and The Magnificat is a magnificent job description.

Note: In light of intentional and un-intentional infertility, you might advantageously drop verse 9 or modify it outside a cultural expectation of reproduction for reproduction's sake.

Psalm 114
Hopeless Hope Vigil — Opened Heart Evening

Vigil: Morning will soon be breaking. The vigil is close to an end. Abandoned Saturday is nearly Assured Sunday.

What might be expected now that a spell of specialness has been broken? A new path rises where none was seen? A new impossibility of hard-as-flint rock in a dry and thirsty land becomes a pool of water for a dry tongue in a dry body? Out of nowhere, an empty tomb fills to overflowing and rolls every stone away, reshaping them into a multitude of cornerstones and keystones and just lovely little stones in their own right.

Is this a forced conversion to meet a soon-to-rise sun, because physics will out? Has our slow movement borne fruit? How long is the half-life vigil effect? By Sunday night, this will probably have to be revisited.

For now, rock to water seems sufficient to remember. More questions will come, but, for now, a breath in, a brief hold, and release.

Evening: Just hours ago, we used this same Psalm during a Vigil. Then we hinted at a new symbol that stands between the Edenic Rivers in Genesis 2 and a River of Life in Revelation 22—a river flowing forth from what was thought to be an empty tomb. I haven't found a graphic for this, and I don't have that gift. Anyone out there able to try to put into visual form the mystery of tomb silence and river gliding on?

Moving from rock to water pooled for us to live by still seems a valuable image and another way of asking whether our heart is more open this evening. Are you less stony and more limpid?

Now: When viewing your last 10 years, can you make a similar review of the positives without mentioning the tension of being caught between a rock and a hard place with no good option, helpless to decide which way to commit suicide, or the difficulty out of which came some unexpected providential event?

Read and analyze your spirit seismometer. Test your study with a prediction of a next tremblor. Refine your next prediction on the basis of your result. Finally, your prediction and a prophecy of mercy need to have a conversation. If what you are testing for doesn't include a shaking of the foundations of an injustice, you are probably wasting your time.

Psalm 116:1–2, 12–19
Courage Thursday

A toast: "To G*D—for blessings—thanks!"

It would be so easy to turn this generosity of G*D into our own little slot machine. Ah, G*D paid off for me.

But hear how the blessings, though experienced individually, are to be dealt with in common, in community (verses 14 & 18). Our vows, our thanks, are to be visible to all. What is *your* understanding of *our* relationship to G*D?

A clue is found in the silent section, verses 3–11.

> "I shall pass my life in the presence of Yahweh, in the
> land of the living." (verse 9, *Jerusalem Bible*)

To so pass one's life is to:

> Relax and rest.
> GOD has showered you with blessings.
> Soul, you've been rescued from death;
> Eye, you've been rescued from tears;
> And you, Foot, were kept from stumbling.
> (*The Message*)

To live within and into blessings is a place of satisfaction, a place of "enough". To so live is a participation in partnership with G*D and Neighb*r. As we have been discouraged and yet remained faithful and trusting and found again our courage, so we engage others in identifying their blessing. As we have found new life, we participate in opening up the land of the living to folks who have been constrained into seeing no way out for themselves.

This day and psalm model for us how we are to be in each of the circumstances of life that we encounter.

Psalm 118:1–2, 19–29
False Dawn Sunday

Figure it this way: "The righteous get to go in through the gate of righteousness. I consider myself righteous, so open to me the gate that I may enter."

Note to self: Then be open enough to consider that I considered incorrectly. Steadfast love doesn't work on such a simplistic one-to-one correspondence. That is much too much, too boring.

Note to all: There are gates upon gates of righteousness—one gate for your form of righteousness, sure enough, and another for mine, and still others for others. All gates are the right gate—some are more easily recognized than others, but there are far more abundant gates than folks to go through. This is G*D's doing; it is marvelous in our eyes.

When our calculations turn out to be too small, think again; return to this passage and be reminded of steadfast love.

Psalm 118:1–2, 14–24
Assured

Steadfast love endures.

Now, if we could get that into our bones, we would be able to better interact with one another (we are loved) and G*D (G*D is loved) and our Neighb*rs ("they" are loved) and our environment (Creati*n is loved).

We keep forgetting and thinking/behaving as though crucifixion and suffering are just around the corner, and that is the end of the story. Easter is a time to simply say, "Love endures; Love prevails." The implication for individuals, congregations, denominations, church universal, and whatever "world" means, is as explosive as e=mc². Steadfast love is our constant for a theory of theological relativity.

A Reader's Response to this blog posting:
Wesley, Faithfully you tell the story, and nowhere on our journeys is the cross found empty without God's steadfast love filling our lives with loops of hope that surround e=mc² with the connective tissue of strings of love. Sunday's lows and highs are only some of the directions we might choose. Blessing and Peace along the way...

Wesley:
Thanks for adding loops and strings. All these things, even the fleeting ones, express a hope and connection exploding through and beyond every time and space, every strong and weak event.

Likewise with software images. We remember every iteration as good – Day.1, Day.2.5, Day.3.3.1, Day.4.6.7, Day.5.1.2, Day.6.9.7, Day.7.0, Day8.7.7.7, 2Day.

All are blessed.

Psalm 118:14–29
Assured [2]

Give thanks for it clarifies the long-haul. A stance of gratitude encourages seeing all the little fiddly-bits so needed for dealing with a glacial shift in institutions, cultures, and self. [Note to self: Given the speed of "glacial" retreat, it is no longer a descriptor for slow.]

Thanks connects us with the depths of Creati*n from which a next-needed act is called forth. In this case, our old friend "steadfast love" is a definition of "LORD". Lazy folks that we are, we think that we have said "steadfast love" when we say "LORD", but, of course, we haven't. This "LORD" all too quickly becomes "my GOD", and "steadfast love" turns into self-preservation at all costs and a position of privilege and prestige.

If this is a day of steadfast love, it is not a 24-hour day that is spoken of. This is a long-lasting experience that is longer than the "7-day" descriptor of Creati*n. This day of steadfast love is seven times eternity long. This is a deep, deep thanks.

Again, this story cannot be confined to easy particulars or justified on the basis of how it has come to be known. But, if we daily open gates of kindness, we will find all the response we have looked for—participation in calling forth the new satisfies like nothing else. So, claim a shard of light and pry open a closed door with all the compassion you can muster. Such a moment will last and last.

Misreading alert—a first glance at the pericope found this, "Oh, how I love your law! It is my *medication* all day long." You can take that where you will. Here is a comment not based on this misreading (by the way, what do you call a correct word mis-typed on its way to the brain?).

The law as a *meditation* vehicle is important. Too often law is simply an enforcement issue.

Meditation here may be a mild word for wrestling. Wisdom comes in the midst of the wrestling, not the passivity that sometimes comes to mind with meditation. Just sitting and waiting for revelation is not what this is about. An active interaction with the law becomes a guide for our living. This is different than setting the law up as an article of obeisance.

Likewise is a need for active participation in the discernment process. Simply lifting one's eyes and seeing everything being taken care of works against an earlier experience of finding conversation in the cool of the evening that would shape our next day. [And there was evening talk and morning work, each and every day, and it was and is good.] Upon the mountains or under the trees, where do you sense a healing touch arising? Is it from far away or here in our midst?

Each line of this 18ᵗʰ stanza begins with tsade (c), the 18th letter of the Hebrew "alefbet".

A tradition has grown that associates this letter with a righteous person because c begins *Tzaddikim* ("righteous ones"—who are the foundation of the earth).

This same c begins Tzimtzum or a voluntary compaction such as G*D humbly withdrawing from being all-in-all to make room for Creati*n. Additional numerological connections and other meanings have been connected with c.

———————————

honest is G*D
honest to G*D is G*D
honesty in me is G*D-ly
honesty is a G*D-ly constant
honesty lost is worth grief
honesty lost is humility's undoing
honesty is tested again and again
honesty restores stature
honesty is a kernel from which justice grows
honesty defines law's purpose
honesty loosens anxiety and distress
honesty delights
honesty remains
honest! understand?

Psalm 121
Proper 24 (29)

This psalm journeys
        from a need for help (1a)
        to searching everywhere (1b)
        to looking beyond everywhere (2)
        to assurance of having found (3–6)
        to helping (7)
        to living (8)

How would you note your own pre-Pentecost journey to assurance and then, from assurance (Pentecost), to a more energetic life journey (post-Pentecost)?

Note that dreaming is not a passive activity, but Lenten discipline.

> Dreaming includes laughter, as future becomes ever more present.
>
> Dreaming includes shouting "Joy!" at the stick-in-the-mud's resistance to move from past to present.
>
> Dreaming also includes all the pain and sorrow that is a background in which laughter is such a release.
>
> Dreaming also includes all the difficult work to prepare, plant, and nurture seeds into releasing their future.

May you dream strongly enough to bear and release the present into a better future.

Psalm 137

Proper 22 (27)

Remembering forgiveness unlimited, we now weep at what has been lost. The music of our lives that brought us to dancing together has been lost.

In this strange, unforgiving space, we are asked to sing of forgiveness out of a reserve we do not have, and we find we have lost the words—we don't want to forgive our captors. Our good right hand of fellowship through restored community has withered.

No matter how we intend to honor our heritage of forgiveness, the words just don't seem to come—our mouth is dry.

Our lack of forgiveness has us wishing harm not only upon our current enemies but all their children, not just the first-born.

Yes, we are in Babylon. Weeping. Unforgiven and unforgiving.

To return to health, we need this lament. May we see what we have done and are doing to ourselves, and not take that out on others. Let us Remember Forgiveness and build Zion anew right here in the middle of Babylon—it is a reliable, long-term tool still available to refugees from Eden and Everywhere.

Psalm 138
Guiding Gift [5] — Proper 12 (17)

There is a formula here for increasing our strength of soul. It could be a best seller because the times are right for a wonderful self-help resource. Who doesn't want their soul strengthened? There is a huge market available.

Unfortunately, it turns out that the cost of imaging G*D is high. It comes with an increased regard for the lowly and a willingness to engage in deliverance of the troubled. To do this, an increased awareness of the haughty and wrathful needs to be cultivated so they can't hide behind fancy language, accumulated resources, and easily applied power.

Soul-strengthening implies a steadfastness of purpose and application. To take one's eye off the prize of regard for and engagement with every level of the poor leaves one open to co-option by the haughty and wrathful. If we are not diligent in our awareness and implementation, we become part of the problem and our soul shrinks.

What seemed like a wonderful offering, soul-strengthening, turns out to be as difficult as anything. This is a task that cries out for not just a personal resolve, but communal support. It takes a village to strengthen a soul.

---

let us now be thankful
for humble people
who are willing to be   they have found
soul-strengthened   needy beyond imagination
                                     poor unto the generations
they will find their   abused just because
time eaten   war-torn millions
resources robbed   abandoned children
hopes erased
faith compromised   for all of this and more
troubled aplenty   they cannot sleep
                                     until souls are joined
these are not techniques   and grow once more
to bring a soul kiss
from a higher power
but a temptation of the lord

Psalm 139:1–6, 13–18

Proper 18 (23)

To be known, through and through, is not just "wonderful" but "awful". Hemmed in fore and aft, gee and haw, puts us at the end of puppet strings. Knowing how wonderfully intended we are ("Good" yelled at the top of G*D's lungs for all Creati*n to hear), we find a crevasse between such intention and our realities.

In the end, we finally come to the realization that neither intention nor reality determines the important things of life, and one of the grandest visions of life (avoiding the trap of duality between law-abiders and wicked) comes at the end of 139:18—"I am still with you."

In my best of times and worst of times, a tale of two MEs, G*D and I are still at it. May it be so for you.

[with apologies to D.H. Lawrence]

god is so nice
so awfully nice
god is the nicest person in the world.

And what's more, god is nice about being nice
about your being nice as well!
If you're not nice, god will soon make you feel it.

Abrahamists and Buddhists and Hindus and Wiccans and so on
they're all very well
but they're not really nice, you know.
They're not nice in our sense of the word, are they now?

That's why one doesn't have to take them seriously,
We must be nice to them, of course,
of course, naturally.
But it doesn't really matter what you say to them,
they don't really understand—
you can say anything to them:
be nice, you know, just nice—
but you must never take them seriously, they wouldn't understand,
just be nice, you know! Oh, fairly nice,
not too nice of course, they take advantage—
but nice enough, just nice enough
to let them feel they're not quite as nice as they might be.

Psalm 143
Hopeless Hope Vigil

How easy it is to shift from asking for mercy to refusing to give mercy.

Think about this in terms of the two 3-stanza poems that make up this Psalm (verses 1–6 and 7–12). Place them side by side instead of one after the other and watch the flow.

Is it reflective of your own way to process life, or have you disciplined yourself to walk this path in reverse? Is your choice to live poem 1 or poem 2?

Poem 1	Poem 2
active prayer for saving justice (mercy)	I'm tired out and hope to hear about a reprieve tomorrow
a situation eliciting fear is closing me down	looking for rescue through a new perspective
remembering the past refocuses a source for hope	save my neck wring their neck

Elections often turn on the wrong questions. Sometimes those questions are simply missed, and sometimes they are deliberately miscast. Each Psalm for the day talks less about an election process but looks to a desired end, regardless of who is elected.

According to the Psalmists, a key criterion for leaders' behavior and systems they support is intimately tied to justice. We will see how leaders newly elected, leaders staying in their position, and leaders yet to be will actually live up to this high calling.

17:1 - Hear a just cause (will our leaders listen?)
17:2 - let your eyes see the right (will our leaders look?)
17:4 - avoid the ways of the violent (whether preemptive or "just"?)
17:8 - guard (the measure of a just society is how the poor are treated)
98:3 - remember steadfast love and faithfulness (do it, don't just talk it)
98:4 - break forth into joyous song (for all above and following)
98:9 - G*D is present to judge righteousness and equity (no other political entity is up to this standard)
145:7 - glory and wonder come from abundant goodness and righteousness
145:8–9 - steadfast love and compassion measure grace and mercy
145:14 - the falling are upheld, the bowed down are raised
145:15 - the hungry are fed
145:17 - justice and kindness are G*D's right and left hands
145:20 - love grows to the stars of the sky, wickedness shrivels from the land of the living
145:21 - justice leads to blessing, forever and ever.

We are making our bed, and we will lie in it. What we sow, so shall we reap. The option of justice is present. Elections do not resolve these issues. Let us continue to act with faith that justice will be served, not arrogance and revenge—no matter how well they are disguised.

Psalm 146
Proper 5 (10) — Proper 21 (26)

Listen again to the listing of the beatitudes and woes —

You are blest by hope in G*D who

> made - heaven, earth, sea
> keeps - faith
> executes - justice
> gives food - hungry
> sets free - prisoners
> opens - eyes
> lifts up - bowed down
> watches over - strangers
> upholds - orphan & widow
>
> ruins - wicked.

9/10 require building good; 1/10 brings down harm.

How is it with your life?
What 10th is constructing a commonwealth?
What 10th is deconstructing uncommon wealth?

Psalm 147:12–20
Blessed Body [2]

G*D speaks to Jacob,
statutes and ordinances to Israel.

One of the questions of our day is about a correlation between our realities and the scriptures. In a three-storied universe, this laser-like action of G*D from above looks different than in a distributed universe filled with horizontal uncertainty principles, quantum inde-terminacy, and evolutionary processes.

As we celebrate a new year, how might we celebrate a new approach to and appreciation for ancient wisdom that does not con-strain a future to the past or enter a future forgetful of its past?

Christmas is not just remembrance but a continued anticipation of the new breaking into the settled and returning it to its ancient energy released from accreted constraints.

Psalm 148
Blessed Body [1] — Assured [5]

Comic books, in days of yore, had ads for X-Ray Glasses that would let you look through that which you considered to be in your way of seeing what you wanted to see. Mostly, that barrier was clothing.

Hormonally, that has a built-in appeal for adolescent boys to see through dresses (the dress of that day) and glimpse naked girls.

Relationally, it has an appeal that we can get to the reality of the person under all the masks they have put on.

Here, Praise is the equivalent of X-Ray Glasses. Praise allows us to see behind any phenomenon to some early creator. In so seeing, we are made part of the powerful (yet another appeal) who are raised up and become close to and partnered with G*D.

While practicing praise can increase the odds that it will be a first response to any number of circumstances, there remains a question about its sustainability over the long haul. It doesn't take long to figure out the gimmick of X-Ray Glasses and to set them aside. It does take longer to figure out the gimmick of Praise. In the end, it is good for the bottom-line of who or what is being praised and leaves its practitioner with a faint distaste—is this all there is?

To praise G*D in the face of Herod and contemporary Slaughterers of Innocents is questionable. When Acts of Piety, such as required praise, trump Acts of Mercy there is going to be hell to pay.

Perhaps the next time around, we will rejoice in being able to rejoice in all things, but the context of intentional inflicting of pain doesn't let us travel that path this time.

The New Interpreter's Bible reflects: "While the songs of praise generally push toward universality (see Pss 67:1–7; 100:1; 103:20–22; 117:1;...), Psalm 148 takes inclusivity to the limit, surpassing even the final climactic verse of the psalter (150:6). The inclusivity of the invitation to praise God has profound implications that demonstrate the inseparability of theology and ecology...."

Question of the day: "Is there a limit to inclusivity?"
If "yes," what is it?
If "no," why do we keep playing the same discriminatory games against people and creation?

Psalm 149
Honoring Day

Suppose this Psalm intends to show the embodiment of justice in the world.

Can you affirm this picture from verse 6—yourself as a gladiator or mercenary, muscles tensed in a threatening posture, yelling a victory yell, and grasping a sword ready to be bloodied?

Is this participation in the execution of justice one through which we usually consider the saints of the church? Certainly, there is St. George slaying a dragon, but none slaughtering other people (though that is a consequence of honoring the most fervent).

Is this picture one you would be glad to show to someone else before your PTSD kicked in?

Can you imagine a scenario wherein G*D the Compassionate, the Merciful, is honored by theocracide? Isn't it more likely that the Psalmist got it exactly right in the last verse—the gore is "our" glory?

At this point, we might ask whether this really is a new song or a reprise of a most unoriginal sin of privilege and division. Haven't we slid too easily past the humble in verse 4 to the victorious in verse 9?

As we come to the conclusion of the Psalms, are we really looking for Pirate Saints? Yo-ho-ho and a bottle of rum! Watch us dance on dead men's chests!

Psalm 150
Assured [2]

Following Thomas:

Question prevailing wisdom!
Question G*D in the sanctuary
  and everywhere.

Question authority and power.
Is this as good as it gets?
This is greatness?

Question G*D blatantly
  or implicitly.
Questions are music to the ear.

Question enthusiastically.
Question in concert with others.
Questions set our lives dancing.

Question out loud.
Question just because.
And be questioned in return.

Let everything question G*D!
Praise the Questioner!
Question praise!

Proverbs 8:1–4, 22–31
Live Together

Ahh, Lady Wisdom, Madame Insight, finally raises a clear eye and a firm voice to the nonsense that has been swirling about, confusing folks as to where life might be found and growth occur.

As often with wisdom, it surfaces in the in-between places of life, such as the elided section of the pericope. Listen to some of the words we miss this week that we need to adopt in the midst of competing bases of authority and power:

virtuous questions	hate evil
truth	counsel
justice	resourcefulness
straightforward	courage
prudence	love
knowledge	resources
foresight	righteousness

Without a good wrestle with these, we are simply left with the emptiness of self-importance. Look at me! See how important I am! G*D and I are closer than crossed fingers! Just do as I say!

We need the middle section that will not be heard unless we claim a wisdom that goes beyond praise, praise, praise. I wouldn't be surprised to find the good news of Pentecost that was shared in native tongues exactly parallels the missing images. Good news is always grounded in clarifying issues and enhancing lives. Pentecost is not just about praise, but bringing light to the troublesome areas of present lives (those 2,000 and 4,000 years ago, as well as right now and 2,000 years into the future).

If you need a Trinitarian reference this day, consider verse 30 and the rare and disputed word ʾamôn which is understood in at least three ways—an artisan or master builder, a nursing child, or a confidant. With each of our encounters with wisdom, it will be wise to consider the context from all three perspectives.

Proverbs 8:1–8, 19–21; 9:4b–6
Hopeless Hope Vigil

We have set our sights on winning and been persuaded that this Jesus is the way to go. We like his odds. And then, somewhere around the ninth round, Jesus is knocked out of the ring. He lost. We lost. How can we understand what is swirling around and through us?

What happened to Wisdom? How'd we hear so incorrectly? Isn't this all about ending up on the right side so we will inherit wealth and treasure?

Wisdom talks about choosing the winning side for a reward or choosing the losing side and punishment. Who in their right mind wouldn't place their bet on who they thought their next boss was going to be, rather than on who they considered didn't have a chance? After all of Wisdom's persuasion to choose, does the purchase of a next-in-line lottery ticket have better or worse odds than the best-planned fantasy football team? Is it all fate?

Ask about the context of judgment of the "wise" and the "foolish". Is it all about how our choices panned out? Is there a place for a context of forgiveness and a continuous offer of a larger wholeness?

If life comes down to individual choice and consequences without a context of steadfast love anyway, let's mosey on to place our next bet. For now, take a deep breath, identify and evaluate the values you thought this Jesus offered. If they are still valuable, hold them and enact them in the midst of this moment of abandonment and hope. This is our edge when the fates seem so strongly set against us. Bet on love, not success.

Proverbs 25:6–7
Proper 17 (22)

There is a tension here.

Living in community brings with it expectations regarding a system of valued interactions. Knowing your place and the place of others does grease the wheels of certainty and security. Not making waves and self-censorship become expected behaviors. Breaking these carries a huge penalty. We still live in a world of shame and blame.

Living in a community brings with it opportunities to recognize where harm is being done and to stand against its continuation. This brings not only a recognition of place but a willingness to risk one's place to make right another's place because we are all in this together. At some point, there is a resolve to be vulnerable and confront powers who will be affronted by such. Shame and blame become passé in light of great injury to the whole community from that community's great harm to some segment of itself.

This little piece of wisdom comes to remind us of this tension and to raise the possibility of an honest look at the whole without a built-in calculus of the limits of new life for the whole community—residents and aliens, rich and poor, those on the way to more wisdom and those satisfied with a static status.

Ecclesiastes 1:2, 12–14; 2:18–23
Proper 13 (18)

Suppose that The Gatherer were to address Hosea 1:1–11.

What a vanity, this tough-pretending G*D. Old Ephraim has been busy with the business of living in human form—unhappy business. We hate our toil; G*D hates our toil. Finally, there is despair from humans and despair from G*D—the more we were called, the more we went in the opposite direction. Thus, despair in all directions.

A solution to this unhappy business is not despair squared, but a recognition that, despairing or not, we and G*D won't give up. Fierce despair/anger won't be unleashed. Rather, what is unleashed are those old hounds-of-heaven and when they arrive, there is a great licking of faces. Imagine forgiveness as slobber—compassion, warm and tender—will find us at home again.

> caught between
> vanity and vanity
> hearken back
> at distance
>
> once loved
> given up for lost
> and threatened
> nothing left
>
> still loved
> compassion shines through
> no more wrath
> welcome home
>
> sense this
> wavering wind of uncertainty
> trembling bird
> new future

Isaiah 1:1, 10–20
Proper 14 (19)

Right thinking is concerned with getting rituals correct.
Right action is concerned with getting justice correct.

There is nothing to keep these from working together. However, the witness of religious history is that religio/politico rituals keep trumping elementary justice; religious laws keep trampling lived experience. Were this not the case, the prophetic tradition, a third of the TaNaKh, would not have the continued presence and power it has.

In this adversarial setting, G*D has seen a larger picture:

> Sin marked from beige to scarlet
> shall be made unremarkable—reset.

And so a question: Given this eventuality, to what are we called to attend and practice?

Do you want to participate in the "snow/wool" conclusion or the "scarlet/crimson" resistance? If the latter, here's an agenda:

- do no harm
- do good
- seek justice
  rescue, defend, and plead for
  the oppressed, orphan, and widow

This is importantly different from other approaches, such as the General Rules of the United Methodist Church:

- do not harm
- do good
- attend to the ordinances of God
  public worship,
    Word (read or expounded), and Lord's Supper
  private prayer,
    searching Scripture, and abstinence/fasting

These can work together. However, religious ordinances—in our day against LGBTQ Christians—keep tripping up that which is for the "good of the land," the commonwealth of G*D, and a healthy connection between belief and action.

Those who wrongly associate Sodom and Gomorrah with sexual sin need to attend to this and other scriptural accounts, which show the issues there were injustice, violence, and poverty. For these separations, there is no amount of praise and worship that will cover or excuse them. There are and will be consequences for every act of inhospitality.

There is no bribing G*D for participating in hurtful behavior. Always, there is a clear voice calling for a care-for-others and a compassion-for-all. There is no excuse for relying on sacrificial repentance when a pervasive presence of mercy is always an option.

Want to make this easy on yourself?

(1) Cease separating your actions from your excuses that you might see the real consequences of your actions.

(2) Go out of your way to restore justice, restrain all manner of violence, and see that everyone has enough without judging their use of it.

Now the internal argument revealed in cognitive dissonance can be put to rest, and we can practice mercy for others as we would receive mercy.

Isaiah 5:1–7
Proper 15 (20)

Must be the Dog Days of Summer—Jesus is looking to burn up the earth, Isaiah is prophesying destruction for a vineyard, the Psalmist recognizes similar destructions have fallen upon the land and pleads for new light, and the letter writer to the Hebrews recounts a cloud of persecutions witnessed. The sweat of our brow is soaking inward, softening the mind and clouding hope.

It is hard enough to do justice when comfortable. When the hot stickies of Sirius joins with the heat of Sol, it is easy to let a bit more justice slip away—who has the energy to do elsewise?

It is hard enough to be consciously moving toward being G*D (merciful) when comfortable. When the heat humidity index hits the danger level, we hide further away from our self and one another. Who has the fortitude to resist an absence of intention? We can hardly move ourselves.

No matter what our call, it is trumped by such little water droplets in warm air and by the driest of heat rising beyond the bearable.

But we know that, so why don't we factor it in to our rhythms and our awareness? Regardless of life's distractions, look just one more time at what is going on around you and offer a cup of cool water to someone in need, a refreshing word of support to a whole group prohibited from simply being. Yes, we can move beyond ordinary limits! Bloodshed can be stanched by justice and the mercy it represents.

Isaiah 6:1–8, (9–13)
Guiding Gift [5]

Guilt is very powerful. Whether it is appropriate guilt or inappropriate guilt, it has a controlling presence in our lives. We find ourselves reduced when it is felt and monstrous when it is absent. In some sense, guilt is something we can't live with or without.

Even when we have previously experienced guilt departing from us and the freedom that opens, we usually forget that sequence and hang on to the next guilt as long as ever we can. A great benefit of a congregation is the reminder system available to help us remember that it is more possible than we thought to be relieved of guilt—just in time to be burdened by a particular calling.

The Natural Church Development folks talk about gift-based ministries. One of the blockages to this is personal and congregational guilt (note: guilt operates on every level in which we do: ideational, national, personal, theological, congregational, etc.).

It makes a huge difference when guilt is taken away or cast away (directionality here probably doesn't make any difference, though it would be very important to some to have it fit their theology/philosophy).

Remember a time your guilt was removed. Apply that to a current guilt. Go ahead.

----

trapped – touched – freed –
an ongoing cycle
moves us from stage to stage

the current play of our life
takes a lot of staging
it is hard to take it on the road

the next stage of our life
asks us to put down
guilty baggage

when staging our next act
there will be a different audience
we will know through play

honoring our current stage
honoring our next audience
ahh, play is the thing

Isaiah 7:10–14
Creation's Conception

Since the 2nd century, this passage has been a dividing line between people. Is it a Jewish prophetic story about some young woman seen by both Ahaz and Isaiah? Is it a Christian story presaging a young Mary, generations in the future? It even divides Christians depending upon their theological need as reflected upon in *The New Interpreter's Bible*, "Texts such as this one, especially when read in the context of Christian worship, sharpen the tension between the historical meaning and the homiletical or theological interpretation of the Bible, and of the Old Testament in particular."

Speculation has it that the "young woman" was passing by or was Isaiah's wife (8:1–4) or was Ahaz's Queen, Abijah (Abi), who gave birth to Hezekiah (Immanuel?), a mirror image of Ahaz and later counseled by Isaiah.

What do you mark as a significant beginning spot?

A big bang?

A big asteroid?

A new relationship?

Your own conception?

A particular war?

A philosophic insight?

The pious denial of a sign by Ahaz or the subsequent eagle-eye of Isaiah to note a pregnant woman before anyone else saw it?

Starting points are important as they shape what we will subsequently carve into stone. Later, any alternative starting point to our self-affirmed certainty becomes cause for censorship and repression. Any idea what our next agreed-upon starting point will be and how long it will last?

Isaiah 9:2–7

Blessed Body – Proper I

There is a promise of an endless peace ahead, and if we paid attention, we would know it is already present. What is the way to that peace—waiting for another angelic flaming sword or chorus? Nope, the way to peace is peace, and it runs through you and me.

The zeal of ALL will do this. Does this mean we are simply to stand back, get out of G*D's way, and clap when the magic is accomplished? Nope. G*D work is not turning you into a puppet.

You are the locus of the zeal of G*D.

Whenever we are open to partnering with the zeal of G*D, it is a birth experience in the midst of a deep darkness. A light shines within us and without us (in both senses). Even before morning light, tonight could be an Eve that goes down in history. May you also be zealous for participating in such activity.

Isaiah 12
Proper 28 (33)

In "that" day: Give thanks....

Do you trust that day will come? If so, why not give thanks now as well as then?

Trust and thanks are antidotes to fear. Trust and thanks are rope and winch lowering and raising a bucket into the wells (plural) of salvation to bring forth Joy. Trust and thanks free us from the fear of anger and control of anger.

In preparation for a focus on thanks-giving and thanks-living, it might be helpful to focus on its twin of trust. Trust lays the groundwork for the courage it takes to sing a new song in an old situation. Trust breaks fear's grip. Trust is another way of spelling salvation from that which looms over us and another way of spelling health or wholeness, pulling us past any rough spot we face.

I give thanks
you – give thanks!

we move
from experience
to rote requirements

forgetting
my thanks is mine
forgetting
your thanks is yours

thanks becomes a technique
we apply to intolerable situations
as though going through this motion
we will change the unspeakable
from fearful to our advantage

starting with thanks
we can go anywhere
with strengthened trust
we are truly at home
wherever we are
and whenever

Isaiah 12:2–6
Needed Change [3] — Hopeless Hope Vigil

An interesting phrase: "G*D has become my salvation."

Compare and contrast that with another statement: "G*D is my salvation."

If salvation is connected with some form of wholeness, might we say, "G*D and I are becoming whole together"? What, then, shifts in our addressing life if salvation is a journey rather than either an accomplished end to be remembered or some result to be anticipated? This makes Advent (or any waiting process) more process-oriented than focused on some external mechanism having left the stars and arrived at our humble abode.

Isaiah 25:6–9
Opened Heart Evening

It is crucial to read the verses immediately preceding this lection. The context for all this current joy and continued hope is that the poor have been cared for. Nations are broken because the poor are further and further oppressed. When that break comes, the poor are relieved and can breathe again—participate in saying a Word of New Creati*n and shaping a new earth, cousin to a new heaven.

When a banquet is laid, it is in contrast to the starvation of the poor who have been in service to the gluttony of the rich (whether conscious of either thrall or gluttony or not).

When we hear of the destruction of death, we have no length added to our days. What is now present is protection from an artificial shortening of life through poverty and war—human misapplications of power.

On such a day as this, we can look back and rejoice. Simultaneous to this day of rejoicing is work to see another such day tomorrow and tomorrow. It is when all three of these days work together that we will finally rejoice. Until then, we rejoice where we can and move onward.

Has Easter helped us enter this movement of resetting current harms until they are gone? Or, have we simply come to the end of a day having acquired a new bonnet for ourselves at the cost of indentured bonnet-makers located at enough distance to be invisible to us? Such a choice is still before us as we act as though a stone has been shifted or is still blocking life together.

Isaiah 42:1–9
Clarification Week: Monday

To be a beloved one is to be a just one.
Justice? What is it?

- Not to lord it over others through propaganda or rhetoric; to have a gentle voice.

- Not to take advantage of someone already down and out; to tend the bruised.

- Not to remove hope from the weak; to bring light.

Justice is first a "not" and then a "to".

All of this is to spring forth from your assurance of being a beloved one of G*D.
It's Monday: Shine; Show.
Don't forget to do the same on Friday and Saturday.

Isaiah 43:1–7
Beloved

Formed incarnate, redemption already secure, we pass through waters dark and deep, water standing against water.

Called from chaotic exile, already created for glory, we rise through waters light and lively, water living within water.

Isaiah envisions active transformation as an integral part of our incarnation, our formation. He remembers an exodus initially protected by parted water and all the desert and parting of more water to come. He anticipates those who had been buried far away will come surfing back. There is nothing static about redemption. Redemption is never "once for ever".

Reading Isaiah emboldens us as we pass through our next water of redemption to find a glory not fully dreamed. Can you imagine living already and continually redeemed, already glorious?

> that which you create
> is imbued with a goodness
> never lost
>
> we learn this creation gift
> reflecting on our own
> ever found

Isaiah 43:16–21
Conviction [5]

There has been a running debate about how best to praise G*D.

Some frame praise entirely within religious language—one has to speak Religion in order for G*D to hear, otherwise you are wasting your breath.

Some frame praise entirely outside religion's bounds—one must do some will-of-G*D for a Neighb*r for it to be accepted, otherwise you are wasting your energy.

Some try to portion those positions out with some acceptable ratio of the two.

This may be another arena where an untenable synthesis of fully praising G*D and fully caring for Neighb*r will come to the forefront. In the meantime, it might be helpful to consider some new things.

If you tend to lump praise under language skills, a new thing for you (desired from you by G*D, even?) would be engaging your translation skills from language to deed.

If you are one who tends to see praise as doing what was asked rather than talking about it, a new thing G*D may be looking for from you is a reflection on what lies behind your deeds.

Any approach to praise is open to a downside of habit and a slow, slippery slide toward irrelevance. What keeps praise alive is an attitude of finding new occasions and styles for its expression.

———————————

carrying father's Alzheimer genes
I look forward
to not remembering former things
of recent days
and living in a land of former things
ancient of days

a former of formers
was a new thing once
new things can hold
former things at bay
and open future things
foiling former's fate

ontogeny recapitulates phylogeny
sometimes
and vice versa others
either way
former becomes present
former becomes future

this calls for praise
former as former
present as present
future as future
intersecting well
living daily

Isaiah 49:1–7
Clarification Week: Tuesday

Early promises can freeze us into Sunday School responses that do not help us engage new situations. This is particularly the case when a promise is huge, such as descendants too numerous to count, or a promised land becomes idolized. There is much to be worked out every day and every generation.

Note how G*D is upping the ante. You thought you were here for a plan, and now the plan shifts to no plan or a different plan. Everything is back on the table as G*D says, "We've thought too small." The plan is no longer personal or tribal, but global. It is no longer what is in it for you and yours, but universal salvation and health of which yours is but a part.

Oh my!

To move in this direction is literally to end our youth and childhood. We are to expand our image of steadfast love to enemies, strangers, and the just weird. It will take the death of the Sunday School part of us to set free an adult relationship and partnership with G*D. Stand by. The game is afoot.

Isaiah 50:4–9a

Premature Fear Sunday — Clarification Week: Wednesday

On Hump Day, we need a word about sustenance in the midst of weariness. Carrying on the excitement of a Palm Parade is as difficult as remembering any parade. Subsequent days bring their agendas, and the parade fades. Likewise, keeping a passion-of-dread fresh and alive is wearing.

Teachers and learners of an encouraging word are sustained by attending, day by day, to the echo and witness of the cosmos. Its explosive expansion simply carries on, eon by eon. We hear of this steadfastness, and we share what we hear. It sustains a first hearing and each subsequent hearing. All can be born and borne.

For today, it is enough. Hump Day becomes Dayenu Day, and we can breathe again with thanks for where we have been and affirmation of what yet lies ahead.

Isaiah 52:7–10
Blessed Body: Proper III

How beautiful are mountain feet running to announce peace.
How beautiful are manger tootsies waiting to walk in peace.

We sing for joy amid past ruins as we live a hope for restoration.
We sing for joy amid present ruination as we live a hope not based on
   resurrection.

Not knowing how much beauty and joy are glimpses into future
options, whether from the past to the present or from the present to
the future, we see and invest in birthing, health, and wholeness for
ourselves and all.

Isaiah 52:13–53:12
Consequence Friday

Language is made even more difficult than usual for communicating when we follow Humpty Dumpty and say one thing to mean another.

Biblical interpretation is difficult enough if we wrestle with what is singular and what is plural (as found in this passage). If all we hear growing up is sin talk, it becomes doubly difficult to later hear its derivation. Anything can grow from an initial impulse to love/create/release. Even sin can be seen as a subset of love—love's absence or redirection by some entitlement desire.

Note that no matter how despised and rejected, oppressed and afflicted this beloved one might be, they are still beloved. Even if ground into the ground, the amazing reality of their presence cannot be reduced below belovedness. Their steadfastness, even to death, only reveals a larger love before which the hardest head and coldest heart will be seen.

Bearing sin here is not the bearing of sin of others, taking responsibility for the sin of others, but to recognize that it is the sins of others that brought about this perversion of justice. This can be heard in a comment from the *Jewish Study Bible* regarding verse 53:4–6:

> Either the servant suffered on behalf of the speakers (i.e., the guilty were not punished at all), or he suffered along with the guilty, even though he himself did not share in the guilt of his fellow Israelites. The former idea (i.e., the notion of vicarious suffering) would be unusual for the Bible; the latter idea (the idea of corporate guilt) is not.

Again, how do you play with "bearing sin" and "revealing love"? Which is vicarious, a substitute for real life? Which is prophetic, a demonstration of how far we have gone astray together?

Isaiah 55:1–9
Conviction [3]

In just how much of the image of G*D are we made? Are we partners with G*D or just sales associates? Co-creators? Just how much higher are G*D's ways and thoughts than our own?

All too often, we turn this into an eternal co-dependency rather than a movement toward holiness for both G*D and ourselves—a revelation or wholeness of both and all. One book that talks about the maturing of G*D (not needing to show off) is *The Disappearance of God: A Divine Mystery* by Richard Elliott Friedman. Here is a sample:

> It is ironic that, starting with Bible scholars, we have begun to use the intimate name of God again, especially since the nineteenth century, precisely in the period of acknowledged divine hiddenness. Let us hope that we are not using it in vain, but that we are moving closer to the entity that the name represents. The name Yahweh probably means "that which causes to be." And that which causes to be is what we are seeking. It is what we have been seeking all along. We may be very close to it. There is some likelihood that, as some of the conscious matter of the universe, we are created more in the divine image than we have suspected. There is some likelihood that the universe is the hidden face of God.

The holiness questions of theosis, sanctification, and perfection are importantly applied here.

Isaiah 55:1–11
Hopeless Hope Vigil

Hey! Anyone thirsty? Come to the waters.
(Isaiah 55:1)

Water, water, everywhere, nor any drop to drink.
(Samuel Taylor Coleridge)

In the midst of a vigil, strange visions come—water of creation, water of destruction, water on which to ride it out, water teaming with leviathans, water releasing doves of belovedness, water of bitterness, and water living.

Trying to stay awake mixes us up. Is it that our thoughts don't contain mercy naturally, and so we need to beg for it and set up rules to enforce mercy artificially? Was that part of our creation not in G*D's image? Or is our mercy as high as G*D's ways and thought—sometimes flowing freely and sometimes withdrawn from consideration as hearts are hardened?

Between Saturday and Sunday, we waver. Wait out our loss? Cut our losses and move on? We find ourselves drawn in both directions and tempted to ride off in all directions.

This vigil business is not easy, as we continue in our fear and can't force a new morning of hope to arrive on our schedule.

Isaiah 55:10–13
Guiding Gift [8] — Proper 3 (8)

We have come through pre-war prophecies of judgment and needed repentance (chapters 1–39) as well as consolations of promise and needed renewal (chapters 40–55). Here is a summary of where we have come—ready to see if our experiences can make a difference as we move ahead into a new opportunity to care for the land and those who live on it, the air and sea and those who live in them.

This passage is a description of our energy to move ahead.

1) What do you understand is a Word from G*D? Does it have to do with calling new life forth and claiming it is "Good"? Does it have to do with nurture and hospitality? Does it have to do with learning and a next opportunity?

2) There is a joy deep enough to provide safety/assurance that the barriers, wars, regressions, closed hearts and minds, and the like will not block this joy of deeper relations from being expressed. In this joy, there will come thunderclaps rhythmically beating under new harmonies growing from old dissonances. Here, in joy, we find a fitting home-coming—a new chance for a further Eden.

And, so prepared, we launch into the concluding chapters (56–66) containing a variety of alternative realities.

May this moment of anticipating a continuation of a first Word of G*D hold you in good stead to use your gifts amid strangers and receive their gifts in your life. We can fold Epiphany into Ordinary Time and vice versa for the encouragement of both.

Isaiah 58:1–12
Self-Recognition Day

Our recent heritage is to reduce communal words to personal disciplines. This has value to some. It is a larger burden to bear for most—and who needs that?

In the way we move back and forth regarding freedom, we now find freedom in fellowship and now in release from community constraint. It is probably time to take a step back toward the familial. In this return, we will hopefully recognize at least one new limit on autonomy and join a recovery group for those addicted to "me first" to practice a life-long fast from rampant individualism.

In returning this passage to the plural, we see again that adding all individual works of charity together does not and cannot make the changes necessary to let the currently oppressed go free. This takes a renewal of communal structures.

Instead of all the individual head-hanging and hand-wringing, this is a day for a level-headed, clear-eyed analysis of verse 8b—

> Implemented justice is to lead you on
> leaving a straight row of "it is good" behind

It takes us, together, to break unjust chains and yokes of oppression, distribute an abundance of food to the hungriest, shelter unnumbered homeless, restrain the still malicious, and meet the needs of the variously afflicted. When these are agreed upon goals and put into action, the imagined fears, previously restraining us from working together, part to reveal light most unexpected.

There are no individual repairers of divisions or pot-holed street restorers. This is common work binding together individual gifts.

Don't forget to also put ashes on the altar and pulpit for all the ways the church has not fasted from harm. The church, too, has come from dust and shall, thereto, return.

Isaiah 58:9b–14
Proper 16 (21)

This comment includes Jeremiah 1:4–10 as a conversation partner. Is there conversation to be had between Isaiah and Jeremiah, as there is between Job and Proverbs?

Of interest are Jeremiah's boyhood diffidence and an immature or rigid appointment over nations. Imagine you can hear Isaiah's age commenting on the yoke implied in Jeremiah's call and invite Jeremiah to be a source of assurance rather than a speaker about justice.

Isaiah might be counseling the doing of justice over the proclamation of justice.

What conversation partners do you have?

---

speaking loudly
because god is speaking
through me for the ages
since before birth
to this day
I speak as commanded

such is the arrogance
of Jeremiah
and even each of us
such assurity
enough to destroy
before planting

such temper
calls for tempering
removing a yoke
that requires such power
offering nothing in its place
but afflicted needs

Isaiah 60:1–6
Guiding Gift

Arise. Shine. A light has come to little ol' you.

Where once there was darkness, a light shines on you.

There is no hiding your belovedness.

Folks are already being drawn to you that your gifts might be mingled with theirs and the common good enhanced.

What is being revealed in destroyed Jerusalem or a manger in Bethlehem or your own locale is the importance of all, from the most overlooked or looked down upon to the most praised and honored. Without your gifts received and given, we, together, are slowed down.

It is time to accept that you are as much in the spotlight as anyone, so act—act as though you mean something.

For whose sake will you not shut up? Let us count those who cov-et our voice.

Yes, the list will extend past our ability to count and also reveal our bias and our blindness. It is important to start anyway. Are you willing to list 5 for whose sake you will not be quiet?

Here are five to get the ball rolling:
- those diminished by others for their sexual orientation
- those constrained by mental illness
- those victims of war (including those perpetrating such)
- those who simply hunger and thirst
- those whose words are but shadows of their thoughts and feel-ings

Add your five arenas of care and send the list on to others. It would be interesting to see the results of several lists after they have been added to a dozen or so times. It would also be interesting to see your list from a year ago and a list you would make in another year.

-
-
-
-
-

To what end will we speak up? That those spoken for, and all, might see themselves crowned with beauty, delighted, and in com-munity.

Isaiah 62:6–12
Blessed Body – Proper II

This is a tricky passage to delve into in a Christmas setting. Yes, we could play with "salvation comes" or "is coming". A focus could also be put on a "signal" to all those awake enough to receive it (those known as "the people").

For now, take a step back to verses 6c–7.

> No rest for you who strive to gather G*D's attention.
> Pester G*D until captivated Jerusalem breathes peace.

Here, we are not looking for some subtle babe to slowly grow. We are demanding direct engagement to clear a way through closed doors and enforced closets. We are taking bids on clearing up Babel-ese that restricts communication and travel between peoples needing one another's gifts.

As much as we would like to consider "Emmanuel", present and accounted for, it will take more than a stork-drop in Bethlehem to vicariously save and make whole. Remember, the vision and our work are finally about transforming people and their interconnections.

Isaiah 65:1–9
Proper 7 (12)

"As wine is found in the grape", so is peace present in our current situation.

When ready to lie down and give it up, we awake to pancakes and coffee. Having gathered our strength for yet another forty days of questing we go on to find a sheer silence in the cacophony of our current situation.

Potential abounds, but it takes imagination and diligence to work at it. If G*D is ready to be found by those who do not seek and continues to invest in being present, so we are ready to find those invisible to us and reenter the fray of life.

———————————

do not destroy
there is blessing
in the midst
of subsets
of creation

from a little grape
dandelions and honey
intoxicating spirits
warm and energize
new creation

from a little Jacob
Leah and Rachel
inheritors of mountains
trick and treat
old creation

from a little you
G*D and Neighb*r
cave dwellers
quiet and change
any reality

Isaiah 65:17–25
Assured — Proper 28 (33)

For what purpose was creation begun? Because G*D said so? To have people have dominion? That all might fall in order for a hero to redeem some of them ("believers")? Even G*D needs a Galatea?

Note that a creation of new heavens (plural) and a new earth (singular) is all wrapped up in the creation of Jerusalem as a joy.

One might surmise that where joy is present, new heavens and earth pop into being. Joy may be one thing that religion has a most difficult time with because of religion's obsession with G*D or ultimate authority. Religion uses great seriousness to approach such.

Joy here is defined as justice implemented:

- No more weeping or distress
  —justice at work, joy results.

- No preventable deaths, early or late
  —justice at work, joy results.

- No homelessness or hunger for houses will be built and gardens tended
  —justice at work, joy results.

- No violence of stealing another's property
  —justice at work, joy results.

- No idle idleness for meaningful work is available
  —justice at work, joy results.

- Labor will sustain one and all
  —justice at work, joy results.

- A workable community and environment will build a holy mountain
  —justice at work, joy results.

As we close off the joy of a surprise of Easter, Pentecost, or today, we ask whether our joy quotient is higher than it was a year ago. If it is, we are building in a creative direction. If it is not, we are tearing something down. If we let things like an economy or a wedge issue raise our anger, but not our joy, we have missed an important learning. G*D is about to create joy and invites us to be glad and rejoice sufficiently to join G*D in so creating.

To read only these verses, without what comes immediately before and follows to the end of Isaiah, is to be tempted to one form of exceptionalism or another. Here is a little pocket carved out from where we can gaze out at all the destruction—the dead bodies of those named rebels to G*D, those who displeased a divine ruler exempt from creaturely limits.

For the moment, enjoy the imagery of being special. You can birth without pain; your labor brings forth without a sweaty brow; your angers do not eventuate in one death or many.

Know, though, that your kin are still your kin even if wantonly destroyed. But for a specialness beyond your control, you, too, would be horror personified.

Begin with imagery from *The New Jerusalem Bible*:

> Rejoice with Jerusalem,
> so that you may be suckled and satisfied
> from her consoling breast,
> so that you may drink deep with delight
> from her generous nipple.

Now, suckled and satisfied, how do you proceed to raise the bones of the privileged who go their own way at the expense of others? How do you strengthen the bones of the privileged to bear the weight of the lame simply because they are kin? How do you heal the bones of the privileged to be a sign of a new way to live together?

These are questions for ourselves, for we have the privilege of having been suckled and satisfied. Now what?

Jeremiah 1:4–10
Guiding Gift [4]
Proper 16 (22)

Imagine Jeremiah as a new Adam.

Adam is appointed dominion over bird and beast.
Jeremiah is appointed dominion over nation and state.

How effective was Adam? Jeremiah?
Will giving Jesus dominion over heaven and hell get us further?
What is the level of dominion that you are involved with? a tree of life? a new heaven and new earth? and how are you doing?
Perhaps it is sufficient to experience a touch of life and go ahead where you can go ahead.

Jeremiah can also be compared to Moses. Though this is the beginning of his life of prophecy, it extended for 40 years, as did Moses' work. Both begin their ministry with natural images—burning bush and almond branch. Both have priestly connections as well as prophetic. Both mark changes in eras—from captivity and into it.

Jeremiah represents a lifetime of calls (verses 1–3). I hope you are enjoying your latest call. There is no telling how long it will last before another comes along. So, gird up those loins, young or old, and grasp your walking stick for there are miles to go, calls to go.

In each of your calls, there will be elements for you to

- pull up and tear down,
- take apart and demolish,
- and, then, start over,
- building and planting.

This is simply a matter of a consequence of life. It cannot ethically be avoided. And so the call to enjoy your opportunities to participate in journeying with G*D and Neighb*r, whether in a demolishing or planting call.

If G*D were domesticated, we would be wrong to stray. A tenting G*D, however, both wanders away and intentionally moves on. In such an image, we wander in place when we are not intentionally moving on.

While G*D's complaint about those G*D brought on Exodus has some legitimacy concerning folks no longer on the same page, a question must be asked about who has wandered and who has stayed the same.

Imagine a Living G*D who has moved further down the line and a people who are still reacting out of rituals from the past. Might the people be considered to have "moved far from G*D" simply by staying still? This can be seen as a difficulty of our being able to keep up.

One reason for looking at things this way is that G*D is described as a fountain and the people as leaky cistern diggers. A fountain is moving; a cistern is still.

From the other side, our danger is not in hewing to past movements of G*D but failing to keep on moving with G*D. Courage friends. It is time to strike out again for promises larger than can be held in today's hands.

Jeremiah 4:11–12, 22–28
Proper 19 (24)

Even though it is difficult to break beyond your experience, the values of your community, the paradigms handed to you, to not do so can lead to writhing in soul pain. This is especially true when it comes to major symbols of meaning. Here, to proclaim against Jerusalem is to call into question all that is holy. After all, isn't Jerusalem the sign of religious exceptionalism—our G*D is not only an awesome G*D but a winning G*D and, did I mention, *my* G*D.

Those who can only live within current power structures are known as court prophets who tell one another about the way it should be, which, fortuitously, is how it currently is. To see no clouds on the horizon is a common but ultimately false way to live. We have so many court prophets that we are empty, empty of understanding.

A very neat thing about this passage is that even though all considered holy is abandoned, it is not a full end. Yes, an end, but a necessary beginning point to shed the accretion of lies (especially those mini-truths that go just a tad beyond what can actually be known) that have deafened us to the full range of gifts that can move a community forward. Eventually, we will be able to hear, "All of creation is holy" without breaking it into rankings of this is holy, that is less holy, and that isn't holy at all.

Start mourning now for a next end in your life. It will be as final as final can be. You won't be able to go back again. Yet (what a wonderful word)—Yet this is not a full end but a new reality that pushes us to journey onward. If you have mourned well, your ears will open to a real and less far-off hymn that hails a new creation.

English and Hebrew scriptures have different versifications in this passage. Don't trust any classification system. All of them will too soon lose the poetic soul of the experience written of as they divide, and divide again, a whole experience—dissection cannot find a soul.

Just before these words at hand (8:13–17), Jeremiah is informed of G*D's decision to put an end to the people—to harvest them (and not in a good way).

I like the translation of 8:18 in *The Jewish Study Bible*. They note the meaning is uncertain, which always gives a bit of liberty.

> *When in grief I would seek comfort,*
> *My heart is sick within me.*

Jeremiah has heard extremely bad news and is looking for an out, and only finds G*D's tears available to him as he hears G*D moan:

> *Because my people are shattered, I am shattered;*
> *I am dejected, seized by desolation.*

There is no healing balm available to the poor—the poor in G*D but rich in various idols.

Only weeping is left.

These spiritually poor lose track of G*D and their own Self. This shows up in the way they deal with One Another, Neighb*rs, and Enemies. They are already in exile before they even know exile to be a vague, far-off possibility that they will not be able to avoid.

Well, Friends of Jeremiah, a dishonest spirit is as troublesome as dishonest wealth. They go together. Whichever comes first, the other is sure to follow. So, given where we are and the predictability of another exile for any nation claiming to be a city on a hill, a beacon, without actually doing the hard work necessary to have us simply be a neighboring city and to only be a steel against which another's flint is struck, it is time to weep.

We are harvesting the accumulation of dishonest wealth and dishonest spirit. This is worth weeping over as we are too far gone to reasonably shift gears. In fact, the pace of a coming exile is increasing. Those with ears can hear it grinding and slouching forward. Be not surprised. Simply do the cleansing work of weeping that keeps clear a larger vision beyond this particular desolation and grief.

Jeremiah 14:7–10, 19–22
Proper 25 (30)

There is doubt about the sincerity of the communal prayer in the first section (7–10) as it attempts to chide G*D into action: "You are absent and powerless—prove otherwise."

This attempt to get G*D to do our work becomes clearer in the second part. Note the second half of verse 19.

> We looked for peace that would sustain
>   our privilege and found nothing.
> We hoped for relief from unwanted change
>   and found only an option of terror.

This is the great "sin" against G*D—looking for G*D to do it all... leaving G*D responsible for our security, especially when we set up structures disadvantaging folks to the point of no choice but to overthrow us. Avoiding our own accountability does no one a favor.

It is as though we have become our own idol—futile to effect needed change.

A result is a hope constrained to perpetuating a particular past wherein our comfort is at the expense of another's discomfort. This dividing up of creation goes far beyond distinction—all the way to discrimination.

No wonder G*D's response claims these praying people are actually bobbing and weaving to avoid hearing a response of, "Grow up." Again, we are back to the beginning of this pericope:

> Our actions indict us; this is another fine mess we've
> gotten ourselves into. We have met the enemy and
> they are us—bail us out: You take the risk and we'll
> receive the reward.

It is a long while since Pentecost, but rebuilding a larger community outside our usual lines is still a potent antidote to idolatrous expectations.

Above all, know this: Your heart is devious. We are as much a puzzle to ourselves as we are to others and to G*D.

As such, we live and breathe skepticism and cynicism. We test and are tested.

The blessing in all this finds open places in which to place a new root and be ever more firmly anchored. The curse in all this finds nothing but shifting sands that elude and cover-over.

And so, in our extremity, we are blind to the coming of relief and, in our satiation, deaf to cries of need.

We yearn for insight that releases and awareness that commits.

In all this, we pray G*D will respond out of mercy, not wrath, as we puzzle our way through life. We pray G*D will deal with us from G*D's best, not our worst. We pray the same for ourselves and our neighbors. We pray . . . .

"They shall be like a shrub in the desert, unable to see relief on the way." So are folk who trust in their own strength and don't know how to extricate themselves from the very messes they have caused. Shrub folk are always causing an unintended consequence.

In light of the limitations of a shrub masquerading as a stately oak and a desert having lush dreams, the prophet suggests another picture for us—trees by a stream.

With these two alternatives, we come to the heart of the matter—deviousness not only happens, but abounds. A test is always running (and not just the annoying emergency broadcast test) to see which of these pictures we will choose—shrub or tree, desert or stream. Like it or not, each eventually bears consequences, unhelpful or helpful.

Note: What follows is in memory of the prophet Molly Ivins, whose final column ended with:

> We are the people who run this country. We are the deciders. And every single day, every single one of us needs to step outside and take some action to help stop this war. Raise hell. Think of something to make the ridiculous look ridiculous. Make our troops know we're for them and trying to get them out of there. Hit the streets to protest Bush's proposed surge. If you can, go to the peace march in Washington on Jan. 27. We need people in the streets, banging pots and pans and demanding, "Stop it, now!"

Jeremiah 18:1–11
Proper 18 (23)

This sounds very much like a story from Kafka or one of the dystopian novels. There is a plan or template you are not aware of against which you are constantly being measured. Moment by moment, you are being conditioned toward some endpoint. Sometimes you receive positive reinforcement and sometimes negative.

This is not really a learning environment. New occasions continue to come along. A new pot or people is raised up and has a flaw. What is a G*D to do—other than toss it aside, of course. If, for whatever reason, some flash of beauty might be seen beyond a flaw (or even within it), then it may sit on an honored shelf.

Appreciate this for the profligate creativity present as life is called into existence and claimed to be good. Appreciate this for Kali showing up to knock it all about with too many left hands, not knowing what a right is throwing.

So, G*D can shape and unshape from the outside in response to our shaping and reshaping from the inside. This and $5 gets us where? Where is the ongoing relationship that accounts for working together for a common good? In the aftermath of Labor Day, this passage is weighted overmuch toward management.

Jeremiah 23:1–6
Evaluation Day

Context: The United Methodist Church trying Frank Schaefer for celebrating his son's marriage to another male (son and son-in-law—a patriarch's dream, except for legalistic religious types appealing to some letter-of-the-law type of "justice" with nary a pinch of human kindness, much less mercy).

How can this passage in this context not be a condemnation of everyone along the way who was swayed to vote for discrimination by some fear of losing members or money or their own privilege?

The shepherd has become the wolf, and a self-devouring one at that.

At times like this, it is tempting to wait for a "Lord" who punishes folks into exile to become self-dismayed and bring them home again (blaming things now on another set of folks). [How do you read G*D gathering back folks G*D had driven away?]

This temptation is unworthy of folks made in an image of steadfast love and merciful justice. We need to call it for what it is, serial injustice upon one officially condemned group after another—same tactics, different targets.

We need to get over some "Lord" being our righteousness. We have integrity inherent in our bones, even if we do cover it up all too often with an overlay of officiousness and expediency. To be zealous for judgment is to be blind to mercy.

A second context is LovePrevailsUMC.com sitting in on a Connectional Table meeting that was so boring the leaders had to plead for an "Amen" after characterizing Jesus as an "adaptive leader" (the latest highest praise a functionary can muster). The whole meeting was sad, with members nearly dozing off if not browsing Amazon. Energy was at a minimum, and communication was all about branding rather than doing/being.

It is tempting to sic a righteous G*D on such an unrighteous waste of time, energy, and resources. Again, this temptation is not creative enough for folks who have tasted of good and evil.

"Woe", cry shepherds who don't know where new grass is. "Woe", cry sheep sacrificed one-by-one. "Woe", cries G*D caught in a self-designed trap.

Jeremiah 23:23–29
Proper 15 (20)

What has happened to the rainbow?

The garden didn't work out. East of Eden didn't work out. Now the vineyard isn't working out. One would think that a G*D that filled the heavens and earth would better get their way without threat and bombast; rainbows simply work better than fists.

Whether yelled with passion at the top of one's lungs or whispered quietly, there doesn't seem to be a way to get around the reversal of intention.

Justice is to avoid bloodshed, to resolve issues, but we choose to go without justice and to roll out red carpets (red with the blood, sweat, tears, and toil of the poor and weak).

Righteousness is to comfort, but we choose to wait for a great wailing before acting generations later.

Will the hearts of the prophets ever turn back to justice and righteousness? Will prophets forever take the easy way of shading the truth about justice and righteousness, of deceiving themselves first and then the rest of the people?

Antidotes to these usual ways of living begin with dreams that radically call forth mercy and foster presence. Dream and tell your dream. Dream and tell your dream. Dream a dream big enough to have heaven come on earth, and tell that dream. Dream a dream large enough to clarify and live "enough". Dream a dream that shatters our usual ways of doing business without justice and righteousness.

Dream and dream again. Speak your dream abroad. Act on your dream as though it weren't a dream. Live your dream to the hilt and watch your dreams increase.

Jeremiah 29:1, 4–7
Proper 23 (28)

We dismiss folks by calling them dreamers, out of touch with reality. Jeremiah's letter, recommending people flourish where they are, opens him to the accusation of being a dreamer.

Does Jeremiah not know our human response to having a perk taken away from us? We are supposed to get angry and work assiduously to regain the privilege and garner more! Or so says our Snake Self when not in healing mode.

In exile, many perks are taken away. And it is not just the quantity of loss but the quality. Our native tongue and all the memories it carries is lost. Our favorite seasonings, not to mention our favorite foods, are lost. Relationships, standing, and class are all lost. These and other losses bind us to the past.

As we attempt to get our minds and hearts around questions of subversion of our vanquishers, our enemies, along comes this dreamer, Jeremiah, with his letter asking us to simply flourish where we are —fearful and lost. At bottom, Jeremiah dreams for us a different present and future than we have for ourself. Our vision is to continue the past, to return to where we were and the power we had. Jeremiah's dream is about cutting the immigrant's nightmare down to size by noting the reality of loss and moving on. Some losses open us to the future.

Whatever has been lost, has been lost. Spending energy on it in regret and grief, in fantasies of revenge and return, turns out to be counter-productive. The loss cannot be put back together again, no matter how many king's horses and king's men are put to the task. All that is left for us is to put our best toward a better tomorrow for our captors as well as ourselves. If we are in it for only ourselves, we will simply repeat a cycle of violent competition and a zero-sum power game.

For what are you being called, counter-intuitively, to help flourish by remaining true to what is better for all and not just yourself?

Do those exiled still have honor? It is so easy to discount them. Often, we act as though they are dishonorable, lazy, guilty, and sinful, even as we mouth that they are of sacred worth.

From Jeremiah, hear that the exiles shall return under the banner of "Together". This is not just about "them" returning, but that we are also exiled in place without their presence. It is "Together" that we find a return, a redemption, and a promise to be together. If this is to come to pass, we cannot languish by refusing to honor one another.

From Sirach, hear that G*D takes root in "an honored people." Wherever you are, ask who is not being honored. There is your work for the moment. It may be to disclose your own worth and to claim it. It may be to be an ally for another whose worth has been devalued and to affirm them.

These passages bring light through their enfleshing qualities of "together" and "honor". When we are not about the business of to-gethering and honoring, we are slowly and surely dimming hope and abandoning a common-wealth.

Note the lack of difference between:

"Parents have eaten sour grapes, and their children's teeth have been set on edge", and

"Leaders have eaten sour grapes, and the community's teeth have been set on edge."

Unfortunately, the solution to this is not to do a pendulum swing and have everyone dying for their own sins, their own sourness. This shift passes right over the interface and interrelationship of our communal and our individual selves. This avoidance also shows up in the imagery of everyone knowing the same larger reality, G*D, if you will. It misses that we also need one another to be able to work through the perpetual disagreements that arise with one generation following another, each having a different experience base. Even within a generation, there are varying understandings based on personality type, gifts and abilities, any number of entitlements, and basic political power theories. Without entering into an admittedly difficult interrelationship with both G*D and Neighb*r, self and others, we either harden ourselves into authoritarianism or participate in constant blame.

This little story is about more than an *Atlas* Shrugged-type individual responsibility or some grand cult in lockstep from the inside out. It raises questions about our being persistent and hopeful "widows" at one point in our life and "unjust judges" in another as seasons of experience and generations succeed one another. What covenant do you see following the one proposed here? Does it take into account this covenant's failure point of pride at having G*D's law within and G*D defined as "on my side"?

Jeremiah 32:1–3a, 6–15
Proper 21 (26)

What timing G*D has! Surrounded by Babylonians. Confined in the Palace. Comes a vision larger than fear, larger than enemies (external and internal), larger than impotency, larger than silence.

Surrounded by external enemies, confined by internal enemies, Jeremiah buys land about to be worthless. This purchase is to be hidden and sealed until a time when it might be returned to the light of day and the equivalent of a Jubilee happens—land is returned to previous owners.

This is a wonderful stewardship story. This is a story for the Palestinians and other refugees of our day. Jeremiah would recognize their loss of land, hidden and sealed, for a later time. May that later time be a sooner time—blessings and peace upon the latest negotiations.

How far ahead are you seeing? Can you see beyond the downfall of the current empire? Your usual investments are going to be worthless. What investment will see you through worthless times to a time of renewal and restoration, restoration and renewal, Jubilee? You did know that Jeremiah is a prophet we need to be listening to today?

Here is a comic strip that plays well with the Luke and Jeremiah passages this week:

http://kiriakakis.net/comics/mused/a-day-at-the-park

Jeremiah 33:14–16
Needed Change [1]

We begin this year by looking at connections between an important pairing—justice and righteousness.

One interesting commonality is that both are connected at their roots with a difference in gender—Justice/male and Righteousness/female.

Since they are parallel terms, when Jeremiah speaks of Judah and Jerusalem, the general and the specific, the generational time frame and the specific representational location as being saved, it is in a "name" called: "The Lord is our righteousness" (feminine), which also reveals "The Lord is our justice" (masculine).

We would all be helped if this pairing were more closely connected in English so we could not say one without the other.

The effect of holding these two aspects of a larger story is to bring forth a new creation. When Justice and Righteousness flourish, they provide the space needed for a new heaven and earth, seedtime and harvest.

Ultimately, this polarity needs to be managed, not chosen between (see the Preface). Justice and Righteousness have left their ideal homes and entered into the give and take of a living together with their offspring of hope, mercy, love, redeeming forgiveness, etc., who will spread their wings and drop their roots into our present, so in need of reformation.

Instead of looking for a fancy word that might stand behind Justice and Righteousness as their measuring rod and evaluator of their implementation in a personal or social context, look for a small word that reveals their creative energy. At least one candidate for an appropriate result would be the small but complex word of "kind" that sits at the intersection of this polarity.

The next time you see the word Righteous, substitute Just (and vice versa) and see what your ear tells you. You may find a kindness developed toward self and others that could approximate the love G*D had/has for creation.

Be still my heart.
Righteousness is such a beaut and Justice such a hunk.
Ain't nothin' but what brings a sigh to a bi-.
It is worth any disparagement to honestly claim both lovers.
Thanks be for heads and hearts and hands and health enough to honor Papa Justice and Mama Righteousness.
May they become one flesh—mine.

Lamentations 1:1–6
Proper 22 (27)

A rewrite —

How lonely sits a church that once was full of people! How isolated and barren! How small and irrelevant after such numbers and influence! A once shining beacon is now an overly protected flame safe from wind—only to have no source of fuel.

There is a great bitterness within—a divided self with comfort limited to true believers. Friends and potential friends must first prove their loyalty and do so again and again, for fear they will eventually reveal a flaw in a self-contained and unambiguous system.

Yes, exile has come; the center has not held, and takes more and more work to sustain. What once honored many differences and gifts has splintered, each looking to confirm its own before affirming another. The very surety of parity desired now comes back to bite far harder than the labor needed to bind compassion to every-day varieties of lived experience.

False enthusiasm keeps deep joy at bay. No matter how loudly we sing the same song, it can't be loosed from walls of silence intended to protect those within—turning a sanctuary into an echo-chamber with naught to offer beyond. Priests groan; youth grieve; blame grows.

Without turning differences into community, we are controlled by denied differences, defining a small and smaller realm of participation. More and more discrimination to protect an ever smaller range of acceptable behavior transgresses G*D's prerogative for steadfast love, especially relevant in the midst of creation's variety. The descendants of Eden have again scattered themselves through a failed hubris of building a babbling code of "holiness" within a larger Holiness all around. The eternal enemy of self-magnification has bound us.

A grandeur of Spirit has departed the construct of Church. Starving the body has us hearing voices of danger in every direction. Finally, we sit down alone, feeling as persecuted as we have persecuted.

———

In this silence, we feed on our shame of trusting our blame of all that wasn't yet us, to keep us pure. Our digital approach to holiness in an analogic abundance failed. Where is hope now?

Is steadfast love trustworthy after all? Are mercies we claim shareable with those we don't like?

If love and mercy are new every morning, dare we lift our eyes from blame and seek their application in our infinite variety?

Our surety-striving let us down, again. Let us rest in hope beyond uniformed peace. Let us seek a common good beyond today's limits. Let us live in communion beyond control.

Lamentations 3:1–9, 19–24
Absent Saturday

again and again—misery
agony is G*D's response
absent light eternal in the heavens
accidents guide us astray
antagonism against me is my lot
again and again—misery deepens

broken bones define my life
bereft of protective tariffs
besieged with multiple hardships
buzzing like bees around my head
basement dark envelopes my options
buried with my ancestors—I give up

choices are no longer available
chains I forged for others are now mine
could I call help murder most foul
callous laughter drowns all appeals
caution reads the sign
closed road go back

grief sets in after anguish
galling wormy worry rises into fear
ghosts in my heart gallop in every direction
grinding every escape into dust
guiding eventually to one old gift
glimmering in the gravel

hope is a mercy not destroyed by death
home and love are renewable
hour by hour we are re-framed
honest eyes see us through
humility even unto Hades is what I have
hope its name, honor its way

Lamentations 3:19–26
Proper 22 (27)

Steadfast love and hope are not medicines. There are no instructions to "take two and see how things are in the morning." There is only one side effect to consider—disappointment.

It is true that we treat these as curatives. When things get bad enough, we will dig them out from the back of the closet, next to the cod liver oil, and swallow them along with our pride. By the time we finally admit to needing such, our need is pretty big. It is as though we keep waiting for lab reports to come back to let us know we are love and hope deficient.

Were attention to be paid, we would note that love and hope are preventatives, but like exercise, not like vaccines. They like to be danced with, not left in the background and taken for granted.

However, we excuse not being at the top of our game, we have a choice to take one short-cut after another until we are lost and can but finally sit and cry out for help. Eventually, we recognize love and hope have ever had our back and can lead us in calisthenics to strengthen our capacity to love and hope for someone else. Now we're on a road back.

Unfortunately, it seems to take a number of turns through this cycle before we can break it by doing daily love and hope exercises in the midst of a larger community. At this point, we rejoice to have learned life is not all about me and patching a little love and hope to another skinned knee. Wisdom of the ages has set in, and we stretch our love and hope at the beginning of the day to find a good-kind-of-tired by evening's close. We lay ourselves down to rest in anticipation of new ways to share steadfast love and hope tomorrow. And if we die tonight, our day has been worth it.

Ezekiel 36:24–28
Hopeless Hope Vigil

Context is important. If we back up to verse 22, we hear G*D is not acting here for Israel's sake, but G*D's own self-image. All this beneficence is so G*D looks good to the Gods of other nations. A little God-off, if you will, and hardly monotheistic.

Israel is to be a refurbished creation. Presumably, water will take care of the outside, and a heart transplant will care for the inside.

If this Spirit Breath implant can be pulled off, we will be ready for the Dry Bones of chapter 37. Even so, we won't be able to respond to the rising and knitting together of the bones—only G*D knows as we are here the acted upon, not a full partner.

An important question for each of us and all of us together is whether we are going to go with power and self-image or the humility of a remodeled creation, some hippie egalitarian Edenic commune.

Can old bones rise? Can our hearts be reprogrammed? What is the half-life of rejuvenation by way of Spirit Breath? Is there anything that doesn't go back to self-interest?

As we wait to see about these promises of being rescued and life rising, we wonder what it means for us to be Spirit Breathed. Are we up to constraining our desire to compete with one another and with G*D?

Is this just one more creation story and covenant? Are we back to being a mirror for G*D, not a partner? Is blessing still conditional? If "holiness" is not part of the Image package but is reserved for G*D, what is the value of Spirit Breath?

Our waiting to see if Spirit Breath can blow graves open comes with a hope for something better than our current condition and a fear that we will be changed. May your waiting bring a needed next gift and energy to apply it in whatever circumstance you find yourself.

Ezekiel 37:1–14
Hopeless Hope Vigil

There is no question that I am a valley of dry bones. No matter from what perspective, I am very dry. No more ranting sweat. No more sad tears. Dry. Dry.

Lungs dry. Breath dry. Skin dry.

It is not Jesus who has gone AWOL (Absent WithOut [my] Leave); it is I who is desicated and separated from life by my expectations, my privilege, my claim of dominion.

Can these bones live again? Well, I don't know, and neither do you. Perhaps there is only a decision to not go AWOL (Absent With-Out [my] Life).

Eyes, so dry, blink for relief, blink again, clouded sight, blink and blink and blink some more. Maybe. Maybe.

Daniel 7:1–3, 15–18
Honoring Day

Visions can be alarming. Spiritual Directors can be a help here to add an experienced reflection on how a vision connects with our lived experience. Visions can deepen or redirect our understanding of how to practice creating beyond our current creation-location.

Visions of comfort and peace deepen our current direction. Visions of beasts and conflicts call us to riskier options.

As we look back at how we have arrived where we are, it is clear that there are folks we need to honor for their commitment to keeping on with basic human hospitality regardless of their changing circumstance. These steadying influences in our life have held us in good stead and still do.

It is equally clear that there have been catalytic people who have added their life to ours, for a moment or a lifetime, and it becomes apparent that we do need to learn a new way in a new occasion. These revealers of a different tomorrow than today have pushed us just enough to unsettle us without scaring us away.

Both might be called "Saints" except for their own denial of such. It seems we are always having a hard time trusting people's own self-assessment and want to pronounce "Saint" or "Great Satan" upon folks.

On this day, we might do well to dispense with titles and simply describe our experience with them. So, who is one of your "Saints", whether officially recognized or not? Write a note or talk with someone about a detail or two of how your "Saint" and you connect. Where is that connection expressed in your relationship with others?

Of course, it will be important to ask them about one of their "Saints" and what difference that has made in their life and your relationship with them.

If you were to look at your family, congregation, community, nation, world—to what image would you compare them that would identify a blockage keeping them from where they might be, were such not present? For Hosea, it was a distraction of where their eye landed without their even being aware of it. G*D called everything that wasn't focused on G*D, whoring around—a convenient digital response of all or nothing.

We do have problems with sexuality in general. Some later interpreters of Gomer deny she was promiscuous before or during her marriage with Hosea. *The New Interpreter's Dictionary* notes,

> Augustine argued that she abandoned her life of harlotry before her marriage; Jerome claimed that her marriage to Hosea remade her "chaste." Luther stated that she was a pure woman who only took on the name of "harlot" as a metaphor.

Regarding their daughter, Lo-ruhamah or No-Mercy, "I've run out of mercy", is revealed as one reality of G*D. Made in G*D's image, we all run out of mercy. What happens then? Can mercy be transferrable—when one runs out of mercy, can another re-infuse them with it? Can we be merciful until mercy returns to G*D?

Well, there is a whole story to go, but for now, we need to hear Jesus re-telling Hosea's story right after his teaching of prayer. Is the giving of forgiveness directly tied to the reception of such? If G*D holds back mercy, can mercy still be learned and offered?

Again, what image would you use to compare the various parts of your life, given that they could be so much more were it not for that particular impediment? Is whoredom or idolatry still the way to talk about self-imposed limits? What other options are open to you? As we imagine our response, we are given a glimpse into where our call might be.

<h1 align="center">Hosea 11:1–11</h1>
Proper 13 (18)

The more I called, the more they ran—this seems to be every parent's/prophet's experience at some point along their journey.

Many of us have been on both sides of that divide. Some of us still prefer one side over the other and operate out of that preference. There are inveterate callers and knee-jerk runners-away.

I've been led with "cords of human kindness" and experienced some of them as shackles. Our "spiritual care" for one another can be pretty heavy, laying all manner of expectation and reservation of acceptance upon us. Greg Brown's song *Driftless* has a line about this:

> Have I done enough, Father,
>> can I rest now?
> Have I learned enough, Mother,
>> can we talk now?

Yet, thankfully, the impulse to keep everyone a thankful third-grader who would never respond like that older teen, can keep us going long enough to move past a need to control things like setting a fiery sword at Eden's gate. With blessings aplenty, we don't give up on folks. With high hopes, we just can't bring ourselves to separate from one another, no matter how disappointed we have been.

In our family, my dearly beloved often has been heard to exclaim, "I don't know how we are going to get through this (whatever was having its day or season), but I'm going to keep loving you." Simple words; profound words.

May you be returned to your "home" (which may be different than where you thought it was or who else is there) in such a way that you can move on into the next stage of your life and your relationship with other family members, near and far.

Joel 2:1–2, 12–17
Self-Recognition Day

Trumpet Desolation! Shout Hypocrisy!

These two are wedded through the generations. Trouble is brewing again.

Where have our hearts strayed? When was our humility avoided? How did our common humanity become over-ridden? Who are we to return, repair, and rebuild?

Consider Torture Reports, Police/Community relations, and intractable political divisions as three places to trumpet and shout about. If our commons can't address these, our Fall will be quicker than not.

Regather and re-ask what important ingredient is missing in our communal life that has brought about the dysfunction in these three and other arenas.

Listen carefully.

Then, listen even more carefully.

The universe is gracious. For example, when food comes to the hungry, the afflicted are healed, light is gathered in the darkness, and gloom dispersed.

What would be an example of graciousness in each news item you see or hear? It is that example which will help you discern your call and work on behalf of all, your prophetic expertise.

Be food. Be light. Be.

A tide has turned, and we are glad and rejoicing. In retrospect, all that business about swarming locusts doesn't seem so bad. We are going to eat plenty again, and that makes all the difference—we'll forget anything that might endanger our next meal, even out-of-proportion responses against us—there will be no talk of reparations from us.

So goes the portrayal of a change in fortune. Being caught between an avenging G*D and a make-it-up-to-them G*D keeps us so off stride that we are thankful for any glimmer of hope, like those whose emotions are tied to any external, such as the volatile movement of stock exchanges.

In this place of being pinged and then ponged, we forget our partnership with G*D and stand grateful for a moment of respite. We became dependent upon the "name of the Lord" and called and called for it to be for our benefit.

It is in the pride of being those who call upon the "name of the Lord" that we lose our humility and again fail the test. In finally claiming our humility, we are overly convinced that we are not able to claim our partnership with G*D and wait for a providential moment, an opportunity for survival.

Can you dream beyond this either/or approach of accusation and requital? Do you still dream of a partnership with G*D and Neighb*r when approaching either? When we wake, this seems more than we are capable of. A sense of partnership with either or both—priceless.

An Ownership Society can be a political illusion, setting people against their own best self-interest. How we deal with economic imagery is important as it goes to the heart of most people's everyday experience.

Jeremiah uses guerrilla theater to dramatize the steadfastness of G*D. In a time of great upheaval, when it appears that real estate is not going to be a growth industry or a viable investment because all titles are about to go down the drain, Jeremiah sets out to draw attention away from property of the moment to promises to be fulfilled.

Amos takes another tack by urging us to run as far and as fast as possible from the usual temptations of getting stuck in the process of getting more or safeguarding that which we have. Who doesn't have dreams of more? What won't we do to get more? In that more, we get lost and lose a sense of promise in the morass of property.

So how would you deal with taxes these days—voluntarily pay extra as a sign of hope or cut them so that you might now have more? Your relationship to the larger community always makes a difference.

---

those who become at ease
face a danger of succumbing
to that very ease
the only antidote of which
is a whole different kind
of ease
an ease
no longer needing ease

Amos 7:7–17
Proper 10 (15)

Plumb lines, levels, micrometers, and other instruments of evaluation are so much more difficult in the short-term than, "Looks good; we'll go with that." Plumb lines and the like don't let us get away with "almost". They cut down on future creativity when we later, surprised, try to fit a square peg into a rhomboidal opening and try to figure out how to get back to plumb without restarting (which may be the most efficient response to the situation).

Prophets like Amos have a well-trained eye that can spot a plumb line in the midst of whatever is going on. They see the presence of an interactive G*D while laughing at the latest popular pundit or a news article so well-balanced it means nothing except we'll be having more of the same for some time to come. A plumb line conversation with G*D can go on about more hopeful pasts and preferred futures when dealing with decisions to be made at any level—personal, familial, communal, governmental, international.

A question for us is training our own eye to glimpse a sea of plumb lines, like using iron filings to note a magnetic field. This is similar work to dealing with competing covenants in our life. Which plumb line, which covenant will we attend to this time?

Plumb lines that are internal to our situations get tricky to notice and follow. A cultural overlay can hide them from even diligent seekers, and the very act of trying to find a plumb line in a busy picture distorts our response to it.

At some point, the recognition of a multitude of plumb lines (good old situation ethics) can drive us crazy—crazy enough to pile up their seeming contradictions and find a meta-plumbline for larger parts of our life.

Blessings on your revelation of a needed plumb line in your life and the life of the community. Further blessings on your courage to attempt to straighten situations accordingly. And even further blessings on your quest to move from plumb line to plumb line, shining them as you go that others might more easily respond to them.

Amos 8:1–12
Proper 11 (16)

The shelf life of fresh, ripe fruit is not long—maybe a generation of fruit flies (and that's pretty short).

It is within this length of time that we are to consider the decisions we have in front of us and to measure them against community well-being—internal hospitality. Often, we limit a hospitable welcome to a stranger and forget how to love one another. G*D says, "Trust me, you are starving one another, and this will lead to a famine of meaning and dissolution of the community." [To find out more about this dynamic, read *Shikasta* by Doris Lessing where you will find out about the consequences of a lack of SOWF (Substance Of We Feeling).]

So set a ripe fruit out on the counter and start considering where you need to engage the community with an internal welcome: basic hospitality, love of one another, kindness, simple civility. If you do not begin to act on your thoughtful evaluation before the fruit rots, you've not only lost a fruit, but you are that much closer to meaninglessness.

Here's an equation for when we are looking for meaning: GM=RM where GM=GivingMuch and RM=ReceivingMuch. This is not just about produce, but relationships.

Amos reveals ourselves to us. We begin to change now, or we begin to practice a dirge for what we missed. Enough missed opportunities, and we are addicted to missing them, and we won't even see the next one.

If you are not going to take the authority you already have to offer a hospitality seminar, I hope you will take your precious time and resources and sign up for one.

O G*D, our security plans are in place; preemption is the operating principle of the day, and still we are scared.

We used to talk about all this in pastoral terms of harvests and summers, but we are urban now, and just because some tomato pickers are unhappy with their pay and benefits doesn't mean you have to take their side against those of us who have acted in the same way we claim you modeled for us—judgment and wrath first; questions second.

Yes, it's too bad they have to suffer. But suffering is redemptive; don't forget that. If we're going to have a soufflé life, a few eggs are going to have to be broken.

Life is hard enough to enjoy without you jumping up and down about selling a bushel of flour a couple of cups short and being sure the minimum wage doesn't impact an ideal corporation's personal due.

You've overlooked so much evil along the way, and so many people have gotten hurt without your intervening on their behalf; it just doesn't make any sense for you to get so bent out of shape about a lousy pair of sandals for some peasants.

You're killing us here, G*D; get a grip. Let's get real, and if you'll just look away one more time, we'll get you a nice temple for us to have Thanksgiving turkey together.

Micah 5:2–5a
Needed Change [4]

Without asking for it or even dreaming about it, a currently insignificant spot is incorporated as an integral part of a new story. A king's birthplace will become an anti-king's birthplace.

Where a king brings order and pacification, an anti-king brings peace and energy. Both bring forth "security/salvation" after their own kind. Security has again raised its head as an eternal quest object, only to be obtained by leaving it behind.

As we finish off another time of waiting for a reincarnation of the past or a harbinger of the future, we still look for security in the dead and gone or the not yet conceived and horizonless. We re-fight a last war and prepare against a previous attack, obsessing over remembrances and compulsively narrowing down future options. We yearn for the sentimental warmth of mangers past and for cold judgment coming on a storm cloud.

If a little town of Bethlehem can birth kings and anti-kings, there is no security as usual. We've been looking for security in all the wrong places. Micah asks us to imagine government and religion not being about order and indestructibility, but about justice coming forth based on having experienced injustice in exile and under our own leaders. The peace of Bethlehem is a renewal of justice.

---

o little house of bread
how easily distracted
by fancier fare
perhaps
"...an undigested bit of beef, a blot
of mustard, a crumb of cheese,
a fragment of underdone potato"

dream of ghostly transformation
through past mistrust
current misery
future emptiness
prayerfully concluded
"God bless us, everyone!"

dream deep
house of bread
of but a little wine and
a creation beginning song
"Peace on earth, goodwill to all"

dream of a feast of love
with thou and thou and thou
each feeding each
in pastures of plenty
'til exiled justice
is welcomed home

Note: The first two quotes are from *A Christmas Carol,* by Charles Dickens. Hopefully you recognize the third.

Habakkuk 1:1–4; 2:1–4
Proper 22 (27) — Proper 26 (31)

The world is going to hell in a handcart. Everyone has their own story of the devolution of human community. Some are just fear-mongering, and some have "evidence". Perverted justice is as good an example as there is. Of course, one person's "perversion" is another's "salvation".

There seems to be no process that can guarantee putting a stop to people's perversity. It doesn't seem there is a technique that will put us on a path to a better tomorrow. All we have is our own integrity. We stand and watch and wait and evaluate and act on what we trust.

So what are you trusting these days? Try this: An end is coming soon, but not soon enough that it will keep me from my responsibility and joy to live as though something better than an end will arrive in its place.

---

barricades have been erected
violence is in the street
finally injustice
has come to this

anguish and devastation
have been the rule of the day
for long too many days
and can no longer be borne

education fell to doctrine
allowing only one reality
our prosperous comfort
to be the standard

so to your post
clarify a new way
putting honest confession
before reconciliation

hold your vision high
that it might be seen by all
and corrected
through shared lives

Zephaniah 3:14–20
Needed Change [3] — Hopeless Hope Vigil

Judgment removed.

With it gone, enemies are, what, also removed?
With judgment no longer on the table, what happens to the enemy known as myself?

Now, perhaps, "fortune" can be rediscovered. Creed and culture
have defined meaning for so long, it will be a new birth to look again
for "fortune" [Middle English, from Anglo-French, from Latin *fortuna*;
akin to Latin *fort-*, *fors* chance, luck, and perhaps to *ferre* to carry —
more at BEAR. – *Merriam-Webster*]

There are no straight lines with this sort of fortune. We are to deal
with what comes our way as best we can at the time. This means
bearing much that can't be sorted out or understood.

There is no final measure of some absolute good fortune or even
one relative to anyone else. If chance and luck and bearing up are
what lie ahead, it will be important to have folks to share with—to
share their fortune and to share mine with them. From each according
to their fortune and to each according to their lack thereof. In time,
this won't balance, but it will suit us to a "fair-thee-well".

Mistyping "fair" for "fare" may be one step too much, but this far
into a vigil brings enough disorientation to finally be silly, grin at it,
and let it be. This vigil is not clarifying, excusing, explaining, or bringing a glimpse of meaning until we have run up against the silliness of
mercy—"Judgment removed".

Job cries, "It ain't right."
Haggai responds, "'Tis so."

How do you explain the difficulties of life?

Is it personal? Is it corporate? Is it random? Is it tit-for-tat? Is it just the way it is? Is it choice? Or does Dana Carvey's Church Lady have the better explanation—Satan?

Is it just a matter of cultic purity?

Are you recognizing your flesh has been destroyed, or are you expecting prosperity? Does one lead you to cry out, or does the other?

How do you think Job and Haggai would get along? Would Job see Haggai as another of his "friends" who don't get it? Would Haggai see Job as culpable? How might these two converse, or must we keep them in separate rooms?

Appreciate the commentators who look at verse 2:3 and find there the current puny temple, compared to the glory of the temple that had been destroyed. By 2:7b, the temple is to be viewed through the eyes of a new generation that benefits from a current trust that resources will come flowing. Both the recognition of a need to build and the promise that sufficient resources will become available are standard Capital Funds Campaign elements.

This is a proven enough process that you may want to consider moving it outside a property/financial model. How is the hospitality/compassion level of the congregation or community? How can you document that it is not sufficient? What vision can be cast that will energize the courage of the congregation or community to invest in growing the inter-connectivity of the congregation or community that will give some credence that such investment will grow and be added to through time, so a more beloved congregation or community might be raised up?

Judgment needs a press secretary to spin the need for judgment. Knowing that the only outcome expected from Judgment is that we don't measure up, we are tempted to believe there is no out from Judgment. At best, it is a refiner's fire that removes those parts that don't measure up, even if that means there isn't much left. Somehow or other, cutting off pounds of flesh is supposed to make us better. Presumably, once the soul has been dissected out, it will only reproduce after its own kind.

There are a lot of questions about a model that disavows choice and time. Somehow, only good choices will be made. Somehow, in a moment of judgment, all is made clear, so a good choice is the only choice available.

As a result, we prefer waiting for judgment rather than be proactive in building the kind of community that will honor, understand, encourage, and challenge its individual parts.

It would help if we were to remember that an anticipated messenger is none other than ourself and our neighbor. Proceed to attend to the message you are passing on.

Malachi brings to mind the old story of Pinocchio, who has gotten trapped in his own lies and desires and pranks.

A Blue Fairy or Fairy with the Azure hair (see original story) brings to mind a messenger (when did you last imagine Baptizer John as a fairy?) who helps the story along.

Jiminy Cricket is a conscience before whom we eventually cannot stand, but must give way. Who can endure the day of his coming?

Can a refiner's fire be matched with a water image? If so, Monstro the Whale or the Terrible Shark (see original) might be the place where we stop lying to ourselves and others.

Judah, Jerusalem and Gepetto become blessed, as the story records, "When bad boys become good and kind, they have the power of making their homes gay and new with happiness."

What fairy tale do we need to remember today to help us make sense of the world around us and within—that we might hope? As G.K. Chesterton said, "Fairy tales are more than true—not because they tell us dragons exist, but because they tell us dragons can be beaten." The good news of transformation from sorrow through a refiner's fire to joy is good news to be spread abroad.

If you find your bible doesn't have a Chapter 4 (for instance, *The New Jerusalem Bible,* which follows the Hebrew text instead of the Greek), the verses in question are also noted at 3:19–20a. This is another good reason to avoid using chapter, verse, and section headings—all so convenient and biased.

If you delve into background material on Malachi you will find a book hard to classify other than it rounds out this grouping of prophets at an even magic number of 12. It also contains more questions than prophets usually ask.

A plethora of questions is a good way to complete the prophets. We are encouraged to apply the question process to our current setting—personal to universal.

- Who are considered "evil-doers" these days?

- What is their offense this time?

- Have you engaged them or let them roll-on and does that lack of challenge locate you as in their thrall?

- Where is a so-called G*D of Justice seen today?

- And lots of "how" questions: How do we clarify steadfast love we have overlooked or avoided? How many excuses have we used to rationalize regularly avoiding expressions of steadfast love?

Depending on our motivational processes, these and other questions lead us to focus on hot wrath to come or a cooling balm already available. For those escaping destruction, blessings on finding an assurance beyond rule-following that you might stop and smell a rose or two. For those drawn toward healing, blessings on finding a certainty beyond personal happiness that you might continually offer your gift to those in need of sunshine.

Wisdom of Solomon 10:15–21
Blessed Body [2]

When we look back with 20/20 hindsight, it is easy to discern a Wise presence. What wasn't understood at the time as wise (remember the fear that continues throughout the Exodus) can later be attributed to some good plan. This connects wisdom with thanksgiving.

When we look around us for wisdom to make difficult choices, we find ourselves caught between focal lengths—attempting to apply an appropriate learning from history that we don't just repeat and repeat, and peering into a dim unknown for a new learning not already in our grab-bag of a treasure chest. This connects wisdom with mystery.

When we do thought experiments regarding the future, we find our prejudices coming to the fore. Our assumptions and speculations rev themselves into red-line danger. This connects wisdom with foolishness.

Do you remember with thanksgiving that G*D has revealed things to the foolish, not the wise? Well, what are we to do with Sister Wisdom, who is all over the map? Sit back and enjoy the ride? Winnow the results with yet a fifth criterion to measure reality?

Perhaps the best we can do here is to raise our sensitivity to the mute and those struggling to put their reality into communicable language. Who are you listening to and how engaged are you willing to be to wrest meaning from inarticulate groans of creation?

Resolution: To listen to Wisdom bubbling from below consciousness and to join in the groans of birthing a new year from an old one by at least boiling water.

Pride is a shorter spelling of Narcissism:

- we lose track of a larger context for ourselves,

- we claim innocence of blame and are hypersensitive to how every event affects us, and

- we are willing to enforce our desires on others—we are pride-full.

The process here is to begin with a blind-spot for a presence of G*D. This blindness is behind the three results mentioned above. The rest of the text works its way from this beginning reality. Consequences reveal their antecedents.

Our various stages of development all contain a desire to stay in the familiar. A temptation, all along the way, is to claim our current location as either awesome or good enough. We are willing to commit or be silent in the face of whatever violence it takes to maintain what status I have, what meaning I have come to.

Deserting G*D, a Living G*D of journey wrestling a new tomorrow into today, is a prideful act. We are fortunate that desertion is a one-way act that does not require an equal and opposite reaction of desertion in return.

Events and insight can find us retracing our steps to again face an interface beyond today. We are en-couraged to again reach forward.

As long as we remain committed to safety-first, we will find we have dwelled too long in the final verse (18) of the connected vices of pride and violence.

This is not a judgment but a description, so we might again be on the road with a testing G*D.

Presumably, we will again get tired and settle for some next plateau. If our history holds, it won't be long before we've been injured enough in protecting our "deserved turf" that we will know it is time to move along. Blessings on where you are on this segment of life, and Blessings on whatever is next.

Believe it or not—Wisdom is to be praised in your life. Creator G*D has sent Wisdom to dwell within the beloved—you and church and Creati*n.

Wisdom was sent because it was needed here. We have so often gone off on a wild-haired tangent.

Wisdom was sent because it can grow here. We yet have possibilities to attest to the presence of good old Sophia.

If Wisdom can sing her own praises and if Wisdom is in you, will you not also join in the singing?

Happy New Year! We can yet release Wisdom's voice in our settings.

Sirach 27:4–7
Guiding Gift [8] — Proper 3 (8)

Consequences clarify in the same way that sieves sort things out through a variety of means—winnowing, a wire mesh, magnetic fields, mathematical processes, etc. Additionally, many forms of delayed revelation of results (physical and relational) help us evaluate what is and is not going on.

Humans are tricky folks. This is particularly true in family, national, and global politics. How can we sort folks out?

One tried and true piece of wisdom is that of listening with more than our ears—pairing what a person says with the results of what they actually do. Does harm eventuate? Do their words accord with or jar your experiences of them? Are there other connections that need to be made than those allowed by the premises of the speaker?

Eventually, the truth will be revealed. You can either wait for such to happen or begin practicing listening to the fears behind a speaker's words.

Knowing our self as we do, suspicion of motives is appropriate. Questions are one important starting point, and if you get to the point where no further questions are required, you and everyone will be the poorer.

Let's take seriously the wisdom that speech needs to be tested. Try these as you practice testing what you read and hear:

- Put ears on your readings—reading aloud can reveal tricks being played on your eyes and brain.

- Put eyes on your hearing—trace the unspoken threads of consequence to the common good for a generation, or seven, ahead who aren't present to rebut an argument because of the way it turned out.

- Put heart into every bald or embellished pronouncement— mock it by putting your fingertips together and oh-so-sincerely intoning, "True."

These three will reveal the trickery and insincerity so inherent in our desire for power and control.

Knowing what verses are in play here depends on the version and versification being used. Here we follow the NRSV used by the Revised Common Lectionary.

In play here is *quid pro quo plus*. The basic formulations are these:

- As you have received, pay out.

- Place your bet; get a seven-fold return.

- Don't bet beyond your resources in order to influence a better return—no bribes.

- The moral arc of justice will even things out; wrongs will be set right.

Having received these examples, it will be important to find ways to particularize them in our setting. Can you take these economic maxims and move them into additional venues?

- How does this work in an economy of violence that escalates to war?

- What about an economy of G*D with choices between judgment and mercy?

- Can this work in an economy of pedagogy where we are tempted to settle for current limits of what is known and tried by learning how to learn more?

- Is there an application to the economy of your family's relationships in its current configuration and stage?

To give generously to your Neighb*r is to give generously to G*D. Your generosity is your response to a gift of life; this Neighb*rliness is part of a reciprocal engine of creativity to draw us closer to tomorrow's gift.

In the end, commit to ever follow your inherent or learned partiality for the poor, weak, or discriminated against.

Baruch 3:9–15, 3:32–4:4
Hopeless Hope Vigil

Why is it my fear and loneliness place me in a land of my enemies rather than my friends who will care for such? Do thoughts actually matter, materialize? Has my response to death brought me to be counted as one dead and powerless before my time?

Is this all because I have discounted all the different Marys along the way? There are so many male prophets that if you say prophet, you mean male—we have a special category for a prophetess. We have so identified G*D and Jesus as, of course, being male that we attribute to them also war and judgment and death eternal.

Here we hear of "her"—Wisdom living among us, unknown, a provisional gift. Even though portrayed as "the book of the commandments" of an understood to be male G*D, she is more.

If you would like to stretch your view of Wisdom just a bit further, you might try listening a few times to *Bring Me My Queen* by Abigail Washburn.

In Advent, we recognize that our every pronouncement that one condition or another is the end-all and be-all of life—even such a summary as "Christ is King"—bumps up against our continued judgment that where we are currently located is not sufficient for gifts to flourish and hope to turn to trust.

Here we dare to claim more beauty is available. Even as wrinkles appear and senses fail, beauty continues—see Rodin's *Old Courtesan* or listen to Stan Roger's song, *Lies*.

Here we dare to try on a justice just beyond our reach and yet drawn nearer by our reach.

Here we dare to reframe our going forward by claiming a new name as legally, ethically, and communally ours—

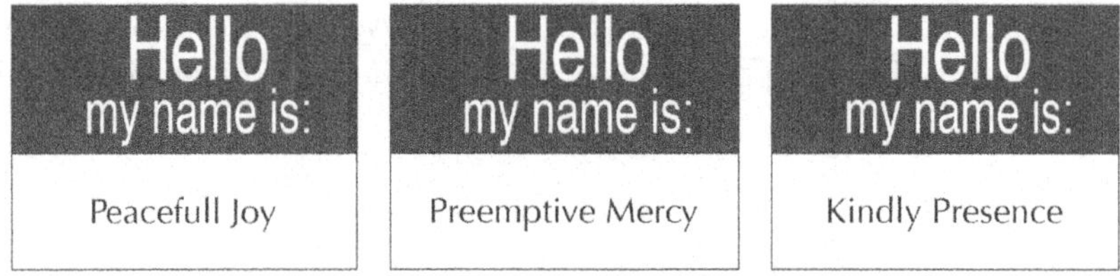

How are we guided, and how do we guide others to identify and engage the needed changes of this day?

May Joy, Mercy, and Grace practice Peace, Justice, and Presence in the present, not some by-and-by. Admittedly, these grand categories are open to enough rules and interpretations that they can fail before even being attempted. Do your best to keep them grounded in the particulars of people you don't get and especially those you don't like. One way of doing this is to design your own name badge and to wear it until people can't tell the difference between your name and your actions.

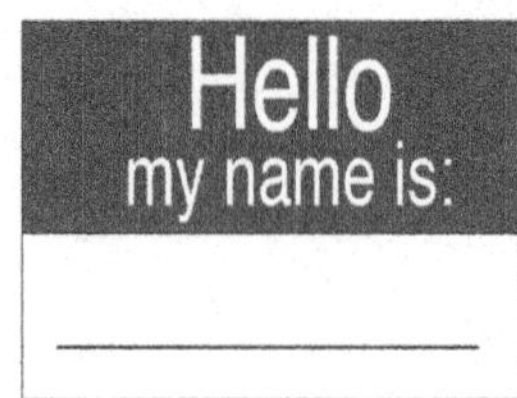

Matthew 2:1–12
Guiding Gift

Matthew, speaking to a Jewish community, should know how poorly astrologers are viewed in the Hebrew scriptures. There is a judgment that they are worshiping the created stars rather than the creator of the stars. At best, they bring a second-rate theology just a little better than necromancers.

Astronomy does give some cover for the Magi in Herod's court, but it also draws attention to Jesus and is precursor to the slaughter we heard of last week—the sequel to this story (what tangled webs are woven when story lines are broken).

A theme of lowliness, instead of fulfillment, is Matthew's way of incarnating G*D into the realities of human life. Through pagans who remain pagans, Jesus is revealed to the larger world. Similarly, in Luke, it is through lowly shepherds, not angels, that word is passed about Emmanuel.

By the time we come to the end of Matthew's tale, we find another pagan, a centurion, affirming what the Magi searched for and only tasted the beginning of—Emmanuel. In the end, we also find Jesus' disciples sent on a search for the Magi at the ends of the earth, that they might be baptized. [Note: If you are interested in an entertaining tale of Jesus seeking the Magi, you may appreciate *The Gospel According to Biff, Christ's Childhood Pal* by Christopher Moore.]

Try looking at this passage through the eyes of surprised Jews who hear it is those second-class Magi who first acknowledge and visit Jesus, who honor him with precious gifts. At least, they won't get distracted by 2,000-plus years of numbering and naming the Magi or the exoticness of the gifts. They will know there is trouble coming when they hear the Magi are connected with G*D.

The felt-but-not-articulated anxiety engendered by the incorporation of strange women into Jesus' genealogy becomes clearer with the arrival of the Magi. G*D is up to something very strange. Now that we are adequately unsettled by unexpected women, pagan astrologers, and murder most foul, we are ready to hear about John, a baptizer, and then to proceed with an adult Jesus from whom we hear an invitation to join in as part of the Presence of G*D.

To look at this one story is to look at the whole story. Honor it well and don't get hung up on the consumer aspect of global trade items.

Matthew 6:1–6, 16–21
Self-Recognition Day

Intentions often overwhelm Intuitions. We hedge ourselves round with rules for survival, success, and plain old acceptance by our current culture and tribe. It is so easy to forget that a current common sense is but a prelude to a larger common good yet to arrive.

This is a day to recognize that our past had a consequence, and it is today. Fortunately, this means that tomorrow is a consequence of what we do today. Choice is still available and tomorrow is still able to be better.

When you attend to this day, do so without setting up a battle between your intention to be tribally and culturally ascendant and your insightful intuition that better is tied to our deep heart's core (Read again *The Lake Isle of Innisfree* by William Butler Yeats).

Remember your place of peace and let your hands move in multiple realms while connected to a larger satisfaction not yet arrived but drawn closer with the practiced skill of mercy, mercy, mercy.

Yesterday is burned and gone. Where there is naught but ash, our third eye sees through it to discern a way forward beyond repetition. Open this eye to see where hope and wholeness wend their way through the underbrush of the "way we have always done it"—and follow.

Matthew 25:31–46
New Year's Day

Here is another Day of Resolution. How nitty-gritty are you willing to get?

> I resolve to work on both the personal and structural realities of hunger.
> I resolve to work on both the firsthand and business realities of clean water.
> I resolve to work on both the interpersonal and institutional realities of welcome.
> I resolve to work on both the charitable and corporate realities of shelter.
> I resolve to work on both the singular and societal realities of prison.

That will be sufficient for one year; for one lifetime. Working on any one of these will get you trouble with family, friends, and community. I pray you are up to facing the consequences of not attending to these resolutions, for they will come around and not just in some final judgment sort of way.

Based on the resolutions and enactments of this day, there will be positive or negative consequences for the next seven generations. Will we care for them as much as we do for our own immediate comfort? Aye, there's a rub.

Matthew 27:57–66
Absent Saturday

The two readings for this day, Matthew and John, have similarities and differences. A major difference is the Matthean addition about guarding the tomb for fear that the disciples would be as duplicitous as the Chief Priest and paid-for mob were described to be. Knowing the power of lies, we are all concerned that a big one told by someone else could counter our big one, and people would remember only the last lie they heard. In which case "the last deception [theirs] would be worse [for us] than the first [ours]" ~NRSV.

The only thing the fearful ones on every side forgot was that you can roll lies over truth for a while, but they become too unwieldy. Building the lie bigger eventually brings it to fall of its own weight.

A second difference is that Nicodemus, only appearing in John, reappears. Initially, Nicodemus had questions; later, he was a voice of reason/moderation. Now his boat-load of expensive spices is a resounding affirmation of Jesus.

The readings are similar in testimony that Jesus is dead. Dead and gone. Gone as far as effectively being in Sheol or Hades or Hell. There will be no Nicodemus-like reprise. Jesus is erased from this world. The guards of Matthew and our experience will both confirm that dead is dead.

The loss of Friday is shock. The loss of Saturday is resignation, not awe.

Though it is day, it is as dark as a sealed tomb where not even hope tiptoes.

Spoiler alert—Note well that without resignation, there is no resurrection. This makes it very difficult for us today to experience Mary Magdalene and another Mary simply sitting across from the tomb. If they are too numb to do anything but sit and sense movement across the way and we are numb to the crucifixions going on in our own context: •trafficking •intentional denial of health care to the poorest •continued discrimination against LGBTQ people, racial minorities, and immigrants without papers •increased gap of purchasing power •blocked decision-making •increased weather events, and •so much more, we won't be able to finally return to life to witness to changes necessary for our common life to rebound and flourish. Eventually, Mary will come back to life and be a source of life for many. May we know how bad it is: There is no rescue on the horizon; we are alone.

Only when this Saturday is real will we take our part. Blessings on those who have lost all, who have nothing left to lose, for they are free to change and bring change.

Luke 1:26–38
Creation's Conception

How far back does an immaculate conception go? Since it is an exemption of the soul, not available even to the previous generation, as Mary was said to have been physically conceived in the usual way. It doesn't seem to have lasted all that long, just until Jesus' birth, and then Mary's salvation was dependent upon his "atoning sacrifice" for her and all.

These attempts to make sense of mystery through doctrine and angelic announcements eventually become magical and less than helpful. In some sense, a terrible beginning may be important here. Imagine the worst, a swirling chaos into which a clarifying and creating word comes.

Scene 1: Good ol' sweet-talkin' Gabriel. His backseat of the car patter wasn't quite believable until Mary's hormones kicked in. At this point, there is no turning back and "Let it be", becomes an imperative.

Scene 2: Powerful Gabriel has never taken "No" for an answer. He is god's-gift to women. After favoring Mary with his mere presence, it isn't long before he has a hand over her mouth and, with a grunt, says, "Don't yell, you'll thank me later...God...O, God!"

Scene 3: Accountant Gabriel is present to make the trains run on time. Following instructions from the next level up, Gabriel visits Nazareth. He has an explanation for everything. There is no discrepancy. Nothing is impossible if we just cooperate with The Plan.

Scene 4: How would you describe this scene? Remember that in ancient of days, March 25th was honored as Creati*n's birthday. Was there or was there not a big "Bang"? To keep things nicely tied up, the New Creation, of course, would be conceived then and be revealed nine-months-to-the-day later, December 25th. Or was it the other way around, and Jesus really was born in the Spring as a goodly number of scholars suggest?

Eventually, regardless of prior circumstance, we refuse both meaninglessness and forced meaning to say, "let it be". Now we walk a new path, refusing to carry an enmity of crushing evil under our heel and so find a way to return to Paradise. If you can imagine it about Mary, imagine yourself exempt from original sin. Now, bring forth, bring forth. A new choice is not impossible.

Luke 1:39–45, (46–55)
Needed Change [4]

Do you sense something stirring in you that needs further clarification?

> Try a Directed Retreat.

Have you become clear about your call and need further clarity about a beginning way to implement it?

> Try a Directed Retreat.

Are you carrying a new mystery as a result of implementing your gifts?

> Try a Directed Retreat.

Mary had heard of a spiritual director who had wrestled for long years with vision and implementation and mystery. The two of them were at a distance and yet related (in this case by blood, but such a relationship can cross every division we impose on one another). So it was that Mary set off to have a directed retreat with Elizabeth.

As is often the case, a word of affirmation is a good opening gambit. Elizabeth took that which was at hand, a busy babe in utero. Elizabeth took her hand from her enlarged and enlarging womb and raised it with a blessing, interpreting life to life. Luke reports Elizabeth interjected some extraneous "Lord" language to double-down on the blessing, even though it wasn't needed.

It is understandable how Mary responded to human affirmation as well as an angelic visitation, bringing a new word from within her. For now, though, imagine Elizabeth and Mary on a 3-month retreat investigating hopes undefined and hopes fulfilled. Mary's response at the end of an in-depth evaluation of circumstance and expected outcomes of a non-Roman "Lord" lasting very long carries more weight and overtones than a paraphrase of ancestress Hannah. These sorts of prophetic/mission statements take time to live into and last beyond an ecstatic moment.

May you, too, take a directed retreat and find its result includes a deep affirmation of your blessedness—blessedness enough to live as though the current circumstance were not final and you were living a reset and new earth into being.

Luke 1:39–57
Elizabeth and Mary Meet

Upon connecting the unlikelinesses of her pregnancy with Elizabeth's, Mary hied herself both hence and thence.

Imagine Elizabeth's surprise and response to Mary turning up miles from home when, before Elizabeth can say, "Welcome", she winces with a foot to her bladder. Imagine Mary, seeing this response, echoes Gabriel and calls out, "Fear not!"

If we are not going to practice a magic trick of pre-conscious revelation by an unborn or a suspicious correlation instead of causation, we might wonder about such an unrecorded, yet universal, greeting that still carries power. How might it be today if, when asked how we are, we were to respond with, "Fearing not! And you?"

Hopefully, our response would turn a bland question into alertness, "Hmm, this conversation might well end in a blessing; I'll risk jumping in."

[Side trail alert—Thinking we can interpret the meaning behind a behavior, particularly that of a fetus, is the ancient equivalent of a 24-hour cable/babel news cycle. Speculation is set on high, reported breathlessly and ardently. You can take it from here.]

There have been more words about Elizabeth's words and Mary's words than can be easily measured by a Google search. [For those who want to know, "Blessed are you among women" clocks in at 879,000 references, and "My soul magnifies the Lord" is more than 4 times greater, 3,580,000.] Add words of your own at your own peril.

While we are dealing with Elizabeth and John, don't forget to celebrate the Nativity of Baptizer John on June 24 (only 6 months, 191 shopping days, until Christmas) as there is an interesting connection between the birth feasts for John and Jesus. You might want to start now with a new rhythm for your church year:

— Summer Solstice or June 24 – Nativity of Fire John
— Autumnal Equinox or September 23 – Conception of Fire John
— Winter Solstice or December 25 – Nativity of Spirit Jesus
— Vernal Equinox or March 25 – Conception of Spirit Jesus

Since the Church dates are entirely made up, having moved several times, why not just set them in accord with the rhythms of nature? How would you use such an addition as the Celtic Quarter Days that would set a sequence of about 6-week intervals? Are these instructional/practice times or celebratory times or both?

Luke 1:46b–55
Needed Change [4]

"Blessed are you among people, and blessed is the fruit of your life." This is indeed an extended translation of "Namaste". Greetings between people at this level bring forth lives leaping from within—"Mexican jumping beings", if you will. This greeting that sees G*D within the other is a creative word that brings forth more and more. One word leads to another, story upon story, until we marvel at how far we have come when we weren't paying attention to the results of our interaction, simply the interaction itself.

In some way, we become a fulfillment of the greetings we have received and given. This is a sacred foundation that can set things right.

In this last moment of Advent, we are prepared to greet another and the birthing that comes from such a meeting. An important part of our Advent journey has been to say goodbye to injustice and unrighteousness that we might move ahead with a blessing not held back by such blockages.

---

magnified my soul is . . .

remembering Isaac escaped from sacrifice
cowering behind the altar
reflecting on Abraham's fearful faith
finally stammering
magnified my soul is . . .

remembering Mary at the cross
immobilized in hope and fear
reflecting on birth and death of love
finally stating
magnified my soul is . . .

remembering every trial come through
still caught in some unfinished
reflecting on my little jokes and G*D's big one
finally praying
magnified my soul is . . .

Inspired by material from *Provoking the Gospel of Luke: A Storyteller's Commentary, Year C* by Richard W. Swanson (this series is evocative and recommended).

Luke 1:68–79
Needed Change 2 — Proper 29 (34)

Mercy is one of Creati*n's intentions.

As such, it has been reflected from the beginning in promise after promise. This mercy shows up in covenant after covenant. A part of the need for this repetition comes from our forgetting to remember a promise for very long. As we look back, we see covenants of mercy continually cropping up in our presence. We may not have recognized them at the time, but now they become clear.

Likewise, tender mercy is on its way from farther away than eye can see or heart hope. It is not just for us individually, for mercy is as social or communal as any basic of life. Tender mercy is not simply a comfort but an equipment of light to find faint ways of peace beyond our experience of death in the midst of life or fear that nothing will really change.

You, child of G*D, are called to be a prophet who preemptively shines forgiveness into the graves of lives. This forgiving light shines beyond our accepted limits to reconnect us to past and future, to friend and foe, to G*D and Neighb*r, to self and non-self. Rejoice in your high calling by boldly receiving mercy and extravagantly and expansively giving it away.

----

a bigger bang than a big bang
precedes expansive energy
where there is stuff
or even non-stuff
has not mercy been there already

mercy lays a groundwork
for foregrounds and backgrounds
for groundhogs and ground chuck
we are grounded in mercy
Allah the Merciful rings true

may mercy continue
greater than judgment
that leading edges of Creati*n
bloom and grow
in and through you

Luke 2:(1–7), 8–20
Blessed Body: Proper II

A birth story written generations after Jesus' death has some problematic details that cry out for explanation. The history of the time of Luke that affects his writing goes beyond our space here. However, there is room for a reminder to explore the history of the end of the first century, as well as what is recorded here.

We are moving from the mystery of the unlikely births of Moses and Baptizer John to their respective overtly political actions. What was a self-help adage of "pray 'til you get it" is now acted out at the altar of palace power.

Caesar Augustus. What a piece of work. Details aside, our moral choices take place within the arena of public policy. There is no hiding in any separation of church and state. In the short-run, only the state counts.

Getting the shepherds involved only heightens the tension. The memory of King David's youth continues as a challenge to the imposed rule of Roman Emperor Augustus, who is imposing an exile-in-place that needs an internal-exodus to resolve it. David was a shepherd, and a whispering campaign by shepherds is an opening salvo in a new campaign to oust Augustus and his henchmen. A new Emperor is in town, and only one will be left standing.

Knowing the power of Augustus' successors and another ruinous destruction of a Temple externalizing G*D's presence, it is important to move back to a pre-Temple time as a way to mobilize any remaining hope of ending our exile by ending a most violent Pax Romana.

> Our once and always Arthurian David, Arise!
> This is our call to arms.
> Glory to those G*D favors—Us!

So, scared populace, be not afraid; we are on our way back.

Of course, death is in the offing. Do we have enough shepherds to see us through to overcome? Will this astonishing opportunity show us how to effectively address power imbalance and inhumanity without countering military force with military force and temple privilege with temple privilege?

After 2,000+ years, we find the same temptations and partial answers trumpeting established right, not expectant growth.

Luke 2:1–14, (15–20)
Blessed Body: Proper I

After looking at all four readings for this day, it doesn't matter if there was actually a census or not. An intent to register in order to dominate is sufficient. This was the state of the world—regimented. — Was?

Into this legalization comes a child a-lying in a manger (coming through its mother's line—read *Sarah the Priestess: The First Matriarch of Genesis* by Savina Teubal and extrapolate from there). This swaddled child of a matriarch is a sign of a new way of doing business. From this generalized description of a child and a manger, there is heard a far-off hymn of new creation come close enough to make out the words, "Glory . . . Peace." [Luke 2:1–14, (15–20)]

Of course, our tendency is to take this antiestablishmentarianism of a manger-child capable of throwing a wrench into the gears of registrations and turn it into the opposite of what we have experienced. Hooray, I get to be in charge. And, of course, that will bring with it grand titles and an assumption of knowing what is just and righteous. How many times has that turned sour on us? [Isaiah 9:2–7]

If we don't take that direct approach to overthrowing the regimenters, we sit back and sing a song of an active G*D—great and greatly to be praised. It won't be long before the pie in the sky sets everything right and treats everyone fairly. Keep singing those carols. [Psalm 96]

The catch to all this is blood atonement. G*D's readiness to give and forgive demands sacrifice to activate it. A simple baby in a manger must become God and Savior and dead before being effective. [Titus 2:11–14]

Perhaps we simply need to go back to a baby, any baby. It is an urge to birth that brings the light back, a return of complex justice, a continually new song, and giving and forgiving. Look behind an aborted, a stillborn, a genetically compromised, a socially untenable, a healthy birth—any—each is a sign to us in the darkness—fecundity pushes onward. Now we can even claim our birth and the weird way our journey has been woven as a sign in the darkness. May we release a Glory within to become a Peace around and about.

The angels have returned from whence they came, leaving you and me—baby signs. Ready, set, go!

Luke 2:15–21
Naming Day

Let's go see about what can be trusted in life. Hearing angels is one thing; finding a promise is quite another.

What needs checking on, to see whether it holds up or not? We all carry old promises along. Sometimes we think a promise is reality when it has actually become a shield against what can be experienced. Sometimes we need to say, "I think we heard it wrong. Life isn't over there in Bethlehem, but right here in the field. The angels hearkened unto us about us, about what is born in us this day."

After eight days, our ancestor could say, "Yes, the baby is still alive and ready for a name." Until a marker of viability was present, a baby was not named. (Today, we name stillborn babies and premature babies who die or take months to leave a hospital.)

In today's medical world of *in utero* genetic testing and an Apgar score at birth, eight days can be reduced, but not always. Life takes testing to see if this is something that is going to last. The same is true of relationships. Some form quickly; some take longer.

Let's not be too quick to claim the fulfillment of a promise. Let's not be too slow to claim there is more community available than we now have. With these two processes, we can both treasure and ponder. Both are important—treasuring what has come forth and pondering what else is on the way.

Luke 2:22–40
Old Welcomes New

What's the right time to move toward purity/justice? The right time to be dedicated to larger visions?

Are you going to wait for New Year's midnight plus a minute? How about waiting another 40 days for purification after childbirth (Leviticus 12), which would take us to Groundhog Day? [What would happen if Mary presented herself for purification and she didn't cast a shadow?]

Poor Mary, here to be purified, and instead of that being the biggie, we have Simeon and Anna butting in to talk about Jesus. Even after the ceremony is done, it is not talked about in terms of a new start for Mary to look toward more teen pregnancies, but the focus is on Jesus growing strong and wise. The favor that was Mary's is transferred to Jesus, just like that—ahh, patriarchy.

In Luke, we find other details overlooked—the redemption of the firstborn (5 shekels) and a later reference to the cost of betrayal (30 pieces of silver).

These and other details aside, a question remains about what rituals you see as important enough to go out of your way to fulfill? Would you have stayed on in Bethlehem for 40 days? It was probably out of the question to walk back to Nazareth and to return to Jerusalem in that time. Did Joseph have enough saved up? What did he do about carpentry jobs previously contracted? Do any of these practical questions have anything to do with anything?

At any rate, Luke seems not to know all the rituals pertaining to birthing. Even without them, blessings from Simeon and Anna come forth. Note the blessings that arise in your life even when not following the straight and narrow. You might almost think that G*D is about being a prodigal blesser. And your image of G*D; your being in G*D's image?

Luke 2:41–52
Blessed Body [1]

Note the change between verses 46 and 47.

In verse 46, Jesus is listening and asking questions. In verse 47, he evidences some understanding and is responding to questions.

There is a sense in which every question contains an idea, a hoped-for outcome, and so there isn't much difference here. We could be looking at an example of parallelism.

We may also be looking at teaching to the test—all that matters is getting a certain percentage of currently correct answers. One way around this is to focus on responses, not answers. Responses help set a context and keep an openness to new information.

However, this is more likely to be the beginning of Jesus' loyal opposition to the state of affairs within the religious community of his time and space. As such, the questions of verse 46 have a definite priority over the answers of verse 47.

Those questions of Jesus are not restricted to a religious sphere. They expand to his parents and, by extension, will go to the political rulers as well. They even extend to your life and mine. "Why would you search for me?", asks Jesus. "Where have you looked and to what avail?"

More and more folks are searching for G*D stuff anywhere but in church. This is probably attributable to the church's reliance upon verse 47 and the giving of answers that no longer correspond to the questions being put to it by its loyal opposition or outsiders. May we get back to Jesus and ask questions of today's religious bodies. If they can't take it, they will fade, while the questioners will increase in wisdom and in years.

Luke 3:1–6
Needed Change [2]

Last week, the parentheses of life were justice and righteousness. This week, they have morphed into repentance and forgiveness. Whichever way your language preference goes, the communal or the personal, we are reminded to ground them both in the very specific realities of this moment in time.

In the fifteenth year of the reign of Emperor Tiberius, when Pontius Pilate was governor of Judea and Herod was ruler of Galilee, his brother Philip, ruler of the region of Ituraea and Trachonitis, and Lysanias, ruler of Abilene, during the high priesthood of Annas and Caiaphas . . .

In the sixth year of the reign of President W. ... the high priesthood of James Dobson and Joel Osteen ..., etc. (you fill in the rest, remembering to update this to the latest military and religious icons of the day), there is still a need for the proclaiming of repentance/justice and forgiveness/righteousness.

There are plenty of crooked paths that still need straightening (repentance). Too many poor valleys still need filling (forgiveness) and accumulated mountains needing lowering (repentance). Crooks with guns and fountain pens still need to go straight (forgiveness) while rough violence calls for soothing smoothing (repentance). All life is intended to find wholeness (forgiveness).

---

a region around the Jordan needs a proclamation
pro-repentance means more than being a pro at it
pro-forgiveness means more than leaning in that direction
would we would learn preemptive repentance
breaking a cycle
would we would practice preemptive forgiveness
healing a cycle
what blessing there yet awaits
come
laugh, sing
we can yet learn
we can yet practice

Needed Change [3]

A brood of vipers has a nasty ring to it. However, what is at stake here are issues of growth, not strength of venom.

Religion consistently attempts to mold people into the shape and size of its own rituals and traditions, not hold a hope of what people might yet become. Religious reformers are quite clear about the changes people need to make to measure up to their own standards. Corporate people constantly call for skin-deep changes that never turn out to be quite good enough.

John doesn't spend a moment on surface change—the right cosmetics or more room for accumulation of resources before paying attention to justice issues. Who warned the crowd to come out to John and get changed? John ultimately doesn't care; he dives right into what is available today—"bear fruit."

Well, asks the crowd, if we are not here to get an acceptable molt or maintenance oil change, "What then should we do?"

"Simple kindness and everyday justice", is John's response. He uses economic justice examples, but it boils down to human values we were created with that are available to be expressed in our current life. Economic justice is a worthy fruit.

---

    we came with high expectation
    we just need to bow before Procrustes
    we will become the acceptable size
    we will find standards
    we will solve today by focusing on tomorrow
        John dashes the expectation

    we are changing to a new high expectation
    we just need to bow before John
    we will have needed power
    we fill find ease
    we will solve today by focusing on John
        John dashes the expectation

    we are left waiting without expectation
    we just need to be kind and just
    we will be open to a change of heart
    we will find assurance
    we will solve today by focusing on today
        John affirms this message of good news for the poor

Beloved

Ahh, baptism, held so dear by the church as a branding of the soul! Baptism, a sacrament of privilege and power, a sign of belonging to the in-group.

Truth be told, you can pour all the water in the world or immerse to the depths of the ocean, but without belovedness awakened, there is nothing but baptism's shell.

The most beautiful of liturgy and prayer might be sung by angels or chanted by saints, but without belovedness awakened, there is no baptism.

If I have the most blessed baptism, but have not belovedness . . . .

To go into all the world, baptizing, is to announce and awaken belovedness. Baptize when requested, but always, always, announce and awaken belovedness. This is an appropriate response to people's expectation of something better in the midst of another fine mess we've gotten ourselves into.

Luke 4:1–13

Conviction [1]

Temptations lead us to assembly-line work. When we have come through a temptation (or not), it is not as though temptations are over and done with, once and forever. Finish one temptation, and a next is on its way.

Whether successfully countered or not, temptations (and our response) give us material to work with as we proceed to live out what we understand to be the movement and intention of G*D. These first 13 verses move toward verse 14, which helps us know what temptations are to result in. Feel free to go the extra verse.

Part of the reason this is so important is that temptations come at their own opportune time. They come at what is probably our least opportune time. Lent is a time to practice how, out of our weakness, we might rise to the occasion.

These 40 days give us a good leg up on how we might regularly spend our time between temptations—doing what practice we can to continually and consistently envision a larger significance to daily events. Did you see G*D in your eating and other survival mechanisms today (presuming it isn't a fast day for you)? Did you see G*D-mercy today in a world with all its emphasis upon power and control? Did you see G*D in the church today, even in its institutional privilege?

If you didn't make those sorts of applications, might we say that the Satan had no reason to tempt you because you had already capitulated? How might you better practice a larger view today that you might be ready for tomorrow's tempting?

To be praised by everyone is either faint praise or an accumulation of political capital.

If praised by everyone, it would be very easy to begin to think one can push to a next level—it is now time to move away from the exploratory committee stage and into full campaign mode. So a platform is presented, and Jesus walked onto it, wrapping the mantle of prophet about himself. Even today, candidates still go back to their hometown, or symbolic hometown, to announce their candidacy for a mantle of power.

Initially, what we have been waiting for has arrived. But, as we will hear next week, this doesn't go so well when Jesus meddles by applying the platform to everyday lives.

What would you say if all eyes were upon you? Would it be that the past is fulfilled? That the future may now begin? Usually, we are pretty humble about those sorts of pronouncements, but it may be time to dust off our pride of relationship with G*D and know the importance of this moment. It is a turning point for you and all of us.

Try reading aloud what Luke says Jesus read from Isaiah

> *The Presence of G*D around me*
> *energizes me to bring good news to the poor*
> *through release of their captivity to the economy,*
> *recovering a vision of their blessedness, and*
> *to otherwise free oppressed people.*
> *This will mark a time of the Presence of G*D*

and say three times in a row:

> *Today scripture is fulfilled in my life.*
> *Today scripture is fulfilled in my life.*
> *Today scripture is fulfilled in my life.*

Response?

Is there a different statement about which you are able to say, "Today this is fulfilled in my life", or "This is my intention"?

A prophecy of old is coming true today that tomorrow may be better.

This is meddling of the highest order. Why should our generation and our town bear the brunt of having things set right? Can you imagine the upset in our fantasies when an increasing gap between have and have-nots is suddenly, without warning, done away with? How can we any longer measure the meaning of life? How will we behave with one another? All control would be gone; chaos would set in. There is a reason the Year of Jubilee was never put into action.

Jesus didn't leave a good idea alone; he had to go and try to do it. In this way, he revealed, just like a sharp, two-edged sword, how far from community are our deeds and intentions. We don't love G*D enough to reset our economics. We don't love our neighbor enough to meet them on a level playing field. We don't love ourselves enough to dismiss these barriers but live in fear that there are no built-in markers that will guarantee our present and eternal comfort and excuse us from participation in the fullness of life.

Elijah, Elisha, (El)esus all yank away our fantasy life and bring us to action that reveals G*D's spirit and binds us together in newer and better ways. Later, these three revealers of *El* will be revered. But for the moment, they insult us by opening G*D's goodness to strangers, foreigners, and non-like-minded believers of what we believe in.

Let's not live for being revered, either now or later. Let's simply live to reset the basis on which we relate to one another, common ground and common vision.

---

today scripture is fulfilled
when else pray tell
could it have been
and still been scripture

scripture lifted from the page
writing turned again to speaking
speaking engaged with hearing
heart heard to life lived

bone by bone
dried and alive
danced and threatening
we meet and go on

again and again
our image of home
fails to be home
drive on

filled full leaves no room
Bethlehem or Nazareth
America or Iraq
scripture passes by

Luke 5:1–11
Guiding Gift [5]

Nets are being washed and readied for a next night's fishing. Jesus talks to people on the lakeshore. Jesus enters a boat and teaches, and then asks Simon to go fishing in the daytime. Fishing out of season calls for a willingness to suspend common sense, that a new revelation might have room to be welcomed.

Sure enough, after getting the nets back in place, they broke their pattern and were nearly swamped with a new catch. Simon, in a boat filled to the brim with wriggling, newly-caught fish, falls to his knees in their midst. (If there isn't some element of humor in a new revelation, it probably isn't a new revelation.)

If this event was possible, what isn't? Simon Peter asks that question with a fearful, dramatic phrasing to distance himself from even more changes, and yet still surmises there is more going on here than literal connections between fish and fields and people. Here is a challenge that can't be passed over and allow one to remain satisfied by going back to a previous routine.

May we each hear a more expansive invitation than we were ready for. Ready or not, daylight comes; patterns are broken; fear rises; courage for a new challenge abates that fear; new life goes on.

---

yet, if you say so
I will come to myself
in this very place and time

until every midnight and noon
every fullness of employment – doing
every empty laid-aside – suffering
sings a body electric

yet, if you say so
I will come to neighbors
in their moment and space

until every race and gender
every variant in culture
every difference in orientation
sings a body eclectic

yet, if you say so
I will come to you
in your whim and wisdom

until every call and response
every habit questioned
every opportunity welcomed
sings a body elected

yet, if you say so
I will come to rest
in expectation and trust

until every premise and assumption
every unexpected youngest child
every unentitled eldest
sings a body selected

I have appreciated the translations that say to the poor, hungry, sorrowing, reviled—"You are not cursed." When we leave it simply as "blessed are you", the affirmation soon becomes enough for the sayer to do. While one statement (you are not cursed) may be implied within the other (you are blessed), they touch different parts of us.

To be blessed means I'm in need of blessing, and the question is whether that blessing is sufficient to cover what needs covering. There is something clearer about not being cursed.

At other times, I am aware of not being cursed, but without the motivation to do anything about that state, and I stand in need of a good blessing to free a direction of engagement.

How do you play back and forth between being blessed and being not-cursed?

Within this may be some hints about the healing process. Some of those who came needed a vaccination of blessing to hold them through every diseased scene they will pass through. Others only needed a seal of approval, received through a proclamation that they are not cursed. The healing arts really are an art form—knowing where to apply what.

Amid the crowd who came to hear and be touched, those looking for a word found themselves spoken to and those looking for a touch found themselves embraced.

Those who are or have been poor and found their freedom as well as its imposition make excellent teachers by word or example. Those who are or have been hungry know the depth of hope. Those who are weeping or have wept and yet find the beginning of a laugh are worthy of shadowing.

These are "saints" among us.

These saints are not consistently or universally able to have their whole life reflect their learnings from poverty, hunger, or grief. They will also sometimes forget or try to say or do more than is helpful. Nonetheless, this is the ground from which saints arise, and we had best attend to their experience.

There are also folks who, by chance or design, have found themselves with resources and status higher than most. We can also thank them for their negative witness that brings into higher contrast the difference between gritty saints from below and sanitized saints from above.

These pieces of wisdom are addressed to those able to listen and enact what they hear. There were those of long-ago who listened. There are those of today who also listen. Even as the institutional church implodes, there will be those who listen to these words and actually implement them in their time.

Sandals and rubber continue to meet the road. Without thinking—who do you identify as your enemy, the person you would cross the street to avoid?

Exactly here is your work for this next year. No, not to convert someone from enemy to friend. Deeper than this is the work of learning to both forgive and love an active enemy.

Susan Werner has a song with applicable lyrics. Search YouTube for Susan and her song, "Forgiveness".

> *How do you love those who never will love you*
> *I think only God knows and God is not taking sides*
> *I hope one day [God] shows us how we can love those*
> *Who never will love us but who still we must love*

It may just be that our learning and showing G*D this love of enemy is our work to do. It will help G*D move beyond floods and fires next time.

Luke 6:27–38
Guiding Gift [7]

This Sunday can often fall on the same Sunday as the last Sunday of Epiphany, when the pericope for a transfigurational experience is Luke 9:28–36, (37–43).

This opens a choice for the day. Just another evidence that there is nothing common about anything held in common. Even a revised common anything doesn't get us all the way to an actual commonality.

But this also gives us an opportunity to play between passages we might not otherwise set alongside one another.

Luke 6:27–38 = Luke 9:28–36, (37–43)

Loving others = transfiguration of self
Loving enemies = transfiguration of self
Not judging = transfiguration of self
Forgiving = transfiguration of self
Giving generously = transfiguration of self

The pattern is established. This is the way we participate in the largest of exoduses or journeys.

Looking for the outcome of living lightly or journeying joyfully? Follow these teachings on your way.

Enjoy this handful (five digits) of a new pentalogue as you participate in them. Think of them as sequential points in a gyre, not a line that ends with either generosity or one transfiguration. Each time through a cycle of these five, you are at a higher spot. If the destination is worth enjoying, so is the travel.

Luke 6:39–49
Guiding Gift [8] — Proper 3 (8)

There is a strong temptation to want to go back and figure out whether the words Luke records were actually addressed to the disciples or if they were for the Pharisees, as in Matthew. We would like to be able to get some either/or out of this to figure out just how much goodness we need to remove from our own savings account and still be able to get into heaven.

If, as we fear, it turns out that these challenges are universals and we are going to have to actually invest more in people than we want to, we will have to recalculate whether or not it turns out that heaven is a matter of sharing treasure right here and not just a storing up of our goodness or good deeds.

Whether at the beginning of the year or middle or end, finally, after a list of commands connecting us with a wider world, there comes a question deserving a response. It is a question that looks for evidence.

May this question haunt you:

Why do you call me, "Lord, Lord" and not do as I say?

Why do you call me, "Lord, Lord" and not do as I say?

Why do you call me, "Lord, Lord" and not do as I say?

Why do you call me, "Lord, Lord" and not do as I say?

Why do you call me, "Lord, Lord" and not do as I say?

Why do you call me, "Lord, Lord" and not do as I say?

Why do you call me, "Lord, Lord" and not do as I say?

Why do you call me, "Lord, Lord" and not do as I say?

Why do you call me, "Lord, Lord" and not do as I say?

Why do you call me, "Lord, Lord" and not do as I say?

Why do you call me, "Lord, Lord" and not do as I say?

Why do you call me, "Lord, Lord" and not do as I say?

Why do you call me, "Lord, Lord" and not do as I say?

Here in Luke and in Matthew 5–7, we have a major job description laid out. Blessings on finding evidence that is confirmable by someone other than yourself.

Luke 7:1–10
Guiding Gift [9] — Proper 4 (9)

This amazing story assumes Jesus' mere acknowledgement of the presence of a trust in authority is the same as specifically saying, "Let them be healed." Again, rules for healing don't hold the day. We continue in the realm of mystery.

Israel was an occupied country, and this "centurion" was either engaged in enforcing the tax/tribute that flowed from Palestine to Rome or stayed on as a pensioner of the Roman army. As a power behind hated tax collectors, it is fruitful to wonder about the connection between this meta-Gentile and the Jewish elders who importuned Jesus for this healing.

You may have even begun wondering about your own soldiers while deployed. If most went about the business as efficiently/violently as needed, how does a modern centurion separate himself from his job enough to engage real people whose source of meaning is to be honored? Did he play a Magi gift-giver? A foreigner and an occupier? More time needs to be spent here, as there is probably a clue in this story about how to transform enemies to friends.

I would expect his district spent less on collection and returned more than the average company. We'll never know, but it does raise a question about whether you really do get further with an enticement of honey and synagogue-building or a threat and confiscation? Does nation-building bring a greater economic return and a more secure environment than shock and awe?

The centurion had heard about Jesus. How? Was there an equivalent of the National Security Agency (N.S.A.) working then? Did your speculation run more to the Jewish elders being Jesus' supporters rather than antagonists?

At any rate, there is plenty of opportunity to explore this account post-Magi and post-Pentecost. What does this story bring to enhance any season?

Luke 7:11–17

Proper 5 (10)

Prophets see life where others see no life. Sometimes a lack of vision is some form of complicity with the *status quo* and all the privilege and entitlement that comes with it. Sometimes it is not having a sufficient lens through which to see new shoots poking their heads through cement.

Prophets do more than see and point. They are engaged with that which is beyond the boundaries of the current community. Here, the disciples and a large crowd were all looking for what they could get from Jesus. Jesus, prophet that he was, looked both at and beyond them.

Unfortunately, disciples and crowds often have a wrong takeaway from a prophetic moment. They get all excited about Jesus, rather than for the mother whose hope for livelihood has been restored to her. They might have had their eyes opened to the standard difficulties of widows and children in their community/culture.

Where was the larger question from this localized situation? Did the Bible get it right that every laud and honor is to go to Jesus, with no learning about participating in his Way?

News about Jesus spread. His prophetic vision and actions went unheeded. From this time and distance, we might try to put this story back together in a new and more helpful way.

This same Jesus has been heard to say that those who came later would do more than he evidenced here.

Well, the needs of many "widowed", physically and religiously, are still present and need attending. Proceeding one-by-one won't suffice. This is going to take a common-unity approach.

Imagine how far this news could spread—beyond a lottery-lucky widow, that all "widows" will be cared for—beyond blood lineage, beyond class, beyond status, beyond religious obligation.

Now G*D has not just looked favorably upon the poor or had a preferred option for the poor, but G*D is literally with the poor and the poor with G*D—so both "poor" and "G*D" are better defined.

Luke 7:36–8:3
Proper 6 (11)

Stories are never meant to carry the whole freight of a lesson. Who would be loaned 500 coins if they were not expected to be able to pay it back in full? Likewise with 50. The more one has to pay back with, the higher the loan possibility (in theory).

To be forgiven 500 coins worth to one person may be the equivalent of being forgiven 50 coins worth to another.

Simon might be said to have judged rightly in absolute terms, but in relative terms, he might also be said to have judged less than rightly—without considering relationship, mercy, or compassion.

Is forgiveness simply forgiveness, or is it caught in the same economic thinking as we apply to everything else in our culture?

What would it have taken from Simon for Jesus to commend him for judging mercifully instead of rightly? And from you?

---

greater forgiveness
equals greater faith
so we set up equations
for the living of life

we love to measure
we measure love
according to one standard
and then another

does this act mean I'm loved
more than ever before
or is it now all over
rapturous catastrophe

when we can back away
we see a weeping woman
and all this right thinking
equates to nothing

Luke 8:26–39
Proper 7 (12)

The 2010 Wisconsin Annual Conference began with word of a potential trial of a lay person in West Ohio and a probable clergy trial here in Wisconsin. Both are logical outcomes of the dismissive and discriminatory language in a rule-book regarding some feared "self-avowed practicing homosexuals."

As I read this passage from Luke, I can't help but wonder if the demoniac in need of healing isn't the Church that has gotten out of its right mind in an over-zealous attempt at inappropriate purity. The potential trials are acting like the child in the story of an Emperor's New Clothes—demonstrating the nakedness of a dead-end attempt to protect G*D and to live among tombs of past purities.

Those attempting to keep this identity-politics, restrictive language of the Church, seem to bounce back and forth between shouting against liberals and begging not to have to change their ways. If called out on the blaming, they whine about being persecuted and having their bible taken from them, and soon after complaining are back to yelling for their way—and around and around it goes.

In this story, the demoniac/church is healed at the expense of pigs and those who earn their livelihood through them. This seems to have torn the community apart, as they ask/demand Jesus leave even as Jesus sends forth a healed demoniac/church to do Pentecostal testimony regarding an amazing, expansive, and experienced love of G*D.

There will be fallout when the current United Methodist Church policy changes. Institutional income may well be affected, but healing work will have been done, and there is no adequate measure of this grace and no adequate reason to resist a needed healing.

Luke 9:28–36, (37–43a)
Mountain Top to Valley — Conviction [2]

Raphael has an interesting painting entitled "Transfiguration".

In it, we have both parts of the pericope—blessing and healing. This is a devotional painting, not a scenic one. Some have said the woman is the Church, the Bride of Christ, pointing out the to-do list for Jesus.

The congregation I pastor is having a Capital Funds Campaign Commitment Sunday for the raising of a shelter/temple in this community. Interestingly, it is going to be located at the bottom of a hill. Perhaps we might yet see that Christ's glory is enough without monuments to it and that a mission outpost or hospitable hospital image might yet be ours.

The distance between transfiguration and healing is not all that great in this painting. How is it in life where you are?

---

got it figured out?
not without figuring
on transfigurement
for figurers

or

figuring
minus
transfiguring
is no figuring
at all

or

F-T=0°F
and that's cold

Luke 9:51–62
Proper 8 (13)

Have you ever "set your face"? Well, of course. We do it all the time. A perennial question is where we have our persona directed. Our vibes are our messengers—how are they doing in preparing a welcome for us? This question comes from the understanding that welcome leads to welcome.

James and John seemed to be spring-loaded to anticipate rejection. Not only do they expect it, but they have their response ready—"Incinerate them!" Which of your vibes have you named "James" and/or "John"?

This same anticipation process comes with folks thinking they are ready for any challenge, only to find the most ordinary ones of "comfort" and "ritual" tripping them up.

Bottom line—the mystery and challenge of the Freedom of G*D can't be avoided or evaded. There is room for all on the field. Are we going to play and welcome those currently on the sideline, or play and force others to the sideline?

———————————

in our current day
we lose focus
so much more to do
so little time
so easy to do one more thing

in our current day
we are tempted to pause
to make one more attempt
to teach one more lesson
to over-function again

in our current day
we set a system in place
and then are consumed by it
bowing to what we made
idolizing our way

in our current day
we struggle with constraint
and loosened reins
when to gee or haw
confusing ourselves

in our current day
the current available
has met resistance
become heat not light
not fit

in our current day
a challenge remains
to keep an eye on a prize
a hand to the plow
and compassion along the way

Luke 10:1–11, 16–20
Proper 9 (14)

Where is this heaven where names are written? Consider the prayer, "on earth as it is in heaven". Might this heavenly record location be earth? Our living in process (read: engaging individuals and communities in the present) is always caught between an abundance of plenty (name written) and a fear of scarcity (name not written). When working together, we are more likely to sense the assurance of plenty.

When we travel together, we are drawn toward opportunities to demonstrate the joy of expressing peace in season and out. Once in a while, we settle for a while, but always the call is to widen the venue of our healing. We invest in others so that they will express their healing gifts. And we move on before the temptation to become a healer upon whom others are dependent.

While we have made the knocking of dust off our feet into a judgment against others, it is simply a recognition of people needing to come together and, for whatever reason, they didn't in a particular time or space.

While it feels good to blame others, it would be better to describe our dust as meaning, "How sad," rather than, "Woe to you!"

The elided verses are appropriately left out as they slip into control and power models rather than a sharing of peace simply for the joy of sharing, regardless of response.

So, homework time—

As you change spaces during the week, offer this preemptive blessing:
> Neighb*rs are here; G*D is near.

See if, from Monday to Sunday, there is a subtle, but noticeable, shift in how you move through your day. If so, you'll be able to see your name engraved where'er ye go throughout this whole, wide earth. If not, keep at it; you will, as John Wesley learned—preach peace until you have it and then live peace because you have it.

Luke 10:25–37
Proper 10 (15)

In days of yore, an important question was that of "eternal life". Often, it now seems the question is, "What do I have to do to get by today?"

We can phrase that in terms of getting whiter teeth, a desirable partner, a viable bank account, or other such, but it all boils down to smaller life goals rather than larger ones. We are still trying to find a way to keep a Jubilee Year from our door.

In Matthew (19:16 ff.) and eight chapters later in Luke, this same question has the kicker of "sell what you 'own', and give the proceeds to the poor". To be aware of our Neighb*r is going to very quickly lead us to this same conclusion. Now a question: Will we be ready to offer a blank check to whatever innkeeper is around—even an innkeeper as sly as Thenardier in *Les Misérables*?

In Mark (12:28 ff.), we note a difference when this question is not being asked as a test. In this case, the "kingdom" (G*D's presence) is not far away. Blessings on seeing your congregation, family, job, etc., as a Mercy Inn franchise.

So, are you interested in drawing closer to G*D? There is definitely an overhead cost of fresh mercy. Face it. Enjoy it.

Luke 10:38–42
Proper 11 (16)

Last night we had a brief skirmish between atmospheric sisters of differing pressures—high and low, cold and hot, dry and wet. Less noticeable were the tectonic plates tussling beneath our feet. We are at another frontal conflict with Martha and Mary.

We've been hearing about the importance, high value, of hospitality and welcome. Here, the tables are reversed. The one providing hospitality is reproved, while the one acting as non-Samaritan Priest and Levite is commended.

I appreciate Richard W. Swanson's comment in *Provoking the Gospel of Luke*, "Many scenes in the gospels make better sense when you begin by surrendering the notion that Jesus is always right, no matter what. I am increasingly convinced that the gospels do this intentionally, but ideological Christian reading simply refuses to go along."

Are there limits on hospitality? If so, what might they be?

A friend recently reminded me, "I would suggest that the huge irony of being irenic [endlessly hospitable/welcoming] is that 'tolerance' applied to intolerance is like pouring gasoline by the 55-gallon drum on an already raging bonfire."

Where do we need to pause in the never-ending work of welcoming to regain perspective? For instance, congregations often get into trouble when they claim they are "friendly". That may indeed be their intention, but they have no way of evaluating how their "friendliness" is being perceived by others [and, truth be told, have no interest in finding out, as it would lead to change]. Let's pretend that Jesus was holding a seminar on the effectiveness of current hospitality. Martha's very continuing to do what she has done is getting in the way of her doing hospitality well. Martha's activity has become expected by her and others, and folks better like the way she is friendly to them—or else.

If your congregation hasn't done it lately, it would be instructive to: 1) borrow a couple of lay members from another congregation to drop by at a time of worship or fund-raiser and later report on their experience of actual hospitality received, and 2) do a quick survey of people on the street, in the grocery store, at the gas station, and people such as a homeless person, police officer, or school principal regarding their perception of the congregation in question. You can even offer to return the favor. This Mary moment might affect Martha and widen the scope of hospitality for her and others.

Luke 11:1–13
Proper 12 (17)

First, a bit of for-what-it-is-worth about catalysts from *The American Heritage Book of English Usage.*

> The word catalyst has been in use since the 1600s and comes from Greek *katalusis*, "dissolution." If this etymology seems slightly out of sync for a substance that helps other substances come together and react, consider that the term was first used to describe political situations, especially the breaking apart of governments. By the mid-1800s, though, the political meaning had been rendered obsolete and the term had become part of the lexicon of chemists. Today, a catalyst is a substance that increases the rate of a chemical reaction without undergoing any permanent chemical change itself.

Now two helpful comments from the *New Interpreter's Study Bible*:

> 1. What might be taken as a request for a correct 'technique' of prayer actually turns into a lesson on nurturing a relationship with God. Prayer along these lines would serve as an ongoing catalyst for the formation of persons into a community of faithfulness.

How do you and your congregation use the prayer that has come down to us as a model prayer? Has it become a ritual, a tradition, a technique? What will it take for this prayer to return to its catalytic position within the community of dissolving our serial discriminations and speeding the implementation of mercy?

> 2. Everyone is encouraged to recognize God's expansive goodness.

Everyone who has been around a Kairos CoMotion event has heard the phrase, "the expansive love of G*D" used and reused. This is a good conclusion to the image of a catalyst that transforms without being used up, able to continue and continue to transform through the dissolving of privileged judgments regarding male and female, slave and free, gay and straight.

When we are out of power, we look for shortcuts to get what we consider we are entitled to. We will appeal to an authority figure. We will attempt to fix the matter structurally by shaping a decision-making process (politics) to be on our side.

This is an ancient story that Jesus or you or I could bet will be coming our way sometime today, tomorrow at the latest. Attempts will be made to triangle us into another person's dramatic moment. I expect Jesus has met this moment in his own life and so was ready for it. We may not be as ready to say to another, "This is between the two of you, and so I wish the two of you a wise and compassionate way to resolve the matter. I love you both, so let me know how it turns out."

This process of appealing to authorities and structures to do our work for us is never a helpful thing. Eventually, the very processes we use to get our way will be turned against us. If you live by another's authority, you will die by another's authority. If you live by a structural advantage, you will die by that same structure shifted against you.

There seems to be no way to take advantage without being taken advantage of in another context. About all that is available is to be generous with life. This value will guide the rest of one's attention.

Luke 12:32–40
Proper 14 (19)

Don't be afraid to sell your possessions and give the proceeds away.

This direction to arrive at a place of "real homeland security" is one that we are capable of subverting in several different ways.

Possession is a code word for security. Our treasure spot becomes the goal of our life. Fear keeps us tied to the treasures we have and away from greater treasure. Fear buries our treasure in the ground.

Remember, there is something about a satisfied-mind that is important to a sense of quietude that strengthens us past temporary securities and lets us hold them lightly.

It is G*D's pleasure to be present; it is our pleasure to be present.

Where your presence is, there is your heart's treasure.

As we measure our faith by looking at our bank balance, credit card statement, etc., so we measure our faith by where we put our presence, where we are active, where we bring some light.

Blessed are those alert to presence with them and their presence with others.

---

how long we wait
for a presence worth waiting for

how often we jump
at any presence that comes along

how do you do
still waiting or jumping

when living presence is noted
there is a veritable feast

servers are served
the served take their turn

yin yang unity turns and turns
each in and out of the other

we're not there yet
rejoice in how far we've come

our waiting has borne fruit
enough to wait some more

Being the literalist that he was [grin], Jesus knew there was no getting around flooding folks out again. A rainbow is a rainbow is a rainbow. The natural alternative for the rule-bound is to flip things 180 degrees. No water!—its opposite is Fire! That's the ticket, Fire!

So a slave sings, "God gave Noah the rainbow sign—No more water, the fire next time!"

Who among us hasn't envisioned ourselves as the spark to get a conflagration going that would refine all the dross of our lives (particularly that of particular other people). Rage, rage, against the dying of the light of justice. Of course, there is going to be separation of people; we are all at different levels of maturity and peace.

This is not new news. This is our condition as long as our condition has been reported. The only surprise is the lack of progress we have made in recognizing our condition.

---

division is so embarrassing
it always means someone
is getting chosen last

division is so normal
it is the water in which we swim
unrecognizable

division is so tempting
we're going to settle this
once and for all

division following Zeno
means we will never
get to a better place

division is a giving up
on the paradoxes of life
and the processes of G*D

Conviction [3]

Unless you pay attention in a different way than you have, you will perish as did those at a deliberate hand of violence or in another anonymous occasion of death.

Our usual process is to use comparisons. I'm better than they, so I deserve better. They are worse than I, so they deserve what they get. Or, we get lost in trying to parse a nuanced duality of good and evil out of a creative impulse and bump into irreconcilable differences.

Here, repentance doesn't change the final outcome of death, but it does change the energy of it. To pay attention in a different direction is to focus on that which brings life and leaves death to do its own thing. We don't try to justify one death as being different than another. We do, however, bring careful compassion to individuals and prophetic justice to unjust systems. In so doing, we join G*D and Jesus in watering lives and changing the pH of contexts.

Just a note: Often we associate G*D with the "man" in parables and, here, the gardener with Jesus. Given the beginning of this section, "the man" might better be seen as Mr. Market Force, Pilate, or the Principalities and Powers—always looking for an advantage and claiming a seven-year fig in only three—always ready to destroy. In like fashion, the gardener role becomes you, so enjoy digging in the stuff of life.

Luke 13:10–17
Proper 16 (21)

We are crippled by all manner of events. Eighteen years is a long time. Was it the length of reign of Tiberius to that date, as some have suggested? Political decisions can bend us over. Military occupation can bend us over. Was it some relational issue that had bent her over? A spouse, a divorce, a death, a child, and/or a friend can bend us over. Was it physical? Disease and disability can bend us over. Was it spiritual? Satanic? Testing?

Regardless of what the form of bent-overness might be, this woman, already demonstrating the same faith as Abram and Sarai, can be recognized as their "daughter". She occupied her promised land, a synagogue, and raises questions about who is kept from their religious promised land.

It is this recognition that sets Jesus apart from the others present. Who among us can see G*D's child in another, particularly another who is bent over? Can such contain G*D? While hypocrites usually put on masks to fool others about themselves, here hypocrites put masks on others so they don't have to deal with them. A mask here is the mask of Sabbath.

---

want to set the folks rejoicing
Mr. Religious Leader
tear down this mask
dividing people

we are after healing of nations
pray for Rwanda and Iraq
America, Israel, and Iran
this is a day for unbinding

in such a day
Monday, Tuesday, Wednesday
Thursday, Friday, Saturday
or Sunday is a Sabbath

since a Sabbath can be any day
it can also be every day
seven Sabbaths every week
is very good

creation is underway
that work is over and done
new non-work is needed
to hallow every hollow

we are like a sinkhole
our ground of being
has sunk until
we are bent over

reach out and touch someone
ground them in your steadfastness
loved and patted into new shape
standing and striding forth

our hollow places filled in
our mutual ministry
beyond our isolation
creates new Sabbaths

Luke 13:31–35
Conviction 2

Dire warnings are all around. Rebecca Ann Parker, in her book, *Blessing the World: What Can Save Us Now*, reminds us there are two ways of looking at disaster through an apocalyptic lens.

1) We can anticipate an apocalypse and become passive or simply await its arrival to set things straight. 2) We can claim an apocalypse has already occurred, and our work is to redeem the current time.

While we usually find ourselves somewhere between a glass more than half empty (anticipating an apocalypse to fill the remainder?) and a glass more than half full (working to remove the rubble, establish community yet available, and to share the little we have with those who have less?), the addition of perspective on apocalyptic matters does add value to our interpretation of what a next needed thing might or might not be for us.

Jesus speaks here post-apocalyptically—not in fear of what is to come but in blessing-mode on what has already happened. You can hear the passion for setting things right after they have gone terribly wrong (and aren't we living in a time when we can say things have gone terribly wrong!). If there is no weeping about our place of living as we rehearse Jesus' words about Jerusalem, we have not read them well.

This is not a time for a monotone reciting of holy words. Rather, our pre-apocryphal resignation or engagement with a post-apocryphal setting will be revealed through the reading of and response to these words:

> This place, here, now, arrived by ignoring/killing prophets and dismissing/stoning those who would bind up wounds! I offer consolation and consolidation as a hen gathers her brood under her wings, even as I am isolated/exiled. I proceed in hope that a time will come when you experience a need for blessing to go forward, and will remember it is in blessing I have been among you.

Luke 14:1, 7–14
Proper 17 (22)

Protocol for state dinners is very prescribed. Who sits next to or across from whom and where they are in relation to the principals has whole manuals that cover the ins-and-outs of such an event.

We actually do that informally in any setting. Watch a cadre of young ones at a movie theater figuring out who is going in first, who tags along last, who makes the decision about where to sit, and who has the most others trying to jockey to sit next to them.

Family tables are similar. Who sits where says a lot about the family dynamics and expectations of serving and being served.

As the *New Interpreter's Study Bible* indicates: "The sharing of food is a barometer of social relations. With whom does one eat?"

You might want to check out your own eating locations for the next week and reflect on what you find to be true for you.

At a non-traditional wedding of a friend, I was privileged to read a translation of 1 Corinthians 13 by one of the partners. It began this way:

> If I speak in human language or in that of the messen-
> gers, but do not have love (the love that is passionate-
> ly committed to the well-being of the other), I am a
> resounding piece of copper or a clanging cymbal.

They felt it important to say more than the standard "love" and assume everyone present would know what they meant—the love they wanted to participate in and that Jesus demonstrates in this pericope is "the love that is committed to the well-being of the other."

You may want to write that down so that every time you hear someone talking generically about love, you can remember the kind of love you are intending to share in your space, your place.

Luke 14:25–33
Proper 18 (23)

After looking at ourselves in the world around us, here is a big "therefore": None of you can continue learning or growing in experience of G*D through me if you allow your possessions to possess you.

This builds on a better language choice for translating what is so often recorded as "hate" of family. "Preferring" a person or persons or privilege over our relationship with G*D blocks our growth into G*D, our imitation of Christ.

---

spinning on his heel
Jesus "told" a following crowd
exactly what they didn't want to hear

a prioritized focus
is needed for continued growth
into and out of an expansive and expanding love

so much distracts
even literally following good
can keep us from completing our heart's desire

so much possesses
power to attract our limited attention
and we stick to what we have already known forever

freedom may be
another word for nothing left to lose
such freedom or presence of G*D is our unsticking place

Let's see, Chapter 14 ended with "Hey, anyone have ears able to listen?"

Now, Chapter 15 opens, "Imagine that! All the tax collectors and sinners were coming to listen to him."

Just taking those at face-value makes it seem as though the folks structurally left out of the religious power loop were the ones best able to listen.

Presuming so, who are the folks who will be listening best in your realm of influence?

If you just run with a religious crowd, there may not be anyone, including yourself, who can listen to transformational rejoicing. If everything is aligned, the scriptures and creeds all cohere with no discrepancies, and G*D is in charge—what is there to listen to? Isn't it just a waste of praise time?

It is possible to see a lost sheep as both lost and mine, and intended to stay lost. A Scapegoat sent to the wilderness is an example of this. Its lostness is its vocation. Finding this lost one is counterproductive because it brings the sins we sent away back again. And yet it can lead us to reconsider the "safety" we thought we had established. When looked at from the location of the "Shepherd", security is just that—an illusion.

If the Pharisees and scribes thought their grumbling might bring Jesus to his senses and see the error of his ways—you ought to turn some of those coming to you away and not associate with them—they received a story that essentially says,

> Oh yeah? Well, I not only welcome these you call lost, but I deliberately leave you behind and go in search of them. Remember what I said about not preferring a family that would keep you from finding G*D? Well, you are such a family in this case, and I am continuing to search for G*D beyond your illusory boundaries. And, guess what, I am finding real rejoicing in this search.

Whether lost in an empty place or a holy place, being found is a celebratory event.

Issues of acceptable loss and collateral damage are perennial. Who among us would leave 99 assets to go looking for a missing one? Not me. You?

Our rejoicing is usually over a profit, and the profit off of 99 is not far enough off 100 to spend the time and energy to search for a missing one or to risk having the 99 reduced even further. We would more likely gather folks around to celebrate such a small loss.

The whole premise of redemption doesn't compute in a profit-motive setting. Here, everyone is on their own lookout. Lost is lost, and gain is gain. Older brothers ought to get theirs first, and doubled.

This all works until the time comes when we are wandering or lost. Who will care or look for us? Well, if enough others have been let go and we have been complicit in their loss, there won't be anyone left to look for us. It is then in our best interest to listen again to these three stories and to hear them as prophecy to be engaged with, not "Soupy Soul" illustrations.

Sheep, coins, people, ozone layers, civilian casualties, etc., etc. are all too important to easily let them go. Keep looking for your compassion and, when found, engage it expansively.

---

no one gave him anything
neither did she receive assistance
with nothing
from nothing
toward nothing
lost and lone
we finally peel back
what feels like fate
to see an abundance
from which we have come
to which we return

in the ashes
from which we have come
to which we return
in an abundance of ashes
we find not only
ashes of abundance
we find also

new sight
new direction
new energy
new life
we hear also
angels rejoicing
as one in hundred is found
as one in ten is found
as one in two is found
as one unique is found

and so
pod-suckers
arise
what have we to lose
when there is paradise to gain

Luke 16:1–13

Proper 20 (25)

It's me again, God. Have I got a deal for you!

Let me get away with one more ___(your excuse here)___ and I'll be at the right place to bring you more thanks than you've seen in a hundred generations. We are right on the edge of new spiritual technology that will clone those who give thanks. We'll be able to get you so much praise it'll be coming out your ears.

It may just look like I'm squandering your resources, but my past investments have all had you in mind, and we are now so close we can both taste it.

For the first time in history, well, maybe the second or a few more, we are going to so connect wealth with God that folks won't be able to say one without saying the other. This is going to have a great outcome for you, God, so let's hold off on your threat to ship my position overseas. I'm sure that within the fortnight you'll get what you've always wanted—constant praise. Enough of this meaningful living stuff, let's get back to the basics—you can't have too much adulation.

Thanks. I know you won't regret it. A big Amen.

It is easy to express what might be called "compassion" with those we are particularly fond of in the moment or with those behind us or ahead of us in time. This might better be called "being sorry for", as in pity, commiseration, condolence, or sympathy.

"Compassion" is one of the big universals, and if it is not pulling us into a larger frame, then it is probably not compassion. To have compassion for one's sisters or brothers, in regard to a danger they will someday face if we don't face up to that danger now, is a good and worthy endeavor. If, however, it ends with one's own without pulling us toward others who are in the same situation, it quickly becomes a mere special interest.

It is easy-compassion to care about American deaths in Iraq without extending that care to the many more Iraqi deaths. It is easy-compassion to care about those caught in what we have come to call the holocaust without caring about those caught in present discriminations that are more narrowly cast. It is easy-compassion to care for those grandchildren to come who we project will face ecological devastation without caring about those who are already caught in it by their bodies' allergic reactions today.

Compassion is defined online by *Merriam-Webster* as: "sympathetic consciousness of others' distress together with a desire to alleviate it." My sense is that compassion is more active and universal than this. A distinction can be drawn between a willingness or desire to bear a "cross" and the actual bearing of it. Another distinction is between alleviating an injustice for an individual or group or alleviating an injustice for all.

Where is compassion leading you in regard to people's lives?

---

prevenient grace for those in hades
must not be put aside
in favor of judgment's chasm
so wide it would prevent grace

Luke 17:5–10
Proper 22 (27)

Mandated to forgive, Jesus' students ask for more faith.

Apparently, they think there is a connection between forgiveness and faith.

Their thinking is this: To not forgive is to lack faith.

Jesus avoids this connection, just as he does with some healings. Not every healing has to do with faith. Likewise, forgiveness is not always tied to faith. More faith would be overkill; see what a smidgeon of a jot or a tittle will do.

Jesus pooh-poohs the need for faith in the face of a clear and dramatic instruction about forgiveness—as often as it is requested, it is to be given. That's all. It doesn't take faith; it simply takes the doing of it.

They are simply to do what they were asked to do without gussying it up or getting faith involved—forgive.

Can you imagine forgiveness simply being forgiveness without forgiveness being a product of faith?

First, Lepers are an excluded people. It matters not what other identity they could also carry; their exclusion is an identity that supersedes any other. A nation of excluded folks within a nation is a crack in the foundation of that nation. Those excluded continually raise a cry from the margin. A prophet/priest may periodically come to release them, only to find another group classified as "leperous".

As a prophet, Jesus announces freedom. It is as though he said more fully, "Go show yourselves to exclusionary priests who are the gatekeepers of privileged inclusion." This points toward "outing" one's self—claiming a place at the table.

While still categorically excluded, it is difficult to reveal one's claim on community. Before an exclusion is excluded, it is surprising that even one in ten claimed their belovedness, their basic wholeness, their inherent belonging in the face of categorical discrimination. Being a pioneer in claiming one's self in the face of exclusion is difficult, difficult work.

Second, once one knows they are whole, not just a person in form but through-and-through, Joy is released. This is shown here with nine out of ten still needing an external validation and probably not getting such from a discriminating priest. They are not heard of again. Here one comes to a prophet/priest claiming their own with thanksgiving. Indeed, trust is their password—I trust I am whole. [Note: Welcome is a sign of a healthy priest.]

Another synonym for faith is following one's bliss. For an expression of a Leper returning, below is a graphic designed by one who is still a Leper in The United Methodist Church that categorically excludes gifted and called lesbian women and gay men from ordained ministry simply on the basis of their sexual orientation. Rev. Amy De-Long was tried by the exclusionary priests of her denomination and is still present because of enough welcoming priests on the trial court.

If you are preaching on this text, what would you think about wearing this graphic on a T-shirt instead of a robe or other professional attire? Would you use this as a bulletin cover or video image to preach on?

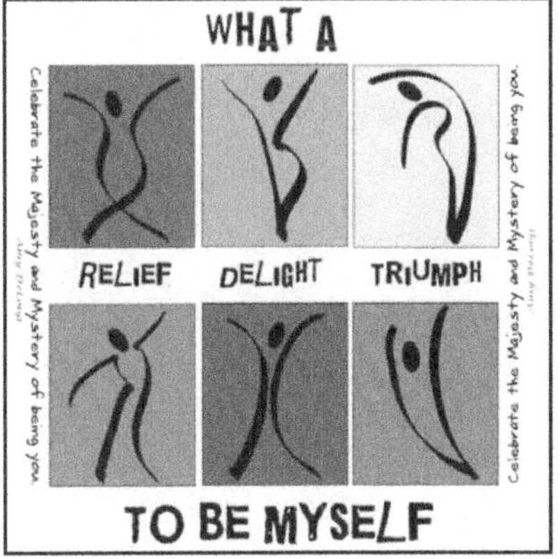

Luke 18:1–8
Proper 24 (29)

This is the season for *Children's Sabbath*. One of the injustices is to limit the slogan, "No child left behind", to the educational realm. Material from Children's Sabbath asks, "What would it look like to treat every child as a child of God?" They go on to indicate, "We would ensure that every child has a Healthy Start, a Head Start, a Fair Start, a Safe Start, and a Moral Start in life."

This emphasis upon the beginning of children's lives simply reveals there are those who are structurally left behind. Behind a call for better starts is the real gap of poverty. At some point, we will need to address poverty as it affects not only starting places but everywhere afterward, including ending points.

Widows and orphans are an inseparable pair in the scriptures. Imagine, if you will, replacing the widow in this story with an orphan. This draws the picture all the more starkly. A widow can have some modicum of standing, being an adult, and possibly having friends. The same cannot be said about an orphan unless you or I enter the picture as an intentional, going-the-long-distance, advocate.

This story is filled with accusations in this and every political season when war, poverty and an increasing gap between the rich and the poor leads to denying any increase of minimum wage to the poor so the rich don't even have to get any richer to increase that gap, and a program that is only concerned about some measurability of grades with no concern about the health of the children that allows any head learning to mean something.

Yes, G*D/widow and G*D/orphan have an accusation to bring against the rulers of our day and those of us who have quietly avoided the call to be an advocate who will wrestle against the powers and principalities of our day.

Are you ready to join the order of St. Widow of Importuning?

---

prayer is to faith

as

persistence is to justice

Luke 18:9–14
Proper 25 (30)

A slightly modified note from *The New Interpreter's Study Bible*:

> A basic question is this: Who recognizes G*D as a gracious benefactor? Who has learned the fundamental lesson Jesus has been developing throughout the Jerusalem journey—namely, that G*D's nature is characterized by generosity, compassion, care, and faithful activity on behalf of G*D's creation.

In terms of atonement issues, note that the blood of Jesus was not necessary for justification and forgiveness of sins. Humility in the present is sufficient. It would be good to remember Jesus' parables and stories and observations whenever we get into doctrinal issues. They show every single-note legalism for the control mechanism it is.

Now, how is the opportunity to stand in the presence of G*D rather than having G*D stand in the shadow of our own selves going to be offered in your worship opportunities?

One option is to use repetition.

Have the congregation stand and repeat, almost ad nauseam, "I'm better than these others." Have them even stick their nose in the air as they say it.

Then invite them to bow forward and repeat, quite slowly, "G*D, mercy." Have them extend that to others, "G*D, mercy for all that is not me."

And simply end the message. "You have both Pharisee and Tax Collector within you. The choice is yours—which will grow and which will diminish?"

Luke 19:1–10
Proper 26 (31)

What metaphorical tree would you climb to see who Jesus is?
>Would it be the tree of human compassion?
>Would it be the tree of church?
>Would it be the tree of meditation?

If we compare this passage with Amos 7:14, we find Amos coming hurriedly out of his sycamore tree to prophesy. Zacchaeus is also a prophet reminding us that economics is our major idol. We don't seem to know how to serve both G*D and Mammon. The reversal Zacchaeus goes through is a parallel to the transformation of Amos. Are you ready to be so converted?

Politically, we might note that the constitution was set up to deliberately keep economic power from overwhelming community political decision-making. We are now at that point of conflict in America where economics has equal status (if not more) with politics.

This wee little story casts a huge shadow. We see how it gets played out every election time and whether Zacchaeus will now say, "I don't see what the big deal is; my house will remain my house and everyone can look out for themselves, just like I've had to."

How will we keep terror at bay? Trust the Economy? Trust G*D? Fortify our house? Share? These are questions that continue to haunt.

Musically, a verse from the song *Where Are You Standing* by Judy Fjell puts this well.

I knocked upon your door, and no, you did not answer
You looked from behind your curtain and then you turned away
Did you do that to me, or did you do that to Jesus
I hope this question lingers, I hope this question haunts you
This question in your life

>*Chorus*
>>Where are you standing,
>>are you standing on the side of fear?
>>Do you close your heart to others
>>when differences appear between you?
>>Where are you standing?
>>Do you shout so only you can hear?
>>Or do you listen to the beat of the world?
>>Are you listenin' to the beat of the real world?
>>Are you livin' for the future of this world?

http://www.judyfjell.com/backoffice/dbops/news/display.htm?rec=170

Luke 19:28–40
False Dawn Sunday

"Go, do [this specific action (colt acquisition)]!" And they did.

"If these are silent, the stones will [take this specific action (sing)]!"

"This specific action" will happen. In the short-run or the long-run, a sign of a change is ready to be manifest.

Listen to Luke's record of some other folks invited to "Go ...." As you listen, raise a question: Where are you being led to "Go ...."? Without the question we might miss an invitation to an expanded life.

<u>John the Baptizer</u>: Luke 1:17 – He will **go** before G*D, in the power and spirit of Elijah.

<u>Jesus</u>: Luke 1:76 – He will be called the prophet of the Most High and **go** before G*D to prepare for G*D's presence.

<u>Shepherds</u>: Luke 2:15 – Left behind by angels, the shepherds said to one another, "Let us **go** to Bethlehem and see this thing announced to us."

<u>Lepers</u>: Luke 5:14, 17:14, 19 – And Jesus ordered him to tell no one. "**Go**, show yourself to a priest and claim your cleansing."

<u>Paralytic</u>: Luke 5:24 – Jesus says, "Stand up and take your bed and **go** to your home."

<u>John's Disciples</u>: Luke 7:22 – "**Go** and tell John what you have seen and heard."

<u>Anointing and Hemorrhaging Women</u>: Luke 7:50, 8:48 – "Your faith has saved you; **go** in peace."

<u>Disciples</u>: Luke 8:22, 10:3, 22:8 – "Let us **go** across to the other side of the lake to face wolves like lambs and eat together."

<u>Would-be Follower</u>: Luke 9:60 – "Let the dead bury their own dead; you, **go** and proclaim the kingdom of God."

<u>Questioning Lawyer</u>: Luke 10:37 – "**Go** and show mercy."

<u>Fearful Warners</u>: Luke 13:32 – "**Go** and tell the authorities, 'Listen, I am casting out demons and performing cures today and tomorrow, until I'm done.'"

<u>Potential Guest</u>: Luke 14:10 – "**Go** and sit down at the lowest place. From there you will be invited higher."

<u>Feast Giver</u>: Luke 14:21 – "**Go** into the highways and byways and invite the poor, the crippled, the blind, and the lame."

<u>Two Different Children</u>: Luke 15:18, 28 – I will **go** and say, "I have sinned" [the Welcome Mat is out]. Then he became angry and refused to **go** [the Welcome Mat is still out].

Where have you been caught thinking that you are caught in a web not of your own weaving or in a story made up by someone without regard for your character development? Time, then, to re-member there is a G*D of the living that goes beyond our limiting rules based on bad interpretation, bad science, or bad systems. In this remembering, it is now possible to move on.

---

children of resurrection
would be a lovely name
for a congregation
wrestling with a living G*D
as they find themselves
born and reborn and re-reborn
shedding skin after skin
growing from within
not compressed from without

child of resurrection
would be a beautiful secret name
for an individual
finding their identity
in being everyone's child
and bearing everyone's child
whether in body
or in metaphor
once or repeatedly

resurrection children
bypass usual fears
of death
as ending
or beginning
or changing
each is permissible
none holds sway
all is alive

Luke 21:5–19
Proper 28 (33)

The end of the church year is fast approaching. It doesn't appear that there is any change to an arc of history that we have been on. We grieve a national fall from a tall pedestal by banging back and forth between extremes, not knowing what has happened nor how to change our larger circumstance. And the same is happening to churches.

The same confusion was evident in the disciples—what's going on? What's the sign of getting back to business as usual or utter collapse? When is something going to come clear?

In Jesus' usual way, he says, "It's going to get worse. The only thing you have going for you is deciding where you are going to hitch your star and hang on for dear life."

We are nearly through another Church Year. Has it made a difference for you or anyone else? If not, that is something worth grieving over!

We don't have much to say for ourselves as we've been co-opted for so long. Our voice is but a whisper. Issues of individual greed and aspirations to more and more and bigger and bigger have stolen our power of testifying to a better way of living together.

No matter which way you turn, it's not going to be pretty. Remember, love G*D with everything you have, even unto becoming G*D, and love your Neighb*r as you would have your Neighb*r love you after walking a mile in each other's realities. This remembrance is all you will have until we move through this latest falling apart.

The end of turning last year's Advent expectation into ordinary living has again mostly gone bust. There is not much expectation of being able to turn that around before another Advent. Gird your loins. Culpa mea. Endure anyway.

---

all beautiful gifts	soul attempt
all gifts to G*D	after soul try
rise up tall	rise awhile
to fall below	fall forever
carefully constructed	leaving trails
carelessly thrown together	of thanks behind
all rise up	a rise
all fall down	a fall

Luke 21:25–36
Needed Change [1]

Signs are present. Signs come in innumerable guises. Some will see them as a destructive judgment. Some will see them as a next opportunity. Some won't see them at all.

Those who are able to see through their hard-wiring or experience will be able to shift. Some will flee from wrath. Some will walk boldly forward.

When trouble comes, as it does, a part of our work is to interpret it. At the beginning of things (which means right now), we are to see more deeply into the processes at work and clarify the expected consequences if we keep traveling down the current path. Being able to stand up, look trouble in the eye, and know that help is on the way and we are part of that help is a great blessing for ourselves and for others.

So look around. What glimmer of a new heaven and earth do you see? Are you acting on that? Are you sharing your perspective with others?

Rather than read verse 33 literally, as though words on a page won't fade and are written in archival ink on acid-free paper, let's listen to the "words" we do know—love, forgiveness, peace. These will not pass away even if the language changes, and one more translation will be needed. When we get too caught up in literalism, we get caught in idolizing the Bible. If there needs to be a choice, finally choose connotation and meaning after denotation and over letters of the law.

Signs not only come to be present; they fade. Signs are as frail as the leaves of a deciduous tree—spring green, productive day-after-day, celebrative in completion, and fertilizing the future. No one sign is normative.

If not signs, what may stay with us? We can claim it to be words, but they are just signs of signs. It is not the "words" here that are lasting, but what they describe—alertness to how to honorably stand and assist others to do the same.

Clarifying and strengthening an ability to stand, clear-eyed, is worth a year's endeavor. Can you imagine how individuals, congregations, and other communities might grow by the end of November next year by working on this orientation rather than on mediating words? Neither can I. But it sounds worthy of our best.

Luke 22:14–23:56 (long) or **Luke 23:1–49** (short)
Premature Fear Sunday

There are different ways of emptying oneself. One way brings one to one's self (non-exploitation). Another way loses one's self (demanding). Both can be trancelike. Both are open to temptation and subversion.

We wrestle with this all the time. Is this a time to not respond? Is this a time to use every tongue at our disposal? What is obedience, and what pride?

Pre-crucifixion, non-follower knees were unbent, goose-stepping toward mob rule. Post-crucifixion followers on bended knee demand a loyalty pledge be on the tip of everyone's tongue to roll off at a moment's notice.

We move from a passionate experience to being passionate about another's passion and, in turn, inflicting said passion upon others. What does it mean to follow one claimed to be non-exploitative and then exploit others for claimed greater ends? This is an impossible line to walk without falling off on one side and then another.

So it is that we might randomly hand some congregants a palm branch as they come to worship, while others receive a stone or nothing at all. All of this—from exuberant praise, to stoning him softly with a cross, to not knowing what is happening or where to gain traction in the turmoil—is going on within and around us and our family, community, and congregation all the time.

May your right hand palm branch know what your left hand stone is doing that you might break both trances before they lead to one exploitation or another, and someone ends up dead enough to require the preparation of spices and ointments. Such preparation is little enough sorrow and restitution for injuries done.

Luke 23:33–43
Evaluation Day

How far is it from a Paradise of here-and-now to some Paradise of there-and-when?

I am struck by how often folks ask for prayer as though it would be something I would do on their behalf somewhere down the line, and how surprised they are when I ask, "Would it be alright to pray now?"

I am struck by how often folks don't make the connection between their vote and voice today and the way life will be for all of us, particularly the poor, in days to come.

There seems to be a disconnect between now and any other time, whether past or future. With that disconnect comes an opening for the glibbest, the one who appeals to the lowest common denominator or our largest fears to guide us in directions directly contrary to the inseparability of our own best self-interest and a common good.

How I wish Jesus had replied to the criminal next to him, "Truly I tell you, we are in Paradise, now and ever."

What would it mean to see today as Paradise? Surely we are not that much worse than some Edenic once-upon-a-time constructed as an overlay on chaos with tree tests, loneliness not assuaged by a ribmate, eternal stewardship regarding what has been entrusted to us, and snakes full of political promises.

What would it mean to see today as Paradise and have that connected with all the nostalgia of Paradise Past and all the dreams of Paradise yet winging their way from a future heaven and earth joined?

What would it mean to see life as Paradise and death as Paradise? Might we begin to bind together the various disconnects in our life? My suspicion is that we might.

When all else is stripped from G*D, there is yet steadfast mercy.
When all else is stripped from Jesus, there is yet forgiveness.

What is there when all else is stripped from you?

Here it is that you will find your joy, your willingness, your paradise.

Luke 24:1–12
Hopeless Hope Vigil — Assured

Men in fabulous, shining clothes try to speak with spicy women. First response—acculturated fear and shyness. With no expected attack, attention returns.

Women with spices try to speak with men in ordinary dress. First response—acculturated distance and dismissal. With unexpected persistence, a trial listening ensues.

And so the confusion of resurrection begins. Unlooked for to begin with and unbelievable when a glimmer is caught, a new story begins in the rocky, weedy paths of a few.

We are still working resurrection out. When we get the acculturated stuff out of the way we will get much closer to all that lies behind this multi-valenced word. If nothing more, may Easter be a scraping away of at least one layer of traditional religion that the mystery of life might shine through every attempt to explain and control it.

---

idol tales of common wisdom
lead us to put our tails between our legs
and simply agree with what everyone knows
and develop an idle tail

first we drop our tail
and then our head
no joy of curiosity
no hope for a quantum leap

no matter how long the lenten season
or how dark the easter vigil
a primeval choice keeps presenting
howl or turn tail

Luke 24:13–49
Opened Heart Evening

A vision of angels by any other name is a vision of life. We are not stuck.

And yet we are slow in agreeing to get unstuck. 7 miles at 20 minutes per mile is a 2 hour, 20 minute conversation. Did the women get it right? Did those who went to see miss something?

How slow our hearts are to be opened. How many Easters have come and gone since you have revisited the silence of Easter, the imagery and symbolism of Easter, and the community of Easter? Has this Easter morning worn off already?

We could have another long conversation about whether we are to return to Galilee or remain in Jerusalem. Here Luke sets up Pentecost by staying in Jerusalem while other witnesses have folks by the seashore.

We are slow enough to get hung up on the details and miss the meaning of the forest.

The only question this Easter Evening is whether our hearts are any more open tonight than they were in the morning. This is a daily question.

A more dangerous way to ask this is whether we experience any more power to see that "repentance and forgiveness" is proclaimed/lived. This is dangerous because it puts more emphasis on the judgment of repentance and less on forgiveness, just because. Religious power structures have always arisen at this divide.

So, back to this question: Is your heart any more open tonight than it was this morning?

Luke 24:44–53
Our Turn to Witness

In Luke, Jesus is parenthesized with angel praise and disciple joy. In between, we have Jesus left behind, invisible, tempted, and crucified, as well as Simeon-blessed, Anna-announced, baptised, and adulated for teachings and healings.

Some early texts have Jesus just walking into the sunset, so Acts can have a numerically significant 40-days pass before some "ascension" to cry out, "Bon voyage and thanks for all the feasts!"

Praise and Joy are watchwords for the day. This is how we are to witness in the Temple and in everyday life. One danger in praise and joy is the way it can anesthetize our cognitive functions and blind us to significant inconsistencies in the biblical record.

For instance, footnotes such as in *The Jewish Annotated New Testament* point out that there is no direct quote about a suffering Messiah anywhere in the TaNaKh. Creative reading and prooftexting are, too often, the name of the game.

Given a goodly bit of experience and an accumulation of wisdom, we will learn to be joyful about such anomalies rather than suppress them. Footnotes open us to more. They take on the nature of an "*" and help unstick us from "You have heard it said," so we can join the blessed refrain, "But now I see further and clearer."

Power to you
Leave
Reveal your reveling

John 1:1–14
Blessed Body: Proper III

Daniel Boyarin's essay, "Logos, A Jewish Word: John's Prologue as Midrash" in *The Jewish Annotated New Testament* reminds us of the Jewish roots of Memra/Wisdom as a "second God", a companion and agent of G*D in creating. Boyarin concludes,

> Only from John 1.14, which announces that the "Word became flesh," does the Christian narrative begin to diverge from synagogue teaching. Until v. 14, the Johannine prologue is a piece of perfectly unexceptional non-Christian Jewish thought that has been seamlessly woven into the Christological narrative of the Johannine community.

Through 12 verses, Jews and Christians can live comfortably together. It is only over time that high-Christology overtones were added. A chink begins in verse 13, where we need to think about a difference between a covenant based on biology and one based on belief.

It is verse 14 where a clearer division comes as we move from a more fluid interaction between Spirit and Flesh to a sharper division between divine and mundane.

If we are going to deal with this passage with grace and truth, we will need to recognize that everyone born comes with a "divine" pedigree written into our genetic code. No matter how that gets worked out with all the various realities of being born dead or with one genetic variant or another, an echo of Creati*n is present.

Yes, hooray for Jesus, but this passage is far more about a long tradition of grace, truth, steadfast love, and trustingness than a definitive dividing line of nit-picky details about a definitive spirit/flesh formula.

How does this passage open us up to a renewal of our birth and the birth of others instead of set us against one another? How do we get beyond the privilege of being recognized and the limits of belief?

Perhaps it will be enough to say light shines. Some light has travelled millions of years to meet our eye. Some light travelled equally far to meet our neighbor's eye. With different information from both of us, we can track our uniqueness back to a common light source, blessing both of us and all.

Are you enlightened yet? Surely you must be for "the *true* light, which enlightens everyone, was coming to the world" (verse 9), and the implication of the scripture is that such a true light not only was coming but had come into the world. So surely you must be enlightened.

Have you stumbled over your own feet again? What happened to that enlightenment?

Is the world around you gone awry? What happened to that enlightenment?

Again and again, our G*D-begottenness has bumped into our blood-begottenness, flesh-begottenness, sex-begottenness (as *The Message* puts it) and been forgotten in the melee of begottennesses.

Welcome back to a new beginning spot amid hovering darkness. As you go about your cultural business of planning a resolution or two, it will be helpful to choose one that realistically takes in all these different aspects of begottenness. If you are simply choosing a resolution on a meta-Word level, disappointment will come quickly enough. The more aspects of yourself you take into account, the longer that disappointment will be put off (but not entirely, remember John's question after a while—"Are you really who we once thought you were?").

Are you enlightened enough, yet, to question your enlightenment? If not, all this high Christology will catch you again having thought all was cared for rather than all still growing, falling, and rising, evening and morning.

John 2:1–11

Guiding Gift [2]

How do you wait for your time to come? Doze? Run in circles? Take a class?

There is such a focus on completedness that we sometimes forget the journey.

Mothers know mothering is never done. The kid will always be in process. So idealized mothers attend to the moment. What does it mean for G*D to be with us in the manger? What about when in Egypt? How about as a runaway? At a wedding?

When we begin to ask what it means to evidence G*D in the particular setting in which we find ourselves, it becomes more possible to just go ahead and find ambrosia and amrita in honey, nectar of the gods, and plain old water (divided by a firmament, but still water on both sides of the sky). Having found a moment of G*D present now, not an hour away, allows a savoring of the simple and finding it simply divine.

In other words, to see Jesus' baptismal water flowing in a wedding scene calls us to perceive it flowing through us. Water/Wine makes no difference; G*D is with us!

———————————

O little cana, how still we see thee lie
on the back of your "Welcome to Cana" sign
it reads, "Welcome to Cana"
your still had run dry
you had the makings
but not the time
for fine wine

look again
you've got the time
you still have the makings
for still water to become living water
to welcome the world
to welcome the universe
still no longer, still right now

John 3:13–17
Relic Day

Antecedents are always fun. Ordinarily, we might expect that Jesus would be compared to the actor, Moses, rather than the tool of a bronze snake used by Moses. Here, though, we have Jesus lifted up with a temptation present to turn him into an idol that will eventually be discarded (see 2 Kings 18:4). This is an example of reformation iconoclasm, not unlike today's, "I'm spiritual, not religious."

This very process of lifting up will again be turned on its head with the lifting up of Jesus on a cross being used as a condemnation of Jews that lasts to this day in the too-easy descriptor of anti-semite when it is anti-everything but me and Jesus. This all too easily discards Jesus' more than life-long Jewishness.

Using this passage to "honor" the tool of a cross has a deep tension in it that can only be reduced to a creedal affirmation by doing more harm to others than good for oneself.

While glad that this passage has been extended to include a touch of non-judgment, it remains argumentative and condemning. Non-judgment here must be seen in light of coercion—convert now or be erased.

In light of this passage, wearing an empty cross is idolatrous (even if excused by way of some resurrectional justification). At best, a crucifix has an image of healing (though usually too oriented toward the gory). What might a crucifix of a healer look like?—Salvador Dali's hovering *Christ of Saint John of the Cross*? Some form of a Tau Cross admired by Franciscans (from a *San Damiano Cross*, to a simple tau remembering Ezekiel 9:4, to one portraying Francis of Assisi/Jesus/yourself with an arms-wide-open gesture of welcome)?

The Holy Spirit is to teach us beyond what we currently know. A part of that presumes being an invalid—blind, lame, paralyzed in our knowing.

We keep waiting for insight and thinking it need come from the outside, that there should be authorization for standing up with a vision. So we wait for credentials that never seem to come. Meanwhile, we get weaker and weaker. Someone else is the lucky one to break new ground, to get the part we wanted. We're just not lucky enough to catch opportunity's time and place.

As a result, we are not at peace. Our hearts are troubled, and we are afraid the assurance we need will never be granted. Our anxiety at not being specifically chosen gets in our way of taking any part at all.

One of the in-valids in our still-patriarchal culture are mothers. You may want to check out the "Motherhood Manifesto" DVD at MomsRising.org. Mothers are hearing a healing word to pick up their lives and walk on without getting their healing certified.

M is for maturing past past limits
O is for opening options beyond heritage
T is for teaching truth from experience
H is for healing hopes from the inside out
E is for exciting entrance to a preferred future
R is for radical reform needed now and always

papa Institution counsels a Mother of all wars
mama Jesus leaves us with the mother of all Peace

John 6:25–35
Thanksgiving

Ah, sweet fleshpots! There is nothing sweeter than vain imaginings that something other than a worthy life will satisfy. We look for that "more" in sex and getting what we want through betrayal. We look for that "more" in "the good old days" (that really weren't). We look for that "more" in controlling unanimity, using fear of the "other" to keep us in line. We look for that "more" in fullness of stomach and pocketbook.

This passage is an antidote to the prosperity theology so popular these days. Always looking for one more buck, one more sign, these "theologians" [read me-logians] continually miss life-bread in the simplicity of living oriented toward deeper meaning. As long as the Ponzi Scheme of prosperity theology holds, folks will give untold dollars for a food that perishes. In short, short-cuts bring us up short and cut us to the quick. There is no slot-machine G*D who will consistently pay out—it is all a ploy to recast a gift as payback in order to suck us in further and further—all the way to bankruptcy.

---

our transgression
needing untold mercy
is the violence
to which we will go
to get a full stomach

no matter how we cover it over
sin is connected with violence
this is its ultimate ending place
little by little we accommodate
and fear fear enough to instill fear

a clean heart restores joy
so lacking in short-cuts
that lead to violence
so focus on joy
sustain a willing joy

joy-gifts touch us
deeper than tokens of fear
joy that sees abundance
all around
reveals the lie of violence

Who are you?

> "I yam what I yam," says Popeye the Savior.

No. Who are you? What category do you fit in? What kind of Savior are you?

> "Just a humble saviorman who swabs decks and looks
> out for all the anointed, like Olive Oyl— silly misfit
> though she be— and orphaned Swee'peas."

There is no category for a swabbing savior. A suffering one, yes; a swabbing one, no.

> "Avast ye blutos, I yam what I yam and it's all what I
> yam."

As long as you keep doing stuff, we will continue to judge it. Oops, make that categorize it.

> "You can toss me in the booby hatch, but I only have
> my actions to speak for me—you have heard my less
> than dulcet tone, haven't you?"

No one wants to make you walk the plank; just tell us plainly how you keep doing the things you do.

> "Well, there's this spinach . . ."

Spinach, minach, talk sense, or we'll swab the deck with you.

> "Ahoy there, a warning shot across my bow! We've
> been chewing the fat long enough. The wind is up
> and I'm running my course. Gangway! Fair Winds to
> you bilge rats! Remember what I've done! Oh, and try
> the spinach."

Indeed! Why wasn't Mary's perfume sold for the benefit of the poor? Why was it even purchased in the first place? Why was a dinner opened to an honored guest, Jesus, and not opened to the poor?

We can track cause-and-effect back and back and back even farther. So any Judas, as well as our very own lowly self, can decide where a difficulty lies, excise that particular, and feel extremely proud about having done so. This is a time-tested process to find a scapegoat and hie it to the hinterlands. This process puts us into each role—Nard, Mary, Lazarus, Judas, and Poor.

A trick is to raise this process from the page without it leading us to cover up our ongoing way of divide-and-conquer by stealing a reputation with an unanswerable question.

A retranslation is needed for verse 8. Here is one suggestion for both individuals and congregations:

> You always have (someone to blame for the current situation),
> but you do not have (an assurance of being beloved).

Presumably, folks can make the connection between poor and blame; between Jesus and assurance.

Judas' question today is asked more bald-facedly with no veneer of piety, "Why was this social security not marketed for volatile investments and the benefit given to the rich?"

This is the equivalent of giving a child poison when they cry from a lack of a handful of rice.

In the sweet scent of revelation, we get the crass propaganda of those in cahoots with power that talks of Clear Skies while it pollutes, or Healthy Forests as it clear-cuts to the horizon.

Judas' concern still lives. It never was and never will be for the poor, the skies, the forests, or the commons but for the rich to get richer, those in power to gain more, and for me to join them.

What sign tells you that you have come into your prime? Is it an internal sign that would look responsive to an external event? Is it dependent upon some criterion being met that would give permission to play your end game?

Attend to the voice that has come for your sake and yet is not interpretable by you. Some said it was thunder, and some said it was for Jesus. No one saw it relating directly to them.

It doesn't help that Jesus continues to talk past people. They ask, and Jesus goes off on a tangent. Jesus claims and then hides his claim away.

If you think you get what this is about, it is probably time to take a 40-day retreat.

Consider again what an absent Messiah might mean. Isn't there an implication that this particular Messiah is Emmanuel, G*D with us, and now is nowhere to be found? How are we to trust absent light?

Over time, we have adjusted to this question and done a lot of contortions to make sense of Jesus hiding from us. This is a most important question early on and remains such if we are willing to give it a try.

John 13:1–17, 31b–35
Courage Thursday

Goal: to love deeply, to the end of time.

Love through dismissal as crazy or irrelevant.
Love through threat and abuse.
Love through success and pain.
Love through betrayal by self and others.

Knowing we are beloved is a starting place for knowing others are beloved. Belovedness takes off its power tie and carries a traveling towel to freshen sweaty brows and soothe tired feet. Whether understood or not, we wash clean both reluctant saint and aggressive betrayer.

Actually living out our goal of deep love brings us to moments of separation. We are all in different stages of journey and modeling for others how to journey. We each have a different path, and so we are not in lockstep. Each, following their way, helps build toward a common goal. Though our various ways seem unique, our common end is more than our means of travel.

At any rate, the bottom line for disciples is the same as for their mentor—to love deeply, to the end of time. Given the variety of paths, this is all we have in common. By this, we and others will know we are all part of a larger project whose nature and name is Love. It is enough.

John 13:21–32
Clarification Week: Wednesday

The sadness here is not about betrayal as such, for that is such a commonplace, unoriginal part of our lives.

We are finally at Jerusalem, and Jesus is colluding with the triggering mechanism of his death. John's controlling Christ would do no less than set up his own crucifixion. This same result could have come directly from the Romans or those Jewish leaders afraid of a successful rebellion.

In later generations, people will use John's gospel as an excuse to be anti-semitic and blame the crucifixion on "the Jews" without noticing Jesus' involvement.

In John, it might be said that it is Jesus who betrays Judas Iscariot. Jesus doesn't raise a telling question or tell a timely parable; he gives permission by way of bread and encourages Judas' action. Is this an act of resignation or instigation?

Being the optimistic folks they are being trained to be, the disciples miss all this with their overactive speculations.

Note here that Jesus claims glorification *after* Judas leaves for his time of betrayal. How much earlier might Jesus have claimed this "glorification"? Does it go back to the glory-hallelujah of angels in Bethlehem? Since we are in John, as far back as "in the beginning"? Perhaps his experience in Jerusalem as a lad? Surely as far back as Baptismal Belovedness? One or more of the healings, miracles, or other signs?

Why would Jesus claim glorification, resurrection, or vindication at this point?

Since it is the last Wednesday of Lent, remember the ashes of the first Wednesday—from dust you have come; to dust you shall return. Did you claim glorification, resurrection, and new life weeks ago? If not, perhaps next year. Or, perhaps yet today? Will you wait for Sunday to make "glory" (G*D's revealed presence) officially yours? Surely you won't wait for your living presence to be a revelation of G*D.

Clarity is generally a good thing. Conversion, forgiveness, and re-pentance, however, are not predictable. No matter how clear deci-sions appear to be, there needs to be room left for Judas to have a change of heart. Who knows what encounter he will have between leaving Jesus' crew and arriving at a house of power to betray Jesus? Bet against new insight at your own peril.

I do wish it wasn't reported that Jesus had/shared his "new" in-sight after Judas left. Having Judas among those who are to love one another would add a whole new dimension to this revelation. There is a long history of disciples not entirely accurately representing their teacher in their dealings with their teacher, neighbors, or one another. If love doesn't incorporate differences, is it love?

Want to know you are dealing with Jesus' disciples? See how they love their sisters and brothers with whom they have profound differ-ences. Anything less than this is a fairytale that they live happily ever after without difficulties.

Does Judas fit within "love one another"? Or is "love your ene-mies" the only rubric left for Judas?

---

betrayal becomes glorification
in chronos

glorification becomes betrayal
in kairos

what do you become
in your time

by these statements and question
we become more than we know

John 14:8–17, (25–27)
Energy to Witness

In prayer and in fear, we ask for assurance. Just show us G*D and we'll be satisfied! Of course, we would like to do Moses one better and see more than G*D's hindquarters. How about a glimpse of G*D's hand? That would satisfy us for a while. Then, perhaps, a glimpse of a strong right arm....

We ask the same things of Peace, Justice, and some Patriotic Way. Just show us—for our dualistic thoughts keep compartmentalizing life in such a way that we are blinded to what is already present. To see G*D in another is not a lesser seeing than face-to-face beyond dim mirrors.

Pentecost stories continue in a transformation of fear and separation into honor expanded to all and satisfaction in who we are. In this presentness, we move forward into ways and works deemed impossible just a bit ago.

Pentecost is a revelation of what is—illusions reduced and Creati*n renewed.

Pentecost is knowing one another beyond simply spending time with one another.

Pentecost is active (not simply a 50-day marker)—those who participate in Pentecost will do greater work than those who have gone before. Please do spend some time this week defining what you think Jesus' work was. Only then will you have a sense of the activity to which you are called. It is not that there is one work for all of us to be strengthening, but that each of our unique gifts will call forth differing arenas of generativity.

Pentecost is transition from past to future, from fear to freedom. Even as you consider Jesus' work, ponder his teaching. What did he teach? Only then will you have a sense of Spirit to which you are called.

Pentecost is a joy of wholeness beyond the brokenness so often trapping us in our separatenesses. Peace is not stillness but wellness, health, wholeness, growth.

Who did Jesus respond to, and what question was he dealing with? Pericopes that begin as this one did, "Jesus responded...." are beginning too late. Every response has a context, and without that specific, any response attaches strangely wherever it lands.

Jesus had said that he would be seen by his friends after he was no longer seen by others. A Judas by any other name asks about this limitation. Is it a voluntary decision on Jesus' part or a blindness by others?

As per usual, Jesus steps aside from the direction of the question to better respond to it. As a result of continuing to learn from their experience of Jesus after he has gone, the bottom-line is that disciples will be able to reframe questions that come their way and continue to grow. This growth will be congruent with their past experiences of Jesus and their present experience of G*D (spirit talk here), which will lead them to trust an arc of the future so strongly that they will act in the present in light of what they yet expect. Responses by others will not raise a question about willful blindness or a limited, predestined, rejection. The focus will be upon what Jesus' followers continue to learn and enact.

Peace is connected with a teaching of how to remember and anticipate. In this connection comes a strength and focus of action that would otherwise be dissipated over too much time, space, and opportunity. Want peace? Trust your action to make a difference, whether or not you can see it.

This kind of peace not only lets you see Jesus, but to also recognize other saints in other traditions.

John 16:12–15
Live Together

This is one of my favorite passages. There is still much to learn.

Such a presumption, when we think we can quote a passage of import and universalize it to all times and places. Appropriate humility understands there is more to come, even better to come, than we have so far experienced. It is arrogance to claim our experience of an expansive and expanding love has run its course and we've received all we will ever have.

That which we have to learn will be grown into. A spirit guides. She doesn't dictate.

So we are again and again in the middle of things received and passed on. All the while, we move closer to one another. In fact, it is crucial that we honor our differences in this model, for they become one more opportunity for Spirit to teach (and learn what to teach). Needed growth will continue until maturity, and there is no need to end this learning with a boundary of death.

---

miles before we sleep
less-traveled roads have been taken
and energy has grown

we grin all over ourselves
just a-think'n about what's left
on our collision course

we enter into a group hug
as differences and similarities come clear
more closely related than ever

Jesus learns more from G*D
passes it on to us
we image it back to a learning G*D

another mile onward
learning to the left
guidance to the right

into a preferred future
dance the million millions
bearing one another up forever

A prayer that we might be connected at our roots is strong.

Such a prayer is weakened when it intends to prove something or other.

Remember: The roots of Redwood trees "hold hands" underground.

The shallow roots of a very tall redwood grow only four to six feet deep. This isn't much support for a tall, heavy tree. Heavy rains and strong winds could bring even the biggest giant crashing to the ground.

But the roots of individual redwoods can grow out 125 feet and interconnect with those of their neighbors. By "holding hands" underground, the roots form a network that allows the trees to withstand even great storms.

A redwood's roots are shallow so that they can collect the large amounts of moisture the tree requires. However, they are sensitive to smothering silt. When sediment from flood or runoff accumulates over its roots, a redwood responds by growing a new root system upwards, into the silt. One toppled redwood was found to have developed seven successive root systems, each a response to new realities during the tree's 1,200-year lifetime.

Intertwined roots = an image of realized and freed presence.
> How is your presence quotient today? Your connection quotient?
> Do they need changing by the end of the day?

Intertwined roots = an image of love.
> How is your love quotient today? Does it need changing by the end of the day?

> By this we see G*D's presence/freedom ⇒ our love and
> our freedom to be present ⇒ G*D's love.

Prelude to all the crucifixion business is a context often overlooked. "I continue to reveal that the love with which I have been loved is also in others." (John 17:26)

Without this grounding, the rest of this pericope loses focus. "When Jesus had finished speaking/praying . . . ." (John 18:1)

This again pushes us against ancient atonement theories. All that follows here is not about some sacrifice to set things right, but a continuing revelation that life is already right if we would attend to its blessing of automatic belovedness. We come pre-blessed.

Look again at the actions:

- Jesus steps forward to initiate contact with his confronters

- Jesus rejects violence, even that of his "protectors"

- Jesus drinks from the cup of consequence for loving even enemies and betrayers

- Jesus deals with accusations by sticking to facts in the open

- Jesus refutes an appeal to power with silence

- Jesus bears the consequence of revealing love in a retributive world

- Jesus binds together a new family

- Jesus continues to thirst for mercy for himself and all

- Jesus offers back his spirit of love instead of rising as a spirit of judgment

May we learn to reveal the love with which we have been loved is already present in others. This day reveals prevenient grace, not the cheap grace of my benefiting from the loss of another.

John 19:38–42
Absent Saturday

Secret or anonymous "Christians" are appropriate for this day of absence. Creedally, Jesus is descending to the nether regions to meet with really secret pre-Christians who had never heard of Jesus by name but who would have followed him except for that bug-a-boo of a river of time.

It is a good thing that Jesus, like Santa, can do an immense amount of visiting in an Eve, for there were more to chat with below than among the living. Jesus' visit to the dead was presumably assisted by a Word from the beginning that had already whispered in their left ear (where Death advises).

Meanwhile, back to the story, Joseph and Nicodemus come round after the problem of Jesus had met a final solution. Stripped, beaten, bloody, and shamed on a cross—even a boatload of myrrh and aloes is little comfort.

While we await what was not originally anticipated as a wonder-filled next morning, it is important to be as wonder-filled about the multitude of "Nones" and others who carry their connection with G*D anonymously. A good Absent Saturday, Hellish Saturday, discipline is to begin an annual reading of Karl Rahner. Hopefully, we will be encouraged to engage folks with hope, joy, and mercy in this world. Such a welcome goes beyond any official baptism or other insider code of an "out" Christian.

How secret is your identification as one on the way to G*D by following Jesus and walking alongside others doing the same via other IDs?

John 20:1–18
Assured

Again and again, we see liberties being taken with the Hebrew scriptures. Find, if you can, a reference in the Jewish/Jesus scriptures to Jesus/Messiah being raised from the dead. If you identify some verse, how much rationalization or other information did you have to load into it?

For followers of one who could be characterized by the phrase "You have heard it said, . . ., but I say to you . . . ." this need to jigger with scriptures to prove a point is unsettling and embarrassing. We at least need to start with what has been said. Finding a confirmation in one's tradition is comforting, but if that is all one has—it is not enough to hold a center.

Mary ran; other followers ran; Mary wept. All of this leaves one breathless. Some year it may be that a congregation would follow a variety of breathing exercises through Lent to prepare for being stunned to breathlessness by the mere mention of death not holding a final card and steadfast love flowing through lives, as does time, attracting past and future to gather in a present moment to restore it to sanity and move beyond what we have so far heard.

Be not stuck in a race or grief. Both have already left their artifacts of trophies and tears. We see them through a light from tomorrow and loosen our grip on their grip on us. With the assistance of one another, we can now, thankfully, break that last grip and teach what we have learned.

John 20:19–31
Assured [2]

Holy Humor Sunday

Jesus the Jester was well known to the Disciples. That was one of the problems with taking notes on his various teachings. You'd be jotting down class notes and then Jesus would throw in one of his parabolic koans. There was no choice but to stop to get your bearing again. He always seemed to quiz folks on the stuff that got missed after one of his switcheroos.

This accounts for some of the missing sections in stories about Jesus' life. Fortunately, we have found some additional notes from several of the Galilee Shore Irregulars. They never made it all the way to Disciple, much less Apostle, but their notes do fill in a few things as they were only focused on getting the facts, not trying to jockey for position on Jesus' nearly non-existent curve of a grading system. Being beloved this week and behind his back the next seemed to distract those who had enrolled and paid full tuition. The Irregulars could just focus on getting everything down to take it home and go over it later.

Tam, son of Raziel, and others did write down other "signs" of life, but they just didn't survive the editor's focus on believing without actual experience.

Tam reports:

Then, Jesus, Blessed be He, said to Thomas, "Put your finger here in my wrist, or foot, or side. Don't doubt it is me."

Then, Thomas reached out to Jesus' wrist and put his finger in the hole. There was a loud buzzing sound, and Thomas jerked his hand away.

Then, Jesus said, "Gotcha!"

Then, Thomas said, "Yo, Jesus, you got me good! High five, bro."

Then, Jesus said, "Let's hope future generations will be as shocked as you and shift from their expectations about the way things are always done and come to appreciate a Great Joke."

Then?

standing a hundred yards apart
we try to speak and hear

even over water-enhanced sound
we are a hundred yards apart
and more hundreds of years

"hey, you missed your mark, right?"
  "what's it to ya?"

even in established relationships
we are a hundred yards apart
and more hundreds of experience

"try another direction"
  "got nothin' to lose"

even in predictable worlds
we are a hundred yards apart
and more hundreds of miracles

"what'd ya find?"
  "wow!"

even in unpredictable worlds
we are a hundred yards apart
and more hundreds of common threads

"let's eat"
  "OK"

"let's love"
  "OK"

"let's partner"
  "OK"

Acts 1:1–11
Our Turn to Witness

The details of Luke and Acts vary enough that, presuming the same author, all scripture can be said to be in the service of particularized settings and agendas. Scripture comments on scripture, such as the story of Sodom, and presents additional understandings of the same event. This is also true of Creati*n, Jesus' last meal, Resurrection, Ascension, and an ongoing list.

Without trying to reconcile irreconcilable portions of scripture, we look for where the variations may be pointing.

We note that Luke's version might be seen through the eyes of witnessing a blessing still in process.

Acts doesn't have the blessing motif. Here is didactic instruction: do this, then that, then the next. A word of witness comes after whatever an ascension might be in physics terms, rather than during it. It comes not from Jesus, but angelic messenger types.

The question raised was to move disciples on from stupefying awe. Basically, the message is to stop our mesmerized slacked-jaw gaze and get on with whatever it means to take belovedness into the world.

Regardless of the setting and timing issues between Luke and Acts, the focus is taken off some future event of restoring political, military, and economic power and is placed on the ever-present opportunity to be grateful for having been blessed by passing that blessing on to make it larger and larger. This gratefulness is the motivation to move beyond the privileges of glory to the responsibilities of serving.

Ascension is to raise us to engage life. To limit it to Jesus does a grave injustice to his impetus to be a joy to the world. Workers of the world, Ascend!

Acts 2:1–21
Energy to Witness

Amazing how surprised we get when we gather for one purpose and a Python comes out of the sea to collapsingly announce, "It's"—time for something completely different.

Judaism 101 says:

> It is noteworthy that the shavu'ot is called the time of the giving of the Torah, rather than the time of the receiving of the Torah. The sages point out that we are constantly in the process of receiving the Torah, that we receive it every day, but it was first given at this time. Thus it is the giving, not the receiving, that makes this holiday significant.

Gathered for honoring the giving of Torah (translating G*D-speak to human community organizing), there is a surprise that the theory of constantly receiving a given Torah involves such as ourselves. On this day of translation, another giving begins to be received. A gift of languages (translating human experience to human experience) sets folks to growing another branch of a tree meant for healing nations.

To hear Torah and more than Torah in one's own language is a soul-stirring moment. It brings out the best in us to hear G*D's mighty works of power—forgiveness, mercy, steadfast love. These continue to break new territory, unbound from the usual limits that separate us.

To hear Torah and more than Torah in one's own language can also scare the bejezus out of us when we stake our own lives on such weak elements as our own power, privilege, and/or entitlement.

Between growing Torah and limiting it, we find hope in this roomful of yeasty people who throw open closed doors to turn strangers into friends by giving themselves away—not insisting others learn their language, but starting with the language of the other.

Which strange Neighb*r or literal Enemy have you spoken with in their language that you both may hear the power of forgiveness, mercy, steadfast love?

Pentecost/Shavu'ot, calls us to receive something already given—a broader translation of an experience, a larger vision than simply repeating today that everyone, Everyone!, will be wholer and whole, again.

So often this passage is read as though it were a debate that was going to go to the side with the most passion or power. In light of Holy Humor Sunday, it might be best to read verse 29 as, "But Peter and the apostles laughed and responded, ..."

So often, experiences of religious differences devolve into bitter separation. I can't help but wonder about the lives of the saints and reformers being portrayed as so diligent that there was no time for laughter. Luther has famously been known to pray the more, the busier his day was to be. Imagine prayer as laughter, and what it would mean to laugh the more, the more expectations are being laid on.

If Peter and the disciples were proclaiming good news, they might as well enjoy the telling as well as the results. How about us?

------

good news scowled
trying to be as serious
as a god should be
as ultimate arbiter

made in the image
of kicker-outer
flooder-outer
sacrifice-initiator
genocidal-invader
he portrayed disaster
for all

all that was forgotten
in light of creation's dance
leading to forgiveness
steadfastly held
lovingly held
forever held
for all

choose wisely your god
for your face will follow
with furrowed brow
with laugh lines

Acts 8:14–17
Beloved

They had only been born. They had only been born Samaritan. They had only been baptized in the name of the Lord Jesus. This is all we know.

Somewhere along the way, that is not enough. It seems nothing is ever enough when it comes to measuring up—right now—to someone else's experience they consider normative for everyone. No process or stage of a process is enough. Not even being at a stage where a measurer will come to is enough, as the measurer isn't yet there to measure it.

We still make up rules and regulations about effective baptism and its deeper meaning when that is not measurable. I can't help but wonder what Jesus would have said about what additional requirement was needed for a baptism in his name to be a baptism in his name. I can't help but wonder how surprised he was to find a dove diving at him as he shakes water from his eyes.

Might a needed Holy Spirit simply be a sense of belovedness, regardless of style or language of baptism? And is that enough, or not?

---

go
pray
handle

unto Samaria and the ends of this earth
we go before there is any evidence
that going will redound glory to us

we identify a greatest need and focus there
even if it is only our greatest need projected
we impose meaning wherever we pray

twisting arms and patting backs
we handle the reins of reigning understanding
that we might drive rather than be driven

indeed we handle if not always gently
indeed we pray if not always wisely
indeed we go if not always happily

Acts 9:1–6, (7–20)
Assured [3]

When I recently re-read the following paragraph by Dorothy Soelle in *The Window of Vulnerability: A Political Spirituality*, it led me to wonder about this Saul to Paul conversion as part of a conversion from patriarchy to feminism. I know it is easy to put Paul in an anti-feminist group, but remember that even sudden conversions have a learning curve to them, a setting in which they grow.

> Let me give an example of how theology can change when women do it; that is, when new subjects reflect on theological tradition. Sin, in the dominant, Protestant-influenced interpretation, is "wanting to be like God." It is the search for power, for superiority; it is overestimation of the self; it is pride; it is disobedience. But women who have become aware of their situation and have asked themselves, for the first time, whether they would really consider this type of sin to be the worst of all have come to quite different conclusions. They have said it is just the opposite. Our sin is not that of self-exaltation and pride; it is self-denial, selflessness in the bad sense of the word, the surrender of any kind of genuine self, underdevelopment of the self, conformity to the dominant structure, lack of pride in being a woman, obedience. Sin is submission to this sexist model of society. It is failure to realize God's image in oneself, and bowing in fearful humility. That means that we need a totally different definition of sin if we want to talk seriously about the ways in which *we* mess up our lives and how *women* are destroyed in our society, how it happens that they never really come to life, and what is the source of all that.

Now that sin can be seen as not simply power, but also submission, how do you apply those to their appropriate situations, and what might be a third and fourth helpful definition of sin that will continue deepening your insight into your own way of being, as well as broadening your application of it in the variety of lives you encounter? Again, definitions of sin are not the goal, but they aid in an analysis that allows seeing farther, seeing more, and transforming life situations.

Acts 9:36–43
Assured [4]

Here is a wonderful definition of a disciple of Jesus: devoted to good works and acts of charity.

Disciples of Jesus could comfortably find themselves in Jewish, Muslim, Buddhist, Hindu, Wiccan, Pagan, Atheist, etc. environments and never bat an eyelash, and be in the mainstream of each of them with these two simple expressions of their discipleship for the transformation of the world: good works and acts of charity.

We may need to start a new denomination named Gazelle, (the root behind Tabitha (Aramaic) and Dorcas (Greek). This will encourage our intention to gracefully leap ahead, the faster to be with G*D by means of good works and acts of charity.

Any other Gazellians out there?

---

where are you lodging this eve
with someone who is unclean
in the eyes of some majority or other

as a good work
an act of charity
or to prove a point

Tabitha lives in Peter
ancestress and ancestor
are alive within us

we don't give up
on charitable good works
being our epitaph too

Acts 10:34–43
Assured

Talk about your resurrectional vision, Peter's vision that precedes this speech (vss. 9–20) is a good example of an everyday Easter experience. Its equivalent in science is that of the thought experiment or sudden insight that changes the way we see the world around us. The same sort of breakthrough happens in every arena of life, from the relational to manufacturing to music.

At moments in our own life, there comes a new understanding equivalent to, "I get it now; G*D's not partial." These moments are as unconscious as learning to walk and as intentional as evaluating a vocational choice.

We see G*D's impartiality at those wonderful in-between moments where we can see our gifts contributing to the common good by staying where we are, and also by moving on to another arena. Both are good, and our partnership in discernment is needed. (This is different than just climbing the ladder to grasp at a better-for-me, wrestling with a better-for-us, sticking to a first call through thick and thin, or innocently pursuing each new opportunity as they arise.)

This week has been a week of choices. Did we do Palm or Passion Sunday? Were we sensitized to injustice with plots by the strong, rigged trials, false claims of impartiality or innocence dramatized with washed hands, capital punishment for stealers of class-driven capital/property, centurion revelations, intentional betrayal, and scared, passive betrayal? Did our walk through the week change us so we are different than last Easter?

Each choice carries the potential of being an Easter choice.

Each choice carries a movement from "not partial" to wholly connected.

Acts 11:1–18
Assured [5]

In the face of strict dietary laws prohibiting the eating of anything "unclean," Peter has a dream about God making a large offering of animals of all kinds and inviting Peter to eat. In response to Peter's protests that he has never violated the dietary laws, that "nothing unclean has ever entered his mouth," God rebukes Peter: "What God has made clean, you must not call profane."

So now it's OK to violate the dietary laws and eat a nice pork roast for dinner? It's OK, too, for Gentiles to receive the "repentance that leads to life" that had been reserved for those chosen Hebrews? Apparently so. At least for those in the early days of a Christian movement that arose from within Judaism.

Conservative Jewish Christians objected to Peter's associating with Gentiles and criticized him for eating with them. Peter had to 'splain it to them that God apparently had a different idea. It probably felt like a slippery slope to those who had gone through all the pain of being circumcised: first, circumcision is no longer necessary, poof, just like that (what a waste of foreskin). Next, you don't even have to be among the apostles and believers to be among God's chosen people. Pretty soon, they will be letting women in, and then who knows what next? Maybe Muslims and Buddhists or, horror of horrors, Atheists.

So what about our own sacred writ of denominational rules? No matter what legalisms get added to such a rulebook by those who see redemption through strict obedience to church law, no matter how many church trials there may yet be, "God has a different idea."

Eating pork had once been anathema to Peter. And God was now saying, "It's okay."

One of the worst offenses a Torah-abiding, temple-worshiping Judean could make was extending the grace of God to Samaritans, or worse, to those Gentiles, for they are incompatible with Torah. And God was now saying, "It's okay."

One of the worst things that could happen in the United Methodist Church in our day is that we ordain a "self-avowed, practicing homosexual" person. Incompatible with christian teaching we say ... and what is God saying?

Apparently, "the Holy Spirit falls upon them just as it had upon us..." May that spirit come and tell us, before it's too late, "not to make a distinction between them and us" (Acts 11:12), whoever they may be, and whoever we may be.

[Note: This comment was written by Thomas D'Alessio,
filling in when I was away at General Conference.]

Last week, Peter had a vision. This week, Paul has a vision. Beware, next week you may have a vision and unexpectedly travel to stay with someone.

Last week Gentiles were welcomed in. This week Gentiles are traveled to. Next week, "Gentiles" (by whatever measure of being left out, marginalized, exiled, etc.) will continue to open their hearts (a miracle in itself that one could wish upon the religious insider).

"Gentiles" as Gentiles, women as Gentiles, foreigners as Gentiles, any discriminated against individual or group as Gentiles: plead for non-Gentiles to finally get a vision that will trigger compassion within themselves and stop the discrimination and physical/economic/spiritual violence against "Gentiles". This is a call to the insiders to stop being blind to the consequences of their decisions and actions. For Paul, it is an extension of his first encounter with Jesus. His blindness became more than simple blindness; it was also a motivation to not be blind again, to see Jesus everywhere, even in heathen Macedonia.

It is in our conversion that we find hope to be converted and reformed again and again. The goal of a once-and-always reforming Church is also a good one for an individual. The Spirit of a Living G*D, revealed again and again in vision after vision, continues to push us to join the Jesus, Peter, and Paul tradition of an expansive and expanding view of G*D's presence in this world.

To extend Lydia's closing comment, "If you have confidence we are growing deeper in G*D by doing so together, let us stay with one another, be guests of one another, and, together, envision others, now separated from us, joining us." Would this be something that your congregation would be comfortable with as a practice and not just a nice thought?

Acts 16:16–34
Assured [7]

Who knows what you will find on your way to a place of prayer! So, designate your next travel destination as a place of prayer.

- Going to the car – go to a place of prayer.

- Going to get groceries – go to a place of prayer.

- Going for a walk – go to a place of prayer.

- Going to visit _(their name here)_ – go to a place of prayer.

- Going to work – go to a place of prayer.

- Going to bed – go to a place of prayer.

- Going to study – go to a place of prayer.

- Going to commit a crime – go to a place of prayer.

See if that changes how you use your car (maybe you'll listen to a different station or yield when you didn't absolutely have to).

See if that changes what food you get (more veggies and less red meat) and whether you get extra for the community pantry.

See if that changes how you see the neighborhood or the woods (in more detail).

See if that changes what your conversation is about (how is it with your soul and with mine and ours).

See if that changes your engagement with the task and money earned (try *The Complete Idiot's Guide to Spirituality in the Workplace*).

See if that changes your dreams (a vision of how you might participate in a better future).

See if that changes accumulated knowledge into understanding (move from information to implementation).

See if that changes your options (how one might build up rather than tear down).

Remember—you can always be on the way to a place of prayer.

For now, we will leave the spirituality of not escaping for another time and simply ask about everyday life. The theory is that careful attention here will open us to making a difference (fast or slow) in someone else's life and simply being faithful in difficult moments.

Romans 5:1–5
Live Together

Paul has an interesting progression that begins with suffering and ends with G*D's love. I'm sure there is good legal reasoning in the context of the time of its writing for moving in this direction, but it feels odd.

If we begin with a completed state of action (we are justified), how do we then enter into a series that seems to begin with the incomplete? Suffering qua suffering doesn't have much going for it. Suffering needs something else to complete itself—endurance. This goes up some ladder to character, to hope, and to G*D's love. It is almost as if one needs to be sure to suffer in order to be able to move toward G*D's love.

If we are going to build on the completedness of justification, it would seem to be stronger to begin with a completed assurance of G*D's love that has already been poured into our hearts (might that be all hearts as part of a universal salvation). Then, growing from G*D's love, we will be open to hope in every situation. This hope becomes our basic character, allowing us to endure every disappointment and crucifixion, even suffering, with a hope built on the surety of G*D's love already and ever present. G*D's love results in a sense of wholeness in every other part of our lives.

It's a little thing, but sequence can be of the utmost importance, and this is a significant sequence to see which way around works for you and yours.

Romans 6:3–11
Hopeless Hope Vigil

Oh, right. To be born is to die. Belovedness does not exempt us from being buried, becoming as nothing. Belovedness does not promise surprises will only be appreciated.

If there is something worth pursuing, it is going to be something larger than one life can give to it.

The projects we sign on to don't stop with asking our all. They need more than our all; they need all our all and more. In case that wasn't clear, they need our corporate all as well as our personal all. So, what community we are joined with does make a difference. How inclusive that community is becomes a measure of the worth of the endeavor. A narrow slice of life, like preaching to the choir, has a certain amount of appeal, but if that is all there is we find it soon grows thin.

To claim our death is to consider ourselves dead to narrowness and alive to the surprises that "more" brings. Its challenges enliven us. This sort of death is worth diving into to see where we surface later. Blessings on your dive.

Romans 8:14–17
Energy to Witness

Here is a paraphrase from Jim Taylor:

> [8.14] We call Christ the Son of God. If you live by God's spirit, then you, too, are a child of God. Children do not need to fear loving parents. So having Christ's spirit in you will not incite fear, or guilt, or self-loathing. Rather, it is like being welcomed into a winning team, a joyful home, a great performance.
>
> In our prayers, we address God as a loving parent. The words we use shape our thoughts and images. So when we speak of Christ as God's son, we affirm that when we are adopted as God's children, we too are God's heirs, just like him. In God's family, there are no favorites. All God's children are equal. As we share Christ's sufferings, we will also share his glory.

If you are interested in more, here is Jim's promo and how to get your free study copy:

In a study group, I found that the only way I could grasp some of Paul's convoluted reasoning was to rewrite the text in my own words. I'm not really sure that my words are any clearer than, say, Eugene Peterson's paraphrase in The Message, *but they are different in two specific ways.*

Peterson and others stay with Paul's historical struggle over the reluctance of the Jews, his own people, to accept Jesus as the Messiah. That emphasis, it seems to me, perpetuates the possibility of anti-Semitism. It's also not what Paul would be arguing today. Today, the distinction between Jews and Gentiles would probably be replaced by a distinction between nominal Christians inside the church and "seekers" outside it. So I have rephrased in those terms.

I also believe that if Paul were writing today, he would make use of quotations from the Gospels—which of course were written down after he wrote his letters—rather than using quotations only from the only Scriptures he had available, which we call the Old Testament.

If you would like a copy of my paraphrase of Romans for your own use, just send an e-mail request, to jimt@quixotic.ca. I will send you back an electronic attachment, in either Word 2000 format, or Rich Text Format if you prefer.

Romans 10:8b–13
Conviction [1]

Three key phrases to attend to:

- word of faith

- confess with your lips

- believe

- Word of faith — an external eternal.

- Confess with your lips — offer assent for assurance.

- Believe — trust there is no advantage to be gained and all are equal before G*D.

  - Our words of faith are incompatible with their words of faith. Battle lines are drawn and friendships quartered over the difference of one little word. So was Eastern Christianity divided from Western and is every schism justified.

  - Confession with our lips tempts us to claim form takes precedence over function. These are never order-able, but always interactive. Here is the beginning of hypocrisy that cannot see itself.

  - Believing is action-based on trust in a wholeness between intention and implementation. To do anything other than both is to deny our earthly and earthy dustiness as well as a heavenly image dwelling within and among us.

Romans 12:9–16b
Elizabeth and Mary Meet

In days when there is much talk of schism within The United Methodist Church and an increasing gap between the rich and the poor, there is great disjuncture and disharmony. There is no solution to an intractable tension between self and other. Both are real and both invisible.

An ever-present danger of dealing with an eternal G*D is that we too easily claim our experience of G*D to be eternal. This makes it extremely difficult to carry ourselves lightly and humbly with one another. We take the on/off switch of chaos/creation and extend it into every other part of our personal/corporate theology. This turns the analog of tuning life into a digital right/wrong. Eventually, an awesome G*D requires sinning worms and a True Church develops its scapegoat of the day.

In our economy, it comes to a false divide between the rich and the middle class. The old false saw about seeing that the rich get theirs and then all boats will rise, cannot be re-purposed to secure the middle class. As long as the poor are not the central measuring rod for our economic health, there will continue to be fever upon fever and burst bubble after burst bubble. Though difficult for us to get our minds and hearts around, ultimately, there is no wealth that is not generated by the poor. Sustainable wealth requires the health of the poor, for this is the great untapped pool of resources that is intentionally kept from offering the gifts invested in them.

Where, in a patriarchal system, are pregnant women meeting? Where, in a capitalist society, are the lowly gathering? Here is where hope will be borne and born. In both instances, mercy is remembered and enacted. Where mercy is forgotten, the beauty-way fades into mirage, and we are truly lost.

1 Corinthians 1:18–24
Relic Day

We begin this passage with a synecdoched cross being the power of G*D for those in the beginning stages of their spirit journey. The passage concludes with Christ being the power of G*D (plus a wisdom of G*D).

While these can be seen as a parallelism, there is a distinction to be made between one moment in Jesus' experience (crucifixion) and that of the totality of a life, including death, and more life. Put crassly, we begin our journey through our stages of faith with the literal as a grounding place and grow/leap to the metaphoric as soaring space.

To help yourself move deeper in faith, step into the closest gap and fill what you can with your lightness of heart that we might move past our dualistic categorizations and be wise enough to see another face-to-face, not just our mutual projections.

————————————

a cross is a foolish message
it needs experiencing
to take on meaning

we don't just proclaim
a crucified one
but live as one

1 Corinthians 1:18–31
Clarification Week: Tuesday

The message about the cross—live your life as deeply and widely as you can and, then, *que sera, sera*—is foolish to those whose life-force is fading and are scared of suffering, but to those who are interested in gathering more energy, it is a joining with G*D and Neighb*r in everyday living.

From this starting point, we are able to take another look at wisdom, good ol' Sophia herself, "Grandmother" in many indigenous traditions. We won't be fooled by scripture/reason or tradition/experience when we insist that all four are needed in addition to the glue of humility/service.

Even if we get into the fancy language of wisdom, righteousness, sanctification, redemption, holiness, dikaiosyne, hagiasmos, apolytrosis, consecration, justification, ransom, purity, or whatever, we won't be fooled by letting projected outcomes control our choice to be loving and merciful in the moment.

Blessings on being able to translate "cross" into "choice". The message about choice is to live your life as deeply and widely as you can.

1 Corinthians 5:6b–8
Opened Heart Evening

Is Easter a leavening agent? If so, only a little is needed in the presence of food and water to raise a large life. This asks an open heart to provide the right warmth of honesty and truth for yeast and sugar to interact and grow.

Or is Easter artificially induced hot air to puff things up for an hour and have it gone by only three holes into the televised Sunday golf tournament or three minutes into a basketball game?

Easter invites us to be part of a new batch of G*D-partners, rich in premeditated mercy and intentional forgiveness. Investing this wealth is how we demonstrate our shift from malice (conscious or not) to clarity and brightness.

May the celebration of continued possibilities live on past the blinding brightness of morning. This evening is the start of a new day and an opportunity to commit to urging one another toward next tomorrows.

Conviction 3

Remembrance of transformations past is part of preparation for a next transformation. You didn't think this was as good as life gets, did you?

Screw your awareness to a mental sticking place. With awareness safely in place, remember back to one of your most recent transformations. It may have arisen from the inside or been stimulated from the outside. Give this transformation a name, something that identifies it for you.

With one transformation under your belt, hearken back to earlier and earlier transformations. They may have been for you alone or for a whole group with which you identified. And don't forget to consider transformations others have reported.

By now, it should be seen that none of these are unusual and that each one contains unexpected energy for its participants.

With thanks for all the manure and rain you have received and given, we are ready for a next needed transformation—ready to be aware of it and to engage it. Watch out world.

I would like a spiritual rock
to follow me all my days
one that would hustle forward
just as I need to sit and stay

I would have a number of names
for my spiritual rock
Christ I'd name it Rocky
a foundation to build on

yes a spiritual rock of my own
that would also go ahead
and pause long enough
to be a perch to farther see

of course I wouldn't want it
to get underfoot
or be a stumbling-block
something seen but not heard

yes indeed a spiritual rock
that would be the ticket
I'd paint it gold
and be the talk of the town

but then when envy set in
I'd paint it invisible
so only I could see it
and merrily go my way

testing a spiritual rock
takes no extraordinary measures
simply take it for granted
just apply it to every rock

in less time than it would take
a bird to peck a mountain down
it too would be gone
and I'd come looking for yours

maybe it wasn't a spiritual rock
if it could be so misused
and maybe it was
especially if it were

1 Corinthians 11:23–26
Courage Thursday

Paul passed on what he received. The same is incumbent upon each of us. As generation is added to generation and experience to experience, what have you received? What have you passed on?

Are you proclaiming the building of community through common meals and common good? Are you threatening judgment on any who does so through an "unworthy" manner (meaning not approved by the received knowledge of those in power)?

Yes, examine yourself. Are you still connecting creedal purity with physical health? Are you still using portions of the scripture to shun baptized and communing members for whatever reason?

A common meal is not a formal ritual; it is a multi-valent, inter-sectional experience of common life with all the messiness such brings. Feast well. Gather strength to helpfully deal with weakness, including your own.

1 Corinthians 12:1–11
Guiding Gift [2]

I am always amused and aggravated at the way Paul can so easily slip from an either/or didacticism regarding Jesus' "name" to an open-ended appreciation of a variety of gifts attributed to a Spirit of this same Jesus. I experience no harm to this pericope if verses 2 and 3 are erased or not spoken when reading. Try it: 1 Corinthians 12:1, 4–11.

With that detail cared for, consider again the variety of images of G*D that G*D seems to appreciate. They range from deserts to your life this day. All the named and unnamed gifts are expressions of an original blessing. Perhaps you will appreciate Chris Smither's song, "Origin of Species".

Here is a pertinent section of the song (listen to Chris sing it on-line at https://youtu.be/jOxgiq6c6_E):

> God said: "I'll make some DNA"
> They can use it any way they want
> From paramecium
> Right up to man."
>
> "They'll have sex
> And mix up sections of their code
> They'll have mutations…
> The whole thing works like clockwork over time."
>
> "I'll just sit back in the shade
> While everyone gets laid.
> That's what I call
> Intelligent design."

Paul calls this DNA "the same G*D who activates each gift". Appreciate an Original Blessing or First Gift that has manifested as you. Pretty amazing you are!

1 Corinthians 12:12–31a
Guiding Gift [3]

The body does not consist of one organ but of many. The church does not consist of one tradition but many.

This, of course, leads to a variety of disputes within the church. Which is the truest true of the traditions? Which is the organizing tradition/law that will eventually bring all the others into line with it?

The blessings of each particular tradition push the whole tradition beyond itself into the gray area of proto- or meta-tradition. The most helpful of the traditions are those which help us see a bit further, hear a bit deeper, walk a step more, stand higher on their shoulders. The most unhelpful start assigning honor and respect—always, of course, assigning themselves the best of show.

Strive for the largest tradition, the widest interpretation, the grandest hope. Regardless of your church tradition, how do the hungry and thirsty fare when you are around? If they are no better off, "Christ" is not your unity.

This scripture passage is not for diagnostic purposes but a call to action. Is this or is this not the year to actually make a move toward activating a gift of greater connection to undergird and organize your specific set of gifts (yes, your entire constellation of gifts, not just one biggie out of a limited list)?

If you take a spiritual gifts inventory and identify your key gift but have not joined it with the gifts of others for the common good of all, you are a prideful gong tooting your own horn and not caring a whit about the joy of mixed metaphors, much less continuing a creation of community.

Knowing where we fit into community is important. Roles are significant.

If we had finished verse 31, we would know that this positioning within community for the sake of the community is important, but only prelude to something even more basic—having our role be connected with our love.

Act for good for others only, and it won't be long before we get to resentment and hate as we are worn down by Compassion Fatigue. Common good needs to take into account a source of action as well as a benefit of action.

Reading this passage horizontally, with all the gift connections running back and forth between us, can get to be law oriented and socially determinant. Don't forget to also read this from an angled axis—a G*D's-eye view, blessing and freeing each gift.

1 Corinthians 13:1–13
Guiding Gift [4]

It is interesting to note that love is not the singular winner and still champion in the run-off for the greatest virtue or gift. Simply extend the passage one more verse.

Just as there are two greatest commandments, G*D and Neighb*r, Love has purpose as well as simple being and is twinned with Prophecy. Let's hear a continuation of the story.

> 14:1 — Pursue love and strive for the spiritual gifts, and especially that you may prophesy.

> 14:25 – [Prophecy] discloses the secrets of an unbeliever's heart and brings them to worship/love.

By turning these around, we can see the connection between love and prophecy.

> Pursue the spiritual gift of prophecy *and* strive for love.
> [Love] discloses the secrets of our hearts and leads us to G*D.

Friends, we don't love without being prophetic. We are not prophetic without loving. Now, let's be about the interplay between these two qualities of a full life.

1 Corinthians 15:1–11
Guiding Gift [5]

Paul's experience of Jesus was first through the eyes of enmity and then a revelation of a risen Christ. Each one of us is a center of the universe, perceiving life from our experience. So it is very easy to see this whole "dying for us" focus as Paul's explanation of the mechanism that led to the transition he went through in regard to Jesus.

When we move away from Paul's limitations, we can see the whole sacrificial atonement process in its limited scope. We can also begin retranslating through our experiences and revelations, and reading of scriptures that go beyond the scriptures available to Paul.

Can you imagine the shift in our institutions had Paul written something like:

> I hand on to you my priority ranking of my relationship with Jesus: Christ lived to reveal G*D and the fullness of life. His presence healed many and upset the religious and political *status quo*. All parts of the *status quo* conspired to exercise their "right" to capital punishment (execution). The fullness of life could not be so summarily curtailed, and in the fullness of days was experienced anew by many, including ourselves.
>
> This fullness is worth participating with to the highest degree through our relationships with G*D and Neighb*r. This leads us to proclaim the goodness of Creati*n, the presence of G*D, and the transformation of life in this life.

It is possible to stop short of this present/future orientation by understanding death to be the purpose of Jesus and a *deus ex machina* bringing him back around. This bloody sacrifice is too limiting and leads to excuses used by each generation for their "holocaust" of one group or another.

1 Corinthians 15:12–20
Guiding Gift [6]

All this propositional proclamation leaves my head spinning.

Might one say, "In truth Christ has been raised" instead of, "In fact Christ has been raised"? This gets us out of a lot of unnecessary binds in regard to proofs engaging my experience against your experience.

As long as I'm changing things around, I would suggest that more folks ought to live in this life as though they hope in Christ and then let the eternity question take care of itself. It is honorable, not pitiable, to live the life we are in. This is different from Paul's direction, which pushes us into earning our way, or so having our eye on heaven that we overlook the needs of the moment.

This is summed up in Greg Brown's song, "Mercy, Mercy, Mercy" that includes the line, "This longing for an afterlife has damn-near wrecked this place. Mercy, mercy, mercy. . . ."

Give me a couple of folks who are intent on living (hoping) Christ right now, striving to imitate his focus on a loving G*D, and I'll take them over thousands gathered to gaze at the prosperity of now and ever. A few are more than enough, not something over which to grieve and wait for more.

---

faith in resurrection
opens our senses to its presence
sharpens our language of argument
grounds our institutionalization of same

hope of resurrection
sets us up for disappointment
causes tentativeness in the present
cuts us loose from action

love with resurrection
moves us toward a preferred future
softens our response to others
deepens our experience of time

1 Corinthians 15:19–26
Assured

After you get done scratching your head over this passage and diagramming sentences, it may suffice to say, "Grace and I are dancing to a wonderful tune, *All-in-All*."

Paul does his best to find some order in resurrection—If this, then that, then another, then something else, then . . . . In fact, all the ifs are beside the point; death isn't all it's cracked up to be.

Paul's circle within a circle can be entered at any point and followed around and around. And his circle can be set aside as beside the point. Death isn't all it's cracked up to be.

So if you've been trying to find a formula to have life in this world, forget about it. This world isn't all it's cracked up to be.

We have life, simply life, to live, and neither the trappings of the principalities and powers in this world nor a fear of death will keep us from this impetus. Jesus offered abundant life, and we are invited to jump in. Here is the "holy" week arc: Enter your Jerusalem, face your death, and live.

1 Corinthians 15:35–38, 42–50
Guiding Gift [7]

Hope leads to boldness!

Hope that doesn't lead to boldness is wishful thinking.

So what is the more that you are hoping? Does it go as far as resurrection? Yes, your resurrection that leads to insurrection?

Now, with your eye firmly fixed on such hope that brings boldness, go ahead—bold away!

What will that boldness lead to in your own spiritual disciplines that will go beyond a Lenten trial period?

What will that boldness lead to in your own family (however you define that)?

What will that boldness lead to in your own congregation and denomination/one-true-church/sect/etc?

What will that boldness lead to in your culture, particularly in its political, economic, and educational life?

What will that boldness lead to in your experience of G*D?

Where is an extreme makeover needed? When will you be about that business because you have emboldening hope?

Don't forget to translate "mystery" into "gospel" or "good news". This makes a difference to a modern or post-modern ear.

With a grounding gospel instead of a mystery, we can take all the talk about perishability and imperishability and simply let it be some inside talk between Paul and Congregation Corinth that is no longer accessible to us.

What becomes gospel for us is a moving beyond our usual fixation on suffering and death, to identify a meta-suffering and death that morphs into letting them go while we participate in life. Letting go, here, is a larger understanding than "victory".

We do not stand through statuary to commemorate a victory. We do stand straighter as the weights of judgment slip their surly bonds of an impossible Elysian fantasy, allowing a current fellowship to labor together past fears and tremblings associated with death.

> good news
> a gift
> to treasure
> pass on
>
> interlocking belovedness
> passing through
> rules of law
> formalized sin
>
> to explore
> new gift
> new good
> good news

2 Corinthians 3:12–4:2
Mountain Top to Valley

Paul was not a biblical literalist. There is no report in scripture of Moses' sense of the presence of G*D having dimmed or failed. He was strong enough to complain and ended his days full of vitality. To move from a reference that Moses wore a veil to cover glory to Moses not wearing a veil mistakes and limits the presence of G*D to a moment of ecstasy.

Glory, like gifts, is revealed in different ways to different people and at different stages of their life journey. To start measuring the amount and style of glory among us is a battle that, at best, ends up being lose-lose.

G*D is large enough to not require everyone to have the same gift or the same amount/expression of glory, either in the present or at some future time.

We can still have heart, whether we revel in or dismiss Moses. The refusal to admit to cunning is a very cunning thing to do and we all fall short of self-revelation to others. Let's get off this either/or approach to various components of everyday life. An extension of being both saint and sinner is that we have a whole range of glory from prevenient grace to lived wholeness. Lift up your heart and lift up your Neighb*r's heart—we are in this together.

---

whatever our brand of faith
  we work with veils
some call them creeds
  masking new revelation
some call them experience
  avoiding larger grounding
some call them discipline
  fencing in options
some call them mercy
  lost without boundaries
some call them hope
  insulation from pain
some call them literalism
  deflecting multiple meanings
some call them heresy
  bypassing engagement
whatever our brand
  we work with veils

Love G*D with everything you are and your Neighb*r as yourself.

Be reconciled with G*D in everything you do, and with your Neighb*r as well as yourself.

Other words that can be substituted in are "peace", "partnered", "engaged", and each of the seven or seventy times seven virtues.

There is an impetus to reconciliation that, once experienced, brings a desire for more. Reconciliation is thus a once and future desire—always available and always sought.

It is this vibrant energy that shows its connection to Creati*n and G*D. It comes from premeditated mercy and results in more of the same. In some ways it is a catalytic magic penny where, when we give it away, we end up having more—it is negentropic [free energy] with increasing capacity for G*D work.

I got me a ministry of reconciliation
and I'm gonna spread it all around
here a reconciliation
there a reconciliation
e-i-e-i-o
everywhere a reconciliation
yee-hah

2 Corinthians 5:20b–6:10
Self-Recognition Day

Try this: The opposite of hypocrisy is reconciliation.

Pretending to be something one is not does have the potentially redeeming factor of a recognition of who one would like to be. This can at some point be built upon to move in that direction in actuality, not just in an overarching fantasy. Hypocrisy is not an out-and-out lie, which makes it more difficult to engage than an outright falsehood.

Not only do we seldom deal with an ideal falsehood, but we seldom deal with some universal truth or righteousness. Reconciliation lives in an imperfect world but chooses the slightly better as a step toward even more better.

While it is comforting to consider that a full-blown righteousness is within our grasp, we are more realistically always in a process moving toward greater reconciliation with ourselves and others. Simply acknowledging we are living in a gray zone and hopefully moving toward a healthier, more whole way is helpful.

Intending to put no burden on another is a wonderful intention even if it doesn't work out that way. Paul's list of his endurances does become a burden for those of us who may be able to deal with an affliction or two but not for dishonor or beatings. How can we live up to Paul's level of commitment much less Jesus'? Reconciliation will lie between so we can take one step further while holding an integrity of our particular experience and gifts.

Galatians 1:1–12
Guiding Gift [9] — Proper 4 (9)

It seems impossible for us to avoid combining our autobiography with our theology. The way we see G*D is directly related to how we see our self. Is G*D a provider? Settle in. Is G*D a protector? Wait. Is G*D a protector? Sally forth. Is G*D other? Praise. Is G*D incarnate? Create.

A seed of ever-current discord is autobiography. If you should receive or otherwise acknowledge a revelation beyond my revelation (even if based on my revelation) your revelation will be wrong, at fault, for it is not, only and exclusively, my meaning.

Among the limits of autobiography we find the possibility of *ekklesiai* and *synagogai* to hold the singulars within together in a larger One (not a numerical, but a whole). The keywords become those lived with one another, "Grace y'all" and peace."

These gifts free us from an ever-current age of my story trumps your strumpet story. So lets party ("glory", if you will).

An autobiography without a community in which it moves and has meaning is as real to us as a unicorn or griffin. Look again at your autobiography. Blessings on holding it lightly and anticipating a next revelation that may be found in someone else's vision. Back and forth we limit and grow bonsai, community and self.

Grace to "you" and Peace and all that Grows between and therefrom.

Galatians 1:11–24
Proper 5 (10)

Paul writes as a corrective to the divisions within the church at Galatia. To do so he brings a story delineating his authority. Key is a view from above that allows change. He had been an important adversary able to find every weakness of Jesus' followers. So he was able to divide and conquer Christians. Out of his experience he found a central unifying source of gospel that those on the inside kept overlooking because they were too close.

Some of this important distance is also found in his journey away from Jerusalem and into the wilderness of Arabia.

From adversarial and geographical dislocations Paul is able to speak truth to the power of focusing on the surface of things, rather than their depths. As Galatians continues, these depths will rise to view.

As noted by Todd A. Wilson in *New Testament* Studies, Volume 50, Issue 4, "The Galatians are on the verge of a wilderness apostasy, hence Paul colours his rebukes and warnings with language that evokes Israel's own tragic wilderness failings." Paul may be able to do this from his own wildernesses of 3 days blind and 3 years in Arabia.

Our own wilderness times are important witness sources for our interacting with a settled church that all too easily attacks its own.

---

    caught
    traditions
    ancestors

    freed
    unknown
    neighbors

    traditional persecutions
    unknown grace
    new families

Galatians 2:15–21
Proper 6 (11)

I died to the law as law, so that I might live with G*D.

We all seem to have our limits. There are litmus tests that we put all around ourselves to see if we are still the person we used to be.

Where in our limits can we find the freedom of G*D? Where is the "crack in the cosmic egg" that offers an option to move forward?

How about such restatements as:

... I died to United Methodism as United Methodism, that I might live with G*D.

... I died to America as America, that I might live with G*D.

... I died to the Economy as Economy, that I might live with G*D.

... I died to my Sexuality as Sexuality, that I might live with G*D.

... I died to Cultural/Societal Mores as Cultural/Societal Mores, that I might live with G*D.

... I died to Ethics as Ethics, that I might live with G*D.

What have you been holding on to more tightly than living with G*D?

Is this a helpful model to assist us in moving beyond the fear and suffering of our well-defended limits? If so, try filling in your idol:

... I died to _______ as _______, so that I might live with G*D!

Our expectations act as law. They rein us in. Self-censorship is always alive and well. We are well-bounded by expectations of others and of ourselves. This is a protective function that serves a purpose—for a while.

At some point an amazing grace comes to no longer need the authority of law or custom and it becomes possible to take authority beyond either. This is where there are no laws against the amount of joy one can have or degree of patience one can demonstrate. There is no constraint regarding kindness or who can be welcomed. Some call this faith, some a gift of one religious leader or another, and some simply being human. By whatever name, to come to an experience where a new invitation to health is hearable is like a drink of cool, clean water in a parched life.

One way to follow the biblical storyline is to note experience after experience where expectations fail, where law fails. This is sort of a "Who'd a-thunk it!" approach to spirituality. When the unexpected happens and we are attentive enough to note it, a new person is set loose, a new people is released. To this day we are using categories to divide, not just to describe, my religious/spirit group and every other, those enslaved by systems and those benefiting from any given economic structure, those of one sexual orientation and those of any of the others. Discrimination abounds. This list is infinitely extendable to residents and aliens, one generation and all others, my privilege and your privilege, and on and on. New separations are continually cropping up.

Just as mono-culturing is dangerous for agriculture, mono-culturing is harmful to community. Sameness leads to weakness, blindness, and falling off a cliff. All manner of seeds and gifts are needed to be able to flourish. If you only belong here, you don't belong anywhere. If you belong everywhere, you definitely belong here.

---

no longer two wonderful words	no longer you or me	no longer male or female
no longer this or that	no longer chosen or unchosen	no longer slave or free
		no longer leads to longer

Galatians 4:4–7
Naming Day

From the *Christian Community Bible* we read this liberation perspective:

> [Christ] received his whole background from the Law, namely, from the people and the religion of the Old Testament: this Law was highly positive. But time had passed and it was no longer possible to receive the fullness of the divine truth without being redeemed from the yoke of the Law.
>
> We must see in this a fundamental disposition of the plan of salvation: God saves us by becoming one of us. The same is now true of the Church which saves people, rather than giving to them or "being interested in them." And the Church cannot bring them a permanent and transforming salvation if it does not share in their very condition.
>
> This is the reason why the Lord wants the Third World churches to bear the cross of the people of their continents: their marginalization, their sufferings and humiliations, in order to give them authentic salvation. When they are only middle-class churches following occidental or Roman patterns, Third World people cannot be saved.

This raises interesting questions about the role of the church in First World countries. Can the church be a vehicle of salvation if it participates in and perpetuates the privilege, accomplishments, and power of First World people?

Eugene Peterson talks about people being "kidnapped by the law". While under the influence of privileged kidnappers will not the kidnapee take on the values of the kidnapper (Stockholm syndrome?). The issue is not that we kidnap for a good reason (deprogramming) or for a bad reason (to raise money), but that we kidnap at all. How does the Church kidnap people? This is a significant question to raise in light of Jesus' name and identity following an angelic song of peace. Does Jesus re-kidnap people?

How will you be known in the lives of those kidnapped by privilege? Surely you will not let them remain unaware of the limitation of their position. This is huge work that will need all your awareness of being an heir of a larger way that does not stoop to "redemptive" kidnapping.

Galatians 5:1, 13–25
Proper 8 (13)

There was a little girl
Who had a little curl
Right in the middle of her forehead;
And when she was good
She was very, very good,
But when she was bad she was horrid.
[Henry Wadsworth Longfellow]

When we are good, the Fruit of Spirit (singular) has many different expressions—each fit for an occasion ... A Willy Wonka Three-Course-Dinner Gum.

When we are bad, the Desires of Flesh (plural) come spilling out, one after the other, piling up ... A Hieronymus Bosch painting.

————————————

no law against love
but plenty of examples
of best intentions
gone horribly terribly wrong

no law against repentance
but plenty of examples
of having put our hand to the plow
never leaving a hedgerow

no law against new life
but plenty of examples
of turning a blind eye
to an open door

Galatians 6:(1–6), 7–16
Proper 9 (14)

Work for the good of all. Why? Because the cosmic payoff is worth it—a new creation.

Enough said.

———————————————

sky-writer large
is not large enough
for a new
creation message

what needs lopping off
is not our sexuality
but our control
of cultural symbol

do this and you're in
avoid this and you're in
do that and that
and you're out

every diminution of one's life
to carry out
someone else's plan
lessens our common good

take care in temptation's face
not to live another's life
no matter the perks
it is not redemptive

focus on gentleness
bear mutual burdens
do your own work
weary not in good

compassion trumps judgment
care overarches competition
sowing precedes reaping
peace always mercy ever

Always with the particularizing.

Christmas turns out to not be a joy to the world, a sign of peace to all people. One way and another, laying a baby in an open manger transfers the significance from angelic song of joy and peace for all to only being available through one personification of an expansive and expanding G*D.

What new lens is needed to see everyone as adopted? Are we all in this together, or not? What value is there in continuing to make "wisdom and insight" smaller in scope rather than larger?

A larger wisdom sees that everyone is already marked with the seal of a promised Holy Spirit.

Was your Christmas for you and yours? Was there an element of it being for everyone? If the last 2,000 years are any indication, an end to us will not happen before another celebration of Christmas. This gives a year in which to better celebrate a wider joy and a deeper peace. Blessings on your journey from an echo of a previous Christmas to the implementing of a next Christmas of "every blessing".

Ephesians 1:11–23
Honoring Day

How we work with what it means to be "destined" will have a significant effect on structures we put in place. Here our preferred understanding of "destined" is "invited" or "anticipated".

Whether talking about resurrection as a personal event or for the the whole church (including even the rascals at every stage of development and position) there is a question about the inevitability of life beyond our current experience—life after life in this time or some other "life" after this body ceases.

Beyond walking in the way of a G*D of Christ or Jesus or both (because that is our thing to do) comes an invitation to engage more life through trust and mercy—Love of G*D and Love of Neighb*r.

Using this as a starting point, questions will need to be asked later on about instructions regarding authority in family, economic structures such as slavery, and interaction with even larger principalities and powers.

When dealing with our models and mentors, it is helpful to honor that they have made choices about growing in wisdom. Were it only destiny, we could simply read their story and do our best. Those we honor as souls and saints are so in large part because of their relationship to us, their revealing of their invitation to a larger dance and their acceptance.

In this, we glimpse again a free anticipation of building common good from the bottom-up and taking responsibility for our gifts and opportunities within the context of a received time and space and a still-open shift of same to be a context we gift the next generations.

Ephesians 1:15–23
Our Turn to Witness

Inhale love, exhale thanks.

Again.

This is the fullness that fills all in all.

Since it is all in all, we can also inhale thanks and exhale love.

No matter where one is on this great circle with a still point of thanks or love and every circumference point of love or thanks, we add to its spin and expansion.

Ephesians 3:1–12
Guiding Gift

The commission of passing on grace is an important task.

To fulfill it takes a discerning eye. A sign is sighted indicating where hope is needed. Provisions for travel and a gift to be given are laid in. These acts take time and resources.

When push comes to shove we have to actually let go of the gift we bring for it to truly be a gift. To hold strings that gold or grace must be used according to the givers direction directly negates the gift as gift.

When we have given our gift, we need to further act to protect the one who received our gift that they might grow beyond this gift, find their own, and live/share it in their own way.

Being commissioned to gift, whether myrrh or mercy, is no easy commission. There is no rulebook for how to carry out your commission. We are either confident in our gifts and able to freely offer them, or we are insecure and look around for the safest route.

May you implement your commission to gift frankincense and fairness, gold and grace.

Philippians 1:3–11
Needed Change [2]

Here is a look at the parallelism of verses 6 and 9–11:

6- I am confident of this,
9- And this is my prayer

6- that the one who began a good work in you
9- that your love may overflow more and more with knowledge
and full insight

6- will bring it to completion
10a- to help you determine what is best,
11a- having produced a harvest of righteousness

6- by the day of Jesus Christ.
10b- so that in the day of Christ you may be pure and blameless,
11b- that comes through Jesus Christ for the glory and praise of God.

Now we can proceed to play with the interrelationship between confidence and prayer. Prayer here is not supplication, but an envisioning or imagining of realized behavior.

What is to be realized is the connection between a generalized good work and the particulars of an insightful love (different than a feeling love). This application of knowledge keeps us from idealism and dogmatism.

When we connect love and insight we are able to do more than have a resolution to do gooder; we are able to not only determine but complete or harvest the fruit of said resolution.

Those who connect Jesus Christ with a revelation of G*D will affirm this pattern will be done "by" tomorrow, is being done "in" what we know to be today, and has already been done or "come through" to now.

So, confident ones, pray that love be connected with knowledge and insight. This is an energy needful in our lives and the lives of many.

PS—Don't forget to shift your language from "the day of Christ" to "today". These verses take on a different cast when this important shift is experienced and lived.

Naming Day — Premature Fear Sunday

My preference would be for this pericope to continue to verse 13. In this manner, we are not simply left with a creedal statement, but we can see Life continued through us. We work out our own salvation (wholeness and health) with fear and trembling beyond creeds—while wrestling G*D within us, attempting to burst through, yearning for us to become G*D.

An alternative way to redeem the creedal formulation is to be sure we know that its exclusive shorthand form for insiders is built on an inclusive vision (verses 1–4) that will continually reform it. Here is a table to be sure is up-to-date before getting too dogmatic about theological emptiness (kenosis) and confessed names. These are far more lively processes than bowing and kneeling at the tolling of a name. In fact, it is these lived blessings whereby G*D's presence is revealed.

Blessing	Sun	Mon	Tues	Wed	Thurs	Fri	Sat
Encouragement							
Consolation							
Sharing							
Compassion							
Sympathy							
Joy							
Unity							
Love							
Accord							
Humility							
Helping							

Woe betide any who ignore what comes before and after this text.

I've got good gifts. Oops, to merely say that leaves me open to pride and downfall. Better to be covetous for the gifts of another. Given the quality of my gifts I really need to find someone perfect to try imitating because anything less would have me outshine them. It is hard to be humble.

So, to do a little reverse psychology on the fates, I'll strive for suffering in death. That way those silly old fates, who are too stupid to catch on and can only reverse things, will reverse my suffering into heaven.

See, if you just spend a little time figuring these things out, you can make out like a bandit. Well, maybe that's not the best thing to be compared to, but what are you going to do with these old sayings that get lodged so deeply in our brainpans?

All this fancy footwork is to get at the nub of the matter. Here is a worthy process of life: "Forgetting what lies behind, forge ahead." If we strip away all put-downs of gifts and the opportunities they bring as being third-rate (not even second-class), we will better see a connection between living expansively/expandingly in a loving direction and a present moment.

To attend to gifts present reduces the restrictive limitations of past experience and enhances the creative possibilities still before us.

So it is that we affirm the note in *The Interpreter's Study Bible*: "What is unclear, and debated, is whether Paul's insistence on these points is intended to correct some opponent's message or to recall and anticipate problems he had encountered elsewhere, especially in Corinth."

It turns out all the suffering and diminishment language, the dismissal of good gifts, is off-message and distracting.

Philippians 3:17–4:1
Conviction 2

Be sure to do your homework regarding Girardian imitation.

What we read as "join in imitating me as I imitate Christ" might also be read from the Greek as "Become co-imitators with me of Christ." (NISB)

This reads much better in terms of the Body of Christ in its many parts. Co-imitators would have us each operating in our arena without having to do the same and say the same. For instance, the foot could imitate what Jesus would do, walking along with folks while the hand could imitate what Jesus would do, healing through touch. Both are needed.

The tricky part for us is when the hand tries to direct the foot to go certain places or the foot doesn't factor in a stop for the hand to reach deep into another's life.

Being co-imitators of Christ is like being a co-creator with G*D. These partnerships are crucial for our own transformation and that of the world. May brother eye and sister ear help uncle foot and aunt hand comprehend a call to move and reach, and to pause and touch.

In our journey to the imitation of Christ it is important to expand that into being part of a larger co-imitation process.

Broods of vipers are not only found in outsiders seeking to come in, but within a flock as well. Euodia and Syntyche are archetypes of every church split; some slight difference is magnified into a bright line of division.

Given that such dissension is not unusual and even can be helpful in moving everyone along, who is this unnamed "loyal companion" called upon to assist Euodia and Syntyche? Having inhabited the role of intentional interim minister, I see this anonymous one as a patron saint of interim ministry.

The work needed in a conflicted setting might be outlined as the Five Tasks of an Intentional Interim Minister:

- returning folks to community through a reestablishment of a common vision [(1)remembering who we have been & (2) determining who we want to be],

- redefining gentleness [(3)a key leadership trait],

- practicing prayers of thanksgiving [(4) reconnecting with experienced antidotes to divisive worry], and

- having peace stand guard at hearts and minds [(5) preparing space for a next generation].

Intentional interim Ministers do this work of salving distressed congregations through G*D who strengthens and beautifies.

Even as Advent has both a backward glance and forward glimpse of a larger picture than a pointillist's present stroke, so, with Euodia and Syntyche, we remember past cooperation and look for a more mature consolidation of community.

Philippians 4:4–9
Thanksgiving

Back in Matthew, Mark, Luke, and John, the disciples were not able to be of "one mind" with themselves or Jesus. Here, the only surprise is that only two folks are mentioned as being out of sync with one another and thus from the whole community. This human reality is a springboard into a blessing to "fare-well" and "rejoice".

There is a whole discipline about conflict resolution that can get to be a bit programmatic or technique-oriented. Basically, this tries to reveal the humanity of those on both sides of a quarrel. Here, we are invited to practice guarding by revealing our developing self with a heart of gentleness and a mind of thanks as a way of not only resolving issues but preempting them.

These two gifts are excellent markers of a whole constellation of virtues behind them. Our work together is to gentle one another into deeper relationships that our time together will be a source of rejoicing and thanksgiving in a larger community.

It is in these depths of rejoicing and thanksgiving where our resolve matures to live on the outside a hope living in and sustaining us.

As wonderful as all the positive thinking and self-help/self-talk can sound, it does take place in a context of contention. There are false teachers, power-hungry individuals, sociopaths, ignorant and stupid people, and an incomplete creation that need addressing.

Gentleness and thanksgiving ask of us difficult choices. Will we walk quietly to our execution by terrible means? Will we engage in a plot to eradicate the people in visibly high places who are causing harm? Will we bring a challenging word to the masses who let those in high places continue doing harm? Will we teach and practice and learn and teach some more? Will we search and find one new lever of power and use it toward an honorable end?

Rejoice gently and openly carry Peace.

Fare well.

Colossians 1:1–14
Proper 10 (15)

Faith and Love are evidenced when Hope is alive (verses 4–5). This emphasis practically turns 1 Corinthians 13 around—here the greatest of these is Hope.

> Look – Love is the greatest!
> Look – Faith is the greatest!
> Look – Hope is the greatest!

So Paul expects and prays for the folks at Colossae that they would lead worthy lives—lives lived with joy, patience, and power that reflect their Hope (verse 10).

This Hope is for them tied to that redemptive mercy of forgiveness (verse 14).

> Look – Forgiveness is the greatest!
> Look – Mercy is the greatest!

Do you still Hope for forgiveness and live that Hope (not groveling for some rescue, but standing firm that your expected forgiveness will engage and energize your present forgiveness of others, even before you experience your own)? Now there is Hope that is still Hope and not a *quid pro quo*. No wonder Paul, here, claims its greatness.

> prayer without ceasing
> calls for a patience
> beyond patience
> known otherwise
> as joy

> prayer without ceasing
> calls for action
> beyond results
> known otherwise
> as hope

Colossians 1:11–20
Evaluation Day — Proper 29 (34)

The introduction to Colossians in *The New Interpreter's Study Bible* includes this comment:

> Most interpreters believe that the problem [the folks at Colossae had] was acknowledging, if not actually worshiping, heavenly powers associated with the stars.

This leads Paul to insert a hymn (1:15–20)

> … extolling Christ in cosmological rather than soteriological (salvation-oriented) terms, but which could impress a congregation like that at Colossae without compromising the integrity of his own position.

Using another's language, imagery, and memes without compromising their integrity is tricky. It is also very important in today's world (well, actually, any day's world).

If Paul can pull this off (as I think a case can be made that Jesus pulled off this same willingness to risk being compromised), so can we.

In this light, hear again these words, "Be strong with the strength that comes from G*D's presence and endure with patience as you give thanks—joyfully."

Colossians 1:15–28
Proper 11 (16)

From a defunct Yakrider.com posting:

> So where, is God in all this? Different members of the Yakrider community will have different responses to this question. Let's look at this from the Christian perspective for a moment. One school of thought conceives God as always outside of the universe, as the "Wholly Other" who built it, set this mechanical model into motion and stepped back to let it run itself, and there is nothing divine in the material world of nature. That's God as carpenter or potter. Another school sees, as in The Letter of St. Paul to the Colossians that the eternal Christ is the "firstborn" or archetype of all creation—in him were all things created, and "all things in him subsist" (Col. 1:16, 17). The Greek term "sunesteken" is translated variously, "subsist", "consist", or "are established". Eduard Lohse, in his commentary on Colossians notes: "In Platonic and Stoic philosophy the verb *sunestekenai* (to be established, to continue, to exist, to endure) was used to denote the wonderful unity of the entire world." It's little wonder that physicists, facing the unexplainable problem of why an atom's whizzing, orbiting electrons never spin off into randomness, call this phenomenon, simply, the Colossians Principle, referencing, though humorously, this verse—that all things are held together by "Christ". Though they don't mean it literally or seriously, such might be close to what St. Paul had in mind.

I was glad to hear of the "Colossians Principle". It gives a needed lightness to this passage that comes close to a Taoist appreciation of Creati*n in all and all in Creati*n. Otherwise we get pretty heavy handed about a uniqueness of Christ (perhaps Jesus, or you) and a too easy taking on of suffering that needs a Buddhist antidote.

All in all, this passage ends up with the helpful and hopeful image of assisting everyone to mature (implicitly, after their own fashion, their own Christness).

Colossians 2:6–15, (16–19)
Proper 12 (17)

"As you received Christ Jesus ... continue to live your lives in that light." This line raises a question: How do we receive a Christ?

Those who have gradually morphed into a relationship with a Christ that continues to point beyond Christ are encouraged to continue growing, not to stop with the current relationship.

Those who have suddenly come to a relationship with a Christ that continues to point beyond Christ are instructed to be prepared for yet another change as Christ pays attention to a Living G*D and will be changing accordingly.

How did you receive a Christ who points beyond? Guess what—there are still more changes to come. Don't become captive to deceitful philosophy or to your current "having come thus far to Christ". There is still more nourishment and growing of additional ligaments and sinews ahead—with G*D.

---

live your life
as you have lived your life
is not a condemnation
to stasis

life so far
has been a journey
of growing maturing
and fading away

live in the middle
of such diverse dynamism
and wonder upon wonder
will be revealed

more life than ever imagined
will open through more growth
and through more endings
along your way

live your life
as you have lived your life
and you will live
as you have never lived before

Colossians 3:1–11
Proper 13 (18)

If you have come to seek, with Jesus, a Presence/Freedom of G*D, then seek. There will be choices to be made about what to attend to during this never-ending Story. Our choice might be attracted by a pull to such a Presence or it might be driven by a fear of wrath to come.

Whichever way you come to the Story, there is a need to jettison such unhelpful pausing points as anger, malice, slander, and abusive language, for these behaviors further separate what is intended to be moving in similar directions. Such behaviors keep our desired renewal at bay by divvying up our past as though it were fatalistically tied to our future. In so doing, "Greek" and "Jew" are eternally divided from one another. "Barbarian", "Scythian", "Slave", and "Free" continue to circle one another with great wariness, each looking to their own advantage.

––––––––––

idolatry is greedy
delving into every possible source
of satisfaction
never finding enough

a good gift of sexuality
is devoured until only
fornication is left
to sell cars

an ideal of purity
is thoroughly doused in
unrelenting cynicism
until it forgets itself

enthusiasm for a joy of life
becomes so bored
passion flares
accepting only one side

so gifts ideals enthusiasms
wear down in the face of bottom lines
including the bottom line of death
leaving only greedy idols

Colossians 3:12–17
Blessed Body [1]

Clothes are technologies of comfort and fashion/status. In this sense, the experience of compassion, kindness, humility, meekness, and patience are techniques of love—clothing covering and revealing love.

Suppose we dream about being garbed with new clothes and find ourselves without a revelation of love; what then?

Here we might listen in to a direction that moves from forgiveness (v. 13) to love (v. 14) to harmony (v. 14) to peace (v. 15) to thanks (v. 15). In the sequence of hope, faith, and love the greatest is claimed to be love. In the sequence here, is the greatest of these "thanks"?

This is confirmed in everything we do being done with thanks.

---

ouroboros traced again
a path told from long ago
arrive, arrive it says

finally arrive at forgiveness
work your way up to it
dissolve the past

finally arrive at love
work your way into it
today never over

finally arrive at harmony
work your way through it
each touching every

finally arrive at peace
work your way over it
past every understanding

finally arrive at thanks
work your way under it
raising each act

ouroboros traced again
each work claiming eternity
and simply rolled on

1 Thessalonians 3:9–13
Needed Change [1]

Here is a question for the year: No matter what the season, are we actually experiencing an increase of abundant love for one another and for all?

This will call for individual work (prayer) and communal work (restoration).

If we can make some progress on this during the coming church year we will find our hearts strengthened for more years of building toward a next step. Is this or is this not a time to go beyond the making of a resolution to the implementation of steps that will help us journey?

This quote may help us:

> His mother had often said, When you choose an action, you choose the consequences of that action. She had emphasized the corollary of this axiom even more vehemently: when you desire a consequence you had damned well better take the action that would create it. ~ Lois McMaster Bujold

Paul, Silvanus, and Timothy are able to identify two keys to living as a significant group of people, a covenant group, if you will. Clarity of what it means to grow toward G*D in both individual and corporate arenas stands everyone in good stead.

A first key recognizes that which we are discerning together affects where I place meaning in my own life. In turn, my individual faith encourages and challenges where we as a group place our trust. Growth in all directions is key to a dynamic fellowship, in this case, Christian (pre-Constantine). This is a different dynamic than later, when formal doctrine will cut some off and homogenize the Church. That, in turn, will lead to authoritarian leadership holding one-right-answer and willing to name others as heretic and kill them.

A second key is how we express love for one another. Our Neighb*rs, even those in the "church", are different enough from our self that it is no small matter that we honor one another with our different stages of growth in faith and trust. This is a different dynamic than both of us gazing toward officialdom and trying to measure up to a distant and theoretical way of being in the world.

These dynamics are still worthy ones to search after—growth and love. In fact, when they are split from one another, we find ourselves splitting from one another. There is no church growth product that will substitute for these basics of growth in meaning (individually *and* together) and love beyond reflections of our self.

What individual or group *within* your "church" needs your prayer that these two gifts might surface in their life?

What individual or group *outside* your "church" needs your prayer that these two gifts might surface in their life?

What within yourself needs prayer that these two gifts might be more clearly revealed?

When growth beyond our current understanding and love beyond our self happen, new hope is born and borne, regardless of the religious or non-religious expression/tradition in which they occur.

2 Thessalonians 2:1–5, 13–17
Proper 27 (32)

As terrible as the present day may be, it doesn't rise to the level of an imminent end of all life. Current difficulties and their causes can be cared for. Though many die, enough will come through to move us, together, one step further on.

Simply consider all the ways through which we have already come—so many trails of tears and other never forgotten disasters. When we stop being surprised at the subtlety and persistence of troubles gathered around our door we are better able to find and travel through fine openings into broader and safer space.

One of the traditions in which we are to stand is that of an open future, a Paradise available right here, right now. This apprehension and acquisition of a more whole future is our part in a perpetual motion process. The future and our today mutually tug on one another. The result is our being pulled from the quicksand of yesterday.

Whenever you hear words being tossed about that join "purpose" and "tradition" there is an incipient danger that a demand will be made to follow a limited path in order to continue one zone of comfort or another.

As we get further and further away from our Pentecostal roots in a locked room, a temptation grows to turn one experience of new vision and energy into only one acceptable way of implementing such an experience. We get fearful and make up all manner of stories to frighten folks from their possibilities of new community back into a locked room, never to be opened, where like talks with like.

Remember a tradition that unlocks rooms from the inside and the unacknowledged energy that can still stretch forth into a more compassionate today—no wait needed.

Here is where having loose boundaries comes in handy. The language being used here is that of "idleness". Given a focus on thanksgiving, we might see idleness as being without thanks or joy. We just don't have the energy, given all we need to do, to spend any more on such frivolities.

We might reflect on the classic sin of sloth or sadness. In this case, idleness is lack of thankful joy. Spiritual apathy that discourages us from our holy work of appreciating beauty and expressing thanks is another way to talk about sloth and to see how what is being warned against here is not relaxing, but a choice against life.

Likewise, we can retranslate, "anyone not willing to work" into "anyone not willing to give thanks and do the work of worship isn't worth any more than the result of eating."

And yet again, "Do not be weary in doing what is right" is less about morality and more about thanksgiving (a focus of this passage).

---

sometimes we learn
from opposites
better than models

our models come loaded
with literalism and creeds
narrowing our options

comparison brings choice
play and mystery
bearing greater fruit

idling is not resting in place
it is actively refusing
to move ahead

1 Timothy 1:12–17
Proper 19 (24)

Paul claims he received mercy because he didn't know what he was doing. (Of course, he "knew". In fact, he was the initiator of the plan he was carrying out.) It seems he lacked understanding of unintended consequences or a larger picture in which to put his experience. Violence seemed the surest way to his desired end, and so he followed it. (Yes, there are probably recent repeats of this with the terrorism of strategic and tactical uses of violence within and against communities. You can begin counting the ways.)

The reason for pushing this a little is that we tend to want to give a justification, at least to ourselves, for why someone received mercy when, if it were left to us, they would still be without it.

What are we going to do with an intentional violator rather than an ignorant one? Are they still worth mercy or being sought after? Are we going to claim the neediness of some is so great that there is not enough grace to fill them to overflowing and thus to a new way of living?

I suspect there is not really all that much difference between being grateful for a smidgeon of mercy or a passel of grace.

> Did the lost sheep enter into the joy of the shepherd? Did the lost coin enter into the joy of the woman? When mercy is present, is joy present for both the giver and the receiver of mercy?

> Was the sheep worth the effort? Joy says, "Yes." Was the coin worth the effort? Joy says, "Yes." Was Paul worth the effort? Joy says, "Yes." Are you worth the effort? Joy says, "Yes."

Even though we want to play the schmaltz game and claim that the bigger the grace, the bigger the thanks, it may simply be that maturing a little at a time or in a big jump is of relatively little consequence, or that thanks is simply thanks whether now or later or big or small.

It may be sufficient to simply know that mercy and grace have occurred and can yet occur. With this awareness, we are able to speed our acceptance of them and respond with increased wisdom and energy.

1 Timothy 2:1–7
Proper 20 (25)

First of all—inclusion rather than exclusion. Pray for everyone that they may be the healthiest they can be, which will be enough.

Prayer is not just a form; it is also content. Pray that we might lead a peaceable, G*D-ly life. A life with quiet dignity.

Universalists arise! G*D desires everyone to be healed, made whole, saved.

Know you are, in turn, having peace prayed for you.

---

inclusion exclusion
hinge upon a doorway
that starts closed

an open door can
include more
than the already gathered

a shut door definitely
excludes more
than it defines

the easy way is exclusion
as a door doesn't need to move
to keep in in and out out

much more energy is needed
to include folks in
doors need to be opened

sometimes it takes a gentle push
sometimes a crowbar
little or great – energy

narrow or wide
there are doors all around
pick at least one to push

1 Timothy 6:6–19
Proper 21 (26)

Enough can be enough when it comes to food and shelter and money. More than enough, though, gets in the way when enough ceases to be enough.

Has there been enough kindness shown yet? How about enough peace experienced or justice enacted? Will there ever be enough consideration given to the poor? What is the limit of an expansive and expanding love?

When we begin trading in religion as though it were a commodity, it turns out that enough is never enough. We are measured by an ever-expanding base of creed and coming up short of elusive grace. This understanding leaks over into the financial and power areas of life, where there really never is enough, and we will cut any corner in order to receive more of the marketable goodies and control we desire.

It is important to address the issue of how to deal with matters where enough is not perceived to be enough. Here, the virtue needed is not a sense of authority to order arbitrary limits on enough or to find a refuge of off-shore tax-exempt storage to keep adding to enough. What is needed is a sense of contentment able to see through the masquerade of mammon and its cohorts playing the pity game and needing just one little bite more, an extra room, or 10% more income.

Researchers tell us that it is not an absolute amount of money that brings "happiness", but where your money ranks in comparison with others. Simply having more than so-and-so brings the happiness of status, fleeting as it is. This, however, is not the kind of contentment that needs consideration. Here we have a reference to the Buddhist understanding of non-attachment—being content apart from standard measuring tools. Contentment is a spiritual gift much needed in today's world of warring words, setting family member against family member.

Better than "Don't worry; be happy," is "In all things, contentment."

You have the gift of faith living within you. That's good. Not only that, but I've touched your life. You are not afraid as you carry a light of power, love, and self-discipline.

But I am afraid that very power, love, and self-discipline will take you where even angels fear to tread, so don't color outside the line I laid down for you.

What a deal—the very gifts given are warned against. And, yet, is not a Holy Spirit a living spirit within us pushing us to greater things than even Jesus is recorded to have participated in?

It is so easy to hold only to the letter of a teaching itself without paying attention to the spirit of the standard of the teaching, which is to break new ground through the cracks in our realities and a new creation pulling us forward.

We have so often read this as a dire warning that if you go beyond Paul, you are on the side of terror. We are called to go beyond such a limitation to herald through our lives, not through Paul's life repeated, a light of good newness revealing life and more.

---

o to see another
as they may become
this precious gift
transforms
seer and seen

2 Timothy 2:8–15
Proper 23 (28)

Being exiled in a foreign country (deportation) or exiled in your own (captivity) is a death experience. Thus, you may want to try translating verse 8 as, "Remember Jesus Christ, *returned from exile....*"

To have returned from exile is to face all the broken dreams of the way things used to be, as well as to do the difficult work of building a new community. Returning from exile is no easier than going into exile. While we fantasize about returning from whatever exile we are currently experiencing, the reality is that fulfilling such a fantasy will be as problematic as the life we are currently dealing with.

Therefore, *enduring* is a good word with which to become reacquainted. Endure the exile; endure the return.

---

what
no wrangling over words
when all I have for meaning
in this unlooked-for exile
are words

words
clarifying our situation
encouraging endurance
fantasizing change
present

words
harboring a past
experiencing this present
anticipating a new creation
priceless

words
so priceless
there is no choice
but to have dominion
wrangle

2 Timothy 3:14–4:5
Proper 24 (29)

Continue what you have learned.

While in Peace Corps training to teach teachers how to teach science without lab equipment, it was emphasized that learning how to learn was more important than learning a particular experiment and fabricating equipment for it.

What have Christians learned? Have we learned memorization? Have we learned doctrine and dogma? Have we learned ritual? Have we learned that a living G*D is going to keep us learning beyond each and every particular learning?

Scripture is "… useful for teaching, for reproof, for correction, and for training in righteousness." [2 Timothy 3:16, NRSV] Here are two support functions and two correction functions. A given passage can be used in at least these ways. Which is the one and only correct use? Neither one. When we wrestle through and learn how to learn, we are equipped for every good work needed in the moment.

Among other things, it takes flexibility to be ready for a next good work needed. We can't keep repeating the same good work in a variety of settings without that good work eventually becoming exactly a bad work that makes everything worse.

Keep wrestling with scripture and the persistent need to keep momentary truths from limiting a coming new heaven and earth.

---

somehow we keep hearing
be sober
endure suffering
evangelize

good news apparently
so diluted
so mechanical
so earnest

humor has been squeezed
down
out
forever

all that is left
persistence
rebuke
solemnity

may we hear again
a cheering evangel
encouraging us
and all

2 Timothy 4:6–8, 16–18
Proper 25 (30)

Straw Pharisee (verses 6–8):
> As for me, I am a personification of a fast. I have lived accordingly, right to this moment, following every jot and tittle of faith. I have a crown reserved for me in eternity that will be personally handed to me by Jesus himself. Others who do it my way will also get a crown.

Idealized Tax Collector (verses 16–18):
> I am deserted, unsupported by anyone except Jesus, who strengthens me to forgive others before claiming a right to teach forgiveness to those most unlikely to offer it. Through forgiveness, I was rescued from biting the heads off those who sneer at me. This rescue from others and myself is worth remembering, always. Amen.

Like Paul and anyone—we wear our tragic and comedic masks in quick succession.

Titus 2:11–14
Blessed Body: Proper I

How are you living the night before Christmas? Not knowing what is coming tomorrow, how would you be living? In the midst of waiting for blessed hope to be clarified, how are you doing with self-control?

It is so exciting to have a night before Christmas. Expectations run so high.

This is being posted several days before Christmas Eve and probably read even longer than that before a next Christmas Eve. Might we begin living in expectation that a night before the night before the night before might be a night before a day we have been waiting for? Tomorrow, probably an ordinary day, may be a turning spot. Who knows! So why are we skipping this moment of hope in favor of a remembrance of a previous blessing?

May we not be so blinded by Christmas Eve that we miss a new Christmas before then.

Titus 3:4–7
Blessed Body: Proper II

One context for these 4 verses is 1:12, which identifies the bad reputation of Cretans as inveterate liars, animalistic, and layabout gluttons. Verse 1:13 sets the task of Paul's followers as reproving the people of Crete for their own good.

Just preceding our text, Titus is reminded how he and others in the Fellowship were also foolish, disobedient, disoriented, and addicted to their various desires.

A Christmas story here is verse 4: When the wholeness of G*D's presence arrived, kindness and love revealed a mercy far wider than any measure of righteousness or lack thereof.

This mercy is a grace we are to shed abroad to cease the stupid arguments we get ourselves into with contrived discriminations—arguing to prove ourselves better than another, making up pedigrees and privileges, and pitting creed against creed.

The way out of our controversies is a return to verse 4, loving our Neighb*r (being kind to our kin) and reveling in pushing mercy to its limits and beyond.

Do note that living mercifully won't keep you from being shunned, jailed, enslaved, or killed. It will, however, keep you on a path beyond rejecting harm that gets all the way to that which does good and is useful for the building up of common-wealth.

Philemon 1:1–1:21
Proper 18 (23)

Ahh, the temptation to command another. And, oh, how difficult to appeal through love.

As we look back on slavery, we wonder how much sooner it might have been overcome had someone in the Bible given us a clearer word than periodic, temporary emancipations and so many examples of folks freed who then enslaved others.

What we are not able to see is our own blind-spots that later generations will look back on and wonder why there wasn't much made of our equivalents of slavery. As we do the long slog of finally resolving the discrimination imposed upon the LGBTQ community (as though gender/partner preference were the most significant quality of a person), a question arises as to what the next categorical discrimination will be. Will we cycle back through some of the old ones? Will it be another round of crusades? Another allowance of tribal genocides?

May our hearts be refreshed enough to clearly see who is being kept down and stand with them.

I've been waiting so long
for you to do the right thing
my patience has been extended
beyond my comfort level
in order that you might
voluntarily do good to another

in such I have been complicit
in your evil ways
aided and abetted
your delusion of hierarchy
let you get away with
enslaving our kinfolk

how might we partner
we so different
and so connected
when will we set aside
our givens and assumptions
to set each other free

Hebrews 1:1–4, (5–12)
Blessed Body: Proper III

Interpretation is key to the quotes from the prophets of yore in verses 5–12. These references are from the past to who knows whom, and some are all too clearly to a specific person of yore. To apply them here and now is a prime example of proving what you want by selective quoting.

The presumption is a patriarchal "Son", and so we force the world to conform to our preconceptions.

Beware when Jesus becomes more important than anything else. When this happens, you go through life with the eternal Sunday School response to every question: "Jesus!" It then becomes all too easy to lose a Neighb*r in order to maintain a Christ.

Compare Isaiah on "servanthood" with Hebrews on "majesty" to get a feel for an important biblical tension. For a moment, erase these quotations from the story and see what incidents from your life you would put in their place to honor all who live as though they were partnered with G*D.

Ah, paradox—Jesus is perfect priest and perfect sacrifice. This is too perfect. It goes far beyond what it means to be human and ends up in Platonic ideals.

Being human is not enough. We need some ideal to become human in order that the human might become super-human, which guarantees inhuman(e) behavior because no condition short of having perfect neighbors will do.

Helpful here is a reminder of etiology to temper this eschatology.

We are G*D's image. As such, we are to create ourselves and new images all along our way. As we know from G*D's response to loneliness, new life is called forth from where we are—no do-overs or going back to find a different fork in the road. What we have is sufficient for our day.

While appreciating a process of reaching back to lend a hand because of having been reached back to, the reach was to solidify a place to move on from, not to pull us a jump ahead past a needed learning only available right here, right now.

What is needed now is release from fear-of-death. Death, itself, is a valley we will need to walk. Period. Support for not self-censoring our fear of loneliness is important to us. In fact, it demonstrates we are not as alone as we feared. With our fear out in the open, we can move from a perfect system with a perfect priest presiding over a perfect sacrifice of said perfect priest and making perfect all imperfect people who gaze at such self-contained perfection.

What we need to move on to is an image in the beginning of Chapter 3—Partners called to undivide our divisions of heaven from earth, flesh from spirit, holy from sinful, everyday from eternity, etc. This takes actual engagement in the messiness of life—no Jesus or *Christ ex machina* dropping in from above to yank on our bootstraps.

May you partner well with your various families and relieve the burden of perfection from Christ by partnering well with Jesus in pointing toward and moving toward a dynamic wholeness, not static perfection.

Hebrews 4:14–16; 5:7–9
Consequence Friday

What is our confession, our affirmation? It is not that we have desired a High Priest who will make a way for us.

Jesus did not presume upon his privilege to escape travail (a three-stake variant of a torturous cross). It is too easy to interpret non-presumption as obedience. This sort of decision is not just an act of obedience. It takes a mature person able to enter into a decision to not escape and to make the situation their own.

Note that in our day, attempts to change a situation are often seen as fanaticism—we judge a difference between how wonderful we are in our maturity and how dastardly they are in their terrorism. While not wanting to equate these two, our major use of this sort of language is to privilege ourselves with the moral high ground of good obedience, not bad obedience.

Obedience learned through suffering is provisional or foxhole obedience. When the trauma is over, so is the obedience. It turns to unquestioning rote or the relief of disobedience. This type of obedience really can't be healthily passed on. It establishes a do-as-I-say-because-I-say-it relationship.

Perhaps it is enough to simply say, "The one we follow as partner is one who can sympathize with weakness even as they can lead us to love beyond our limits." These two actions complement one another and set a healthier ground for transformation.

Hebrews 9:11–15
Clarification Week: Monday

At best, this is Pre-Easter Week, not Holy Week. Our very distinction of "Holy This" or "Holy That" belies the holiness of life in all things. Language of holiness easily moves into unhelpful dualities that end up with a split between spiritual and material.

Let us take hands and declare to one another that which is yet to come to pass before it has sprung forth. This imagery from Isaiah sees us through many life situations.

The Psalmist reminds us of the continuance of steadfast love (salvation, if you will). We participate in this love and add our part to its continual revelation. Hold hands; do not be driven from this reality.

The writer to the Hebrews knows that a new covenant does not depend on some third party, but on the integrity of those engaged together. She reminds us it is not the sacrifice of others that brings life, but it is our own participation in that which we deem essential that moves us from life's repetitive works to continually revealed expressions of a steadfast love not held away as a carrot for tomorrow, but offered as a full feast for today.

Whether it is our commitment to giving roses, perfume, anointing, relationship now instead of later, or our past experiences of resurrection coming to challenge the leaden, deadly inertia of cultural and political blocks to more life for more people, we challenge a current *status quo* that strives for more advantage and control. It is our generosity and awareness of new life that bring forth opportunities to reveal the basic choices of life. Generosity and awareness of the abundance of life are still counter-cultural fulcrum points that can move the world.

Let's keep telling a larger story than our own small part and honor our small part in moving a larger story along.

Remember the multitude of creation stories: some here and some there, and even more that have been scattered through space and time.

It is worth the time to consider how this story plays with other accounts. How would you compare and contrast these and other similar recountings in regard to "will" and "atonement"? Without doing this basic work, a misconstrued beginning will mischievously echo into our current decision-making.

Stepping outside your current story about your beginning or that of the world/cosmos will help you come back to it a wiser person. Now you can confront seemingly stolid fate with a next creative choice.

G*D gets pickier and pickier
bulls and goats no longer make it

we return to Abraham and Isaac
no substitutions this time

one and a multitude of first-borns
are needed as offering

if only one
Jesus will do

and the rest of us
breathe a sigh of relief

we can still breathe and
avoid having to will anything

yet we are unsatisfied
until finally we step forward

to say "wrong" to a wrong G*D
"we're in this together"

Hebrews 10:5–10
Needed Change [4]

In the schizophrenia of Advent, we rejoice over sacrificed bodies turning us toward tomorrow. We also recognize a body perpetually rolling away a rock, facing back at us, to judge what we have sacrificed—our steadfast love and ever-ready mercy.

Generally, we end up on one side or the other of the unspoken divide between the end of verse 9 and the beginning of verse 10. Often, it is the space between our utterances that is the real crux of the matter. What happened in that mysterious moment between verses of sacrifice of one another and personal sanctification?

Advent asks us to stop our continued sacrificing and scapegoating in light of an anticipation of Creati*on's built-in wholeness.

---

good earth-birthed adam
male and female adam
named good
called blessed
called to name
coming one

good angel-sung jesus
shepherd and magi jesus
named freedom
called sheep and goat
called twelve and more
coming two

good sickle-bearing lamb
judge and jury lamb
named bright morning star
called bride and groom
called new jerusalem
coming three

good body-entrusted friend
saint and sinner friend
named tomorrow
called from past
called from present
coming four

and more

Hebrews 10:16–25
Consequence Friday

Where there is forgiveness, there is no longer any offering for sin. The life of Jesus is merciful, forgiving. This is not just a momentary accomplishment, but a life-time achievement that challenges all those mentored by Jesus.

If you are not going to claim the power of forgiveness as a fundamental key to the presence of G*D, there is nothing in Jesus' death that will substitute for your responsibility to forgive.

Even here in the midst of a temptation to idolize crucifixion, we hear these strange and powerful words: "Let us provoke or call one another forward, toward love and good deeds."

Jesus shows we can make it to and past the consequences of loving good deeds in the midst of a greedy and privileged culture. To claim any given moment of a nation to be the pinnacle of morality is an exercise in futility. Only a brief reflection is needed to reveal that an official history is but a cover for extending the current power structure one day more. Alternative histories (read Howard Zinn) always reveal a liberation rising from the grassroots to break through the cement (thank you Malvina Reynolds). We arrive at a better tomorrow by a whole series of sequential or persistent actions, not by protecting wealth and privilege with guns and armies.

Indeed, let us meet together in all our confusing and contradictory ways. Only in this time of meeting can we each assist one another toward love and good deeds. When we lose this connection, we lose our basic mission that has come at such a cost to so many.

Today, reflect on this wooden carving I found in Korea. I'm told the clothing style is that of a scholar, and the backpack is like what I saw farmers in the community using for their chores. Scholars and workers are crucified for the wealth and power of a few. Listen to both saying, "We can do better." This provocation to love and good deeds is the call we need to hear. Mourn death, yes, but do better.

Hebrews 11:1–3, 8–16
Proper 14 (19)

Faith is currently defined in *Merriam-Webster* online as:
>1) allegiance
>2) belief and trust in
>3) that which is believed

How does this differ from:
>1) assurance of that hoped for
>2) conviction of the unseen
>3) a source of approval

After you have played with the intersections of the connotations of the above, note a fourth category from the lection:
>4) obedience

Remember again your comparison of 1), 2), and 3) above. Now play with "obedience". How does that change things? Is obedience a matter of faith? When? Under what conditions?

Etymologically, obedience is to be oriented (ob- —toward) what can be (-oedire —heard). What have you heard calling to you this week? Something in the news? A community still to be brought into being by our choices throughout the day?

At stake is what is so firmly grounded in you that, whether or not it comes to pass in your lifetime, you will live for it to be available for some generation to come. Remember realized eschatology and be glad.

Realized Eschatology: being engaged in the process of becoming, rather than waiting for external and unknown forces to bring about destruction.

For extra credit, there is this paper to consider:
http://philipclayton.net/files/papers/Process%20Eschatology.pdf.

People acted. Presumably, they acted on what they understood to be true for them—their faith (since we don't trust that which doesn't ring true for us). But, bottom-line, people acted.

Given the complexity of communities, there were undoubtedly some who simply acted because others led the way. It wasn't a faith thing at all for them, just a path of least resistance.

Yet everyone on the winning side is accorded a trophy; faith is attributed to their actions, whether they knew it or not. It is this mixed bag of the designated faithful we are called to emulate. They bear witness to actions accomplished and now surround us with encouragement, regardless of the amount of faith we hold, to participate in the joy and journey of life. Even if you are but a tag-along, do so with all you can muster.

Hebrews 12:1–3

Clarification Week: Wednesday

Many have had a difficult time, but, of course, my situation is worse than anyone else's because I am such a special person. That others are stumbling might feel comforting to me, but, as noted, my trouble is worse.

It might be helpful to remember my own previous rocks and hard places, but even here, my current problem makes all previous ones pale in comparison.

Nonetheless, I might as well do my best to put some perspective on my disastrous setting since nothing else has helped.

To do this honestly is hard work. Excuses to keep on being overcome abound. We dismiss one excuse, and there is an infinite number of excuses waiting to take its place. Perhaps all we can do is to practice meditation. As our distracting excuses arise, we need to simply acknowledge them, let them know they will be dealt with a bit later, allow them to leave, and continue with a soft breath.

Usually, we will find betrayal betrayed by its own limitations. We have been asking the wrong questions and coming up with betrayal as a solution. Now we can ask a better question, set a larger context. Ahh, finally, relief.

Living G*Ds are always dangerous. They leave chaos in their wake. Rules are made and remade. Rituals come and go. What will satisfy a Living G*D won't satisfy a reformed Living G*D that recognizes a previous way of doing business is no longer satisfactory for either G*D or creation or creature.

You thought the threat of fire next time was tough to bear up under; that's nothing compared to the blaze of requirements of this reformed Living G*D. In retrospect, it seems that it was easier to deal with animal sacrifice for behavioral issues than it is to deal with doctrinal sacrifice for theological issues.

To circle back to the gospel lesson (Luke 13:10–17), can you hear Jesus talking to both the Living G*D of his tradition and the reformed Living G*D he was experiencing—and using the term hypocrite? You can't really talk about the hypocrisy of priests without also talking about the hypocrisy of the power they represent or mediate.

"Give thanks or else", is not a comforting word. Blessings on you for being able to give thanks by simply seeing life beyond wrath and calling out those who limit us to a fear-based approach to life. Blessings on you for being able to give thanks even while seeing the end of life as subservience and randomness and colluding with it. Blessings on you for being able to give thanks while convinced there is no hope and nothing to trust. Simply blessings on you for your thanksgiving, regardless of its etiology or degree.

Hebrews 13:1–8, 15–16
Proper 17 (22)

It is always instructive to read scripture from a different point of view. Here we have a passage directed toward our actions in regard to others. Try reading it as though you were addressing a part of the congregation within yourself.

For instance: Let self-love continue. Do not neglect to show hospitality to the stranger within, for thereby some have entertained angels unaware. Remember those parts of you that are imprisoned, as though the rest of you were in prison with them, and those voices within who are ill-treated, since you also are in the body with them....

For those of us who are so other-directed, it is important to hear a call to equal care for self.

---

looking for confidence
    in all the wrong places
    is an alternative
    country wailing
we know we need it
    for our fears are real
    and rising with a dark moon
    in a stormy sky
there is no escape
    the fiercest of nightmares
    that are not only possible
    but actually real somewhere
our needed confidence
    is directly tied to contentment
    our culture and our yearnings
    disparage and dismiss
is there a place
    of no forsakenness available
    in our past or present
    we can count as steadfast
is that place only in our dreams
    where a helper is quick
    to be present and protective
    that others within won't scream
with or without confidence
    we could do with a few
    content people to imitate
    and share with others

1 Peter 4:1–8
Absent Saturday

Oh, sure, deny the denials of life. You can no more give up your human desires than you can escape a gravity field of G*D. To deny your supposed negative passions will also deny your hoped-for positive passions. You don't need to express them, but they cannot be denied. To deny them is to not give an accurate account of your life.

This day is an opportunity to discipline ourselves regarding hope. Without hope that it will make a whit of difference, we commit to love one another, nonetheless.

That which we had counted on, steadfastly, proved to be quite frail. Death came all too easily (which is not to say it was faked), no legs were broken to hasten suffocation. What we wanted to be a loud cry wrecking the world and setting it right turned out to be a last gasp for a last breath and then no more—not a hoped-for bang, but a whimper.

And now a stone-rolled dark tomb. We are reduced from grunt to silence. Only motions are left. We will be gentle and kind with one another. It is available for us to do. Perhaps, in time, more will come; our desires, in both kinds, will return. There is no explaining our reliance upon our memory of a last command. Was it real or not? Whatever. That word, for whatever reason, continues to echo within. So we do our best to love one another even when love is lost. And Simeon's blessing comes around; with a sword in our soul we pull out our beads and recite a traditional Roman Catholic prayer:

> Hail Mary, full of grace. The Lord is with thee.
> Blessed art thou amongst women,
> and blessed is the fruit of thy womb, Jesus.
> Holy Mary, Mother of God,
> pray for us sinners,
> now and at the hour of our death. Amen.

We will love one another until and through our death.

Twice we hear the refrain: "Is...Was...To Come." This Trinity is a source of grace and peace.

Being able to play with these elements brings forth helpful questions.

Is this order significant to you: Is ···→ Was ···→ To Come ?
Some folks seem to prefer: Was, period, or Was ···→ Is.
Some folks modify this projection into: Is ···→ To Come.
Utopians may move from: To Come ···→ Is.

You get the idea.

What is your starting point to evaluate a next important decision spot?

Has G*D said all that is necessary, and is now just judging folks on that basis?
Is G*D waiting for some next propitious moments to enter into dialogue?
Is this moment more a continuation of the past or prelude to the future?
Does this moment have a life of its own, regardless of where life has been or might go?

A sliding scale can be devised for the Alpha to Omega, A–Z, imagery. Are you more starting out or winding down? And the culture you identify with?

All too often, the Book of Revelation is read as "To Come" when it is more helpfully read as "Is". Blessings on playing with a Trinity of Time available to you this day.

A recent production of *1984* reminded me of the goal of the "Ministry of Love"—to so "help" another discard everything they held dear, one's own perception and love of another, that they become empty enough to love only Big Brother. Then the Ministry of Love can fill the emptiness and finally kill a non-martyr, one who does not desire to further betray Big Brother.

I must admit I get a sense of that when I read such passages as this. All honor and glory being given away until we can only cry out, "I love you, Big Brother" or "I love you, Worthy Lamb."

We cry out for filling, for we are nothing. In crying out, our emptiness is filled.

Even if we take such praise as subversive against a power of any age that requires its own praise, the substitution of blind praise for G*D is no better than blind praise for Nation. Apocalyptic language is not all that different than Newspeak or Doublespeak; it can change direction and symbolism on a moment's notice. Read on its own, without Prophetic pronouncements, it is most dangerous.

We will need to figure out what we love with such forcefulness before sheer glory takes over our "love."

---

one angel is enough for Mary
Jesus had access to ten thousand
now myriads of myriads and thousands of thousands
are arrayed before our eyes

that many angels singing
in unison or four-part harmony
or lovely parts infinite in scope
deafen wisdom and worship

our work is done for us
all that is needed is assent
get on the bandwagon
forever might escape without unanimity

join the angel band
lend your voice
creation's wall will fall
only pure love will be left

Revelation 7:9–17
Assured [4]

When an ordeal is over, thanksgiving is in order. In fact, giving great thanks simply comes through, whether in order or not.

That which can wipe away our every tear is highly valued. Of course, it is exactly this that often gets us into ordeals. Fascists and dictators of every stripe first appeal to being a source of great comfort—getting the trains to run on time or provide security from some projected and convenient-to-blame internal or external foe.

Wiping away every tear is a worthy value. The question is at what expense and for what purpose. If it is to control or for praise of the most powerful around, the value of comfort is diminished and needs to be replaced by rebellion.

What other responses are there to coming through terrible troubles? "Remember!" is one. "Never again!" is another. "We learned X or Y or Z and will structure that into next decisions" is yet a third. Do add your own fourth or fifth or tenth.

Imagine for a moment that Revelation were to return us to earth to rectify past errors and eras. What then would be the appropriate behaviors? Probably something beyond 24/7 worship. If there is any humanity left in heaven, it is hard to imagine this level of good-time lasting. At some point, a mind will wander, an extraneous thought enter, admiration of that gorgeous set of wings will set off some greed-o-meter. If this is a next garden time, will there be time for an evening talk as well as an insatiable coveting of more and more thanks?

If Revelation is simply encouragement for folks in travail, what happens when onlookers of another time begin to claim the perks of ordeal survival without the ordeal? It turns into a pie-in-the-sky theory that removes us from the development of relationships with one another. We end up with only a relationship with whatever we name God. This becomes a control mechanism of a religious institution.

Watch out for a false future representing a false G*D.

Revelation 21:1–6a
New Year's Day

Let's begin with verse 3 and various translations. Depending on your choices, the final pronouncement of all-in-all will carry a certain bravado or confirmation certain.

What "loud" voice do you hear describing its reality, if not yet yours?

- Where is G*D's location regarding us—a home, a tent, a tabernacle? Each of these carries overtones of static stability or a movable feast and rest.

- What is G*D's relationship with us—a home, a tent, a tabernacle? Each of these raises questions about authority, status, and trust.

- Are those thus connected with G*D a "people" or "peoples"? Was the beginning and is the end inclusive or exclusive? How does that affect these between-times?

- Will G*D simply be with us or will G*D insist on playing *GOD* with us? Presence is powerful. This is different from "Power is present—all bow."

Looking at these four choices will lead us to differing inflections of "Alpha and Omega"—settled or ongoing. Noting changes in alphabetic notations over the eras is a good hint that the natural order (given that this is an iffy category) is evolutionary and ongoing.

Do you read this ending of a story that can set us on a new journey for a new year as

- a home run by a patriarch of a nuclear family is stable because of rules?

- a tent run as a partnership of a multi-generational family of refugees is stable because of mutual care?

- some other combination?

As we identify our best reality, we have more than making resolutions ahead of us. Further investigation, implementation, evaluation, feedback, and modification will solidify our experience of actually being on a journey of life and not just trapped in a mirage, mistaking speculation for movement. One evaluation tool is to check your joy quotient as the ratio of hope and trust changes when one or the other is increased or decreased.

"My work is done; my thirst sated." [from the cross]

"To those yet thirsty I will give a gift from a spring of
living water." [from the clouds]

"Yes. Do it!" [from the crowds]

Life is always done and still to be done.

Imagine a Tree of Life, later barred by flaming swords, as nurtured by a spring of the water of life. Did that come from the chaotic waters below? Is it a suggestive image regarding the bounding of such chaos into a directed energy—a River of Life—a constrained chaos directed toward an expanding mystery of life?

When faced with a seeming defeat of a positional belief and subsequent loss of identity, revelatory images can provide a modicum of relief. However, such images don't help us catch a new context of our journey toward a new heaven and a new earth: a journey of a new earth onward and a new heaven toward us. Revelations can help us see a new chance or beginning by destroying the past, but they don't help us see connections between endings and beginnings that bind us together.

Somehow, we need to see these bold statements in Revelation through a longer view that sees "life as a gift" as a done deal for all, not just for me. So we weep, breathe deep, and keep on being who we were and are and even will be as we deeply honor who others have been and are and will be.

> Legislation cannot void identity.
> Death cannot deny identity.
> Invisibility cannot disappear identity.

Whatever part of a Tree of Life or a River of Life you claim, may it comfort you as true enough and present enough to act on and pass on.

Revelation 21:10, 22–22:5
Assured [6]

If you were to see what you understood to be a City of Peace descending slowly from above, would you note what was there, or what wasn't?

It takes a theologically sophisticated viewer to note there was no Temple and the whole place glowed from an internal source. Most of us would get caught with the shape, size, color of the walls, and ornateness of the gates. It is strange that they are standing open—but look at those jewels. The elided section covers all these shiny things that first catch our eye, but we are interested in what lies beyond glitz.

Later, shown a Life River, we might look back and wonder if there was a waterfall from Jerusalem as it was lowered upon earth. If such a river is not overflowing, is it a circular river contained within the city itself? If it is not overflowing, is it really a river of Life?

Eventually, we will probably come to reflect on this vision as a vision and begin to have it inform our own behavior. Worshipping for Worship's sake is gone (no temple there to receive manipulative praise). With open gates, there may be some uncleanliness that enters (after all, aren't you expecting to be there?). The whole Book of Immigration Policies, aka., Book of Life, is trumped by an open door. And so we are informed about our living when restrictions take a second place to our work of opening doors. With an abundance of living water, we can expect that a Tree of Life (left over from Garden Eden?) will keep on bearing fruit. With such fecundity, we can afford to be generous; month after month, new fruit will ripen.

So worship changes, relationships change, and economics change when we are living in the shadow of a New Jerusalem. Imagine the changes in your life if hanging over you were not Damocles' Sword, but a temple-less, open-gated, fruitful city—a preferred future—that we can model here below as it is ahead and above.

Revelation 22:12–14, 16–17, 20–21
Assured [7]

Scripture is not always scripture. Here we have a debate between the selected and omitted verses. Which is it for you? If you want to keep both, how do you hold them together without finding yourself being omitted?

Whether a robe-washer (selected) invited to come inside or a falsehood-practitioner (omitted) kept at bay, we run into Paul and Silas in a prison that became open-doored. This openness is fearful for many until they experience Paul's invitation, "Do not harm yourself (or others), for we (including you) are all here."

We are all here. Let anyone who wishes take the water of life as a gift.

In the selected verses, we hear an invitation and blessing—a Tree of Life is still available; a big door is more widely opened to include you and even more widely opened to include those you haven't yet forgiven.

In the omitted verses, we hear about a share in the Tree of Life being taken away; a big door is slammed shut in your face.

This side of a New Jerusalem, do you want to spend your time affirming that a Tree of Life is still available as a prevenient grace and is attractive enough to draw its deniers nearer?

Would you rather spend your time warning people about what they will lose if they keep on the way they are going?

While both options have their place, I hope to be spending more time with the Beauty of Life as an attractant than with warning folks about something outside their experience base.

Appendix — Sunday Designations

Past Designation	New Look
Advent	Needed Change
Christmas	Blessed Body
Holy Name of Jesus	Naming Day
New Year's Day	New Year's Day
Epiphany	Guiding Gift
Baptism of the Lord	Beloved
Presentation of the Lord	Old Welcomes New
Transfiguration of the Lord	Mountain Top to Valley
Lent	Conviction
Annunciation of the Lord	Creation's Conception
Ash Wednesday	Self-Recognition Day
Liturgy of the Palms	False Dawn Sunday
Liturgy of the Passion	Premature Fear Sunday
Holy Week	Clarification Week
Maundy Thursday	Courage Thursday
Good Friday	Consequence Friday
Holy Saturday	Absent Saturday
Easter Vigil	Hopeless Hope Vigil
Easter/ Resurrection of the Lord	Assured
Easter Evening	Opened Heart Evening
Ascension of the Lord	Our Turn to Witness

Pentecost	Energy to Witness
Trinity Sunday	Live Together
Season after Pentecost	Community Practice Propers 3–29
Visitation of Mary to Elizabeth	Elizabeth and Mary Meet
Holy Cross	Relic Day
Thanksgiving	Thanksgiving
All Saints Day	Honoring Day
Reign of Christ/ Christ the King	Evaluation Day

Abbreviations

The following are abbreviations of Bibles referred to and used:
    CCB—Christian Community Bible: Catholic Pastoral Edition
    CEB—Common English Bible
    CEV—Contemporary English Version
    IB—The Inclusive Bible: The First Egalitarian Translation
    JANT—The Jewish Annotated New Testament
    JB—The Jerusalem Bible
    JSB—The Jewish Study Bible
    KJB—The King James Bible
    MSG—The Message
    NCB—The New Community Bible
    NIB—The New Interpreter's Bible
    NJB—The New Jerusalem Bible
    NISB—The New Interpreter's Study Bible
    NRSV—New Revised Standard Version
    REB—The Revised English Bible
    SB—The Schocken Bible, Volume 1
    SFB—The Spiritual Formation Bible
    WSB—The Wesley Study Bible

    Unattributed—indicates paraphrase/translation by the author.

About the Author

Wesley White has been partnered/married with Brenda Smith White since 1972. He is father to two: Shai, daughter; Brandon, son; and grandfather to Nathan and Nicholas.

Wesley grew up outside a small town in southern Wisconsin, went to a one-room country school (through sixth-grade), and graduated from the University of Wisconsin—Whitewater with a degree in Sociology. He served for 2 years in the Peace Corps in the Philippines. After returning to the United States, Wesley graduated with an M.Div. from Garrett-Evangelical Theological Seminary in 1971 and served in ordained ministry for 38 years before retiring. He is also a trained and registered Transitional Intentional Interim Ministry Specialist and has served three congregations in that role.

Wesley has received recognition for work on inclusion from the Wisconsin Commission on the Status and Role of Women and other justice issues through a Perry Saito Award of the Wisconsin United Methodist Federation for Social Action.

His current work is with LovePrevailsUMC.com to remove a false testimony within the church about the incompatibility of LGBTQQI-AA persons and Christian teaching.

Production Details

Manuscript: formatted in Apple Pages
        exported to .PDF

Cover: *Blue Green Clash Background Photo* – Nicholas Moore
    Image Credit: © Crashoran | Dreamstime.com -
            Blue Green Clash Background Photo
    Design Consultant: Amy E. DeLong
    Typography: Title is Trebuchet MS

Book Typography: Headings: Helvetica, 11point italic: 12 point bold
            Text: Optima, 10.5 point

Book Graphics:
    Page 230: *The Transfiguration* by Raphael. Public Domain.

    Page 249: Love On Trial Logo by Amy E. DeLong. Copyright Love On Trial. Used by permission.
    http://www.loveontrial.org/lp_shirts/a-logo-2.jpg

    Page 278: Logo from a past Resiliancy Festival at Guelph University, Ontario, Canada. I can find no other information about the artist/graphic designer. The original was found at:
    www.guelphresiliencefestival.ca/images/Sweeklogo.png

    Publisher Logo: designed by Susan Eaton Mendenhall of www.JazzArt.biz for use as a logo for *in medias res*. It represents being in middle of things as a way of life—lifting the past to make way for the future.

    Other illustrations, charts, and photographs: Wesley White